THE $100 BILLION MARKET

How To Do Business With The U.S. Government

HERMAN HOLTZ

on

The federal government spends more than $100 billion a year on practically every product and service known to man—but fewer than 2% of America's 13 million businesses are sharing in it. Why? The government market is so diverse, so complex, with dozens of purchasing instruments and methods, that many of the businesses that could participate in this vast and continuing enterprise are too baffled by it to try.

Your business may be one of them. If so, here is the help you need; a complete education on what the government buys and how you can sell your own product or service to it. Discover what and who the government is...how it is organized...how it works...where the sales opportunities are for *you* and how to pursue them. Let Herman Holtz tell you how the government evaluates costs and how it wants cost figures from you analyzed and presented. Learn about special government programs designed to help small businesses succeed—and the special areas of government buying it's easiest to succeed in. Where is the competition—and where isn't it? When should you bid, when should you negotiate, and how can you make yourself seem the low bidder when in fact you may not be? What does the government offer free, and how can you get free many of the things it usually charges for?

The entrepreneur will find this a priceless invitation to opportunities that could become a major source of business. In fact, it could become your sole business, a business in itself. Proposal writers

HERMAN HOLTZ

The $100 BILLION Market

How to do business with the U.S. government

A DIVISION OF AMERICAN MANAGEMENT ASSOCIATIONS

Library of Congress Cataloging in Publication Data

Holtz, Herman.
  The $100 billion market.

  Includes index.
  1. Government purchasing—United States.   I. Title.
JK1671.H64   353.0071'2   79-54836
ISBN 0-8144-5578-6

First Printing

To two unsung heroes,
my wife Sherrie and my daughter Julie,
who put up courageously and patiently
with a man who works at home.

Foreword

Before discussing the content of this book, some observations on the nature of federal acquisitions should be helpful. Those in the private sector who are not familiar with the bureaucracy tend to see the federal government as a monolithic, amorphous organization, pumping billions of dollars into the economy through the federal procurement process. Viewed from this position, federal acquisition is a means of exerting a large amount of economic and social influence on contractors, on state and local governments, and in general on the private sector of the economy. Its efforts are pervasive, and the government contract is something desirable or abhorrent, depending on one's point of view.

The economic significance of federal procurement is truly massive. In fiscal year 1978, the government spent $81 billion on the acquisition of goods and services through the procurement process, and during the same fiscal year distributed $86 billion through federal grants. Generally speaking, any time the government receives a benefit, whether in the form of a product or a service, the document extant is a contract. This book concerns itself with federal contracts and the federal acquisition process. It provides priceless information to help you understand every facet of government procurement.

Today, thousands of government activities are involved in acquiring products and services or supporting programs that affect millions of people. The impact of government acquisition on the nation's economic and social well-being can be even more far-reaching than the figures I have quoted suggest. The award of a major contract can stimulate the growth of localities or even entire states; conversely, withdrawal or termination may cause the decline of or, in some cases, the collapse of whole communities.

The magnitude of government procurement provides leverage for achieving national and socioeconomic objectives that are not directly related to the goods or services being contracted for. For example, procurement is used to assure equal employment opportunities, improve wages and conditions of employment, and to channel employment and business opportunities into labor surplus areas. In fact, every major and significant social achievement in the history of the United States was first introduced through federal contracts. Over the past twenty years, procurement has increased sixfold. More than 80,000 federal employees are involved in the federal acquisition process, and many more are employed in private industry, awarding subcontracts to support large government contracts.

Government procurements are incredibly diverse, encompassing everything from brooms to missiles, from paper clips to computers, and from hand tools to vehicles. The government contracts directly for research in both refuse disposal and interplanetary space travel. And government construction procurements include warehouses, missile silos, and atomic energy plants, among other structures.

These various and sundry situations require a variety of contracting techniques, complex skills and procurement knowledge, and adherence to many different rules, procedures, regulations, and guidelines. How on earth can one crack this vast maze of procurement procedures? Where does one find the answers to so many questions?

My colleague, Herman Holtz, has painstakingly put forth a tremendous and, I might add, successful effort to inform you honestly and clearly of the "ins and outs" of government procurement.

I have spent 17 years in federal service, and during that time I have held a variety of procurement-related positions. I have taught many

courses on the subject for the U.S. Department of Agriculture Graduate School, the General Services Administration, and the National In-
will learn about the entire procurement process (NIGP) I've also served on nu-
and will be shown how to make their proposals th procurement topics.
win. Engineers and other professionals who write stantly bemused by the
proposals themselves will learn the step-by-step nding government pro-
procedures and the fine points that can turn a competent but unpersuasive proposal into a first-rate
one. The general manager, doubling as sales or
marketing manager, will learn how to evaluate man Holtz, endorse his
proposals in light of realities, and how to correct r procurement profes-
the common mistakes that so often mar even the is wealth of information
best ones.

All this and more in an easygoing, readable
style—with case histories and anecdotes from the
author's wide personal experience. More than a
book to help you save money, it's a book to help **Kent Goodger**
you *make money* in a market that's not only wait- *ager, Procurement Branch*
ing for you, but *needs* you. *eau of Government Finan-*
al Operations
Treasury Department
hington, D.C.

HERMAN HOLTZ knows his business—and
his business is the government's. Consultant, lecturer, and seminar leader, his own proposals and
bids have won more than $100 million in contracts
from such diverse government agencies as
NASA, the FAA, Departments of Labor and
Commerce, the Army, the Navy, and HUD. An
electronics engineer by formal training, Holtz has
worked in various capacities for RCA, IBM, GE,
and other large, successful outfits. From this it is
clear that he knows the government procurement
process intimately, and how it can be made to
work for *you*.

Preface

Some years ago, I was an executive with a small firm which supported the large government contractors who build missiles, aircraft, radar, and the like. We wrote their technical manuals, drafted their drawings, and did all the other such chores. When I went in pursuit of our own government contracts, other executives in the company jeered at me. They *knew* that we were too small, at $8 million a year in volume, to compete for government contracts.

Several years and several million dollars' worth of government contracts later, those other executives were still shaking their heads disbelievingly. I must be engaging in some kind of sleight of hand to get those contracts. Wasn't it an established fact that we were too small to do business with the government?

Prejudice dies hard with some people, especially those who believe myths. Yet even I was not totally immune to the disease. When I left the company to strike out on my own as a freelance writer, it was a contracting officer who knew me from "the old days" who asked me why I wasn't bidding to him for some of his smaller contracts. He laughed at my protest of being just a one-man enterprise and assured me that I was entitled to and would get full and equal consideration for any bid or proposal I submitted.

Thus it was that I became a small, independent government contractor, often burdened with more work than I could handle. And thus it was that I began to learn many details of government contracting which I could never have learned as an executive in even an $8 million firm, much less in my earlier experience as a consultant to or an employee of the huge corporations (for example, IBM, GE, RCA, Philco, Sperry-Rand, and so on).

I learned that while the huge contracts go to the huge firms (which are the only ones who can handle them, of course), the vast majority of government contracts go to medium-size and small firms. I also learned that in many cases, small firms have a great advantage over large firms. But the most surprising thing I learned was that my own experience with that $8-million-a-year firm was not at all unusual: Ignorance of government marketing and the opportunities to be had in the government markets is the rule, not the exception. I recently listened impatiently to a lecturer, who was supposed to be a government-marketing expert, smugly assure a group of near-neophytes that proposals play an almost insignificant role in contract competitions. And he was preparing to teach them how to write good proposals for winning contracts! In addition, I just finished reviewing a manuscript which claims that proposals play a relatively small role in the contract-award decisions—yet the manuscript explains how to write winning proposals!

Somehow, the paradox always seems to escape these cynics, who know so many things that aren't so.

Less than 2 percent of the 13 million businesses in the United States do business with the U.S. government, and it is a fact that on many occasions, federal contracting officials are hard put to attract enough bidders to constitute a fair degree of competition. No doubt such myths as the one referred to here are at least partially responsible. But there are at least two other reasons:

- The government market is not *a* market; it's a large and complex *set* of markets—impressive in its sheer diversity. Those markets are scattered throughout many agencies and many geographic locations, and represent countless needs, many of them unique (the U.S. government is the *only* customer for numerous items and services), and so many kinds of purchasing arrangements.

- The government is extremely limited, by the nature of bureaucracy, in its ability to educate and inform the businesses of the United States about its needs and business opportunities. It is confined principally to its own publications to make announcements, which reach only those already aware of and usually actively engaged in marketing to the government!

This book has, then, two main purposes: (1) to make more business people aware of the business opportunities available from the many government agencies, and (2) to try to place these diverse government markets into some sort of framework, and perhaps bring order to what appears to the newcomer as pure chaos.

This is not a philosophical work; it makes no political commentary and engages in no economic theorizing. It is offered strictly as a how-to book. It is based on my own experiences, not on any official publications. In fact, I have scrupulously tried to avoid including those mechanical details which may be found in other, usually official, publications, and have made it a goal to bring you information which can be gained *only* through experience.

Will this book make you an expert on government markets? Of course not. Only your own continuing experience can do that. But it will put you on the right road. It will reveal to you information and inside facts for which I paid dearly. It should save you a great deal of time. It should spare you a great deal of shin-bruising stumbling in the dark. And I hope it will teach you techniques, strategies, and methods which you might never have learned otherwise.

I am indebted to many people for my education in government marketing and for their help and encouragement of my work. I wish also to note that despite occasional abuses and improprieties in government procurement, the sincerity and dedication of most government officials continue to make our purchasing systems the best in the world.

Herman Holtz

Contents

1

The
U.S. government paid me
$6,000
to answer its mail

(Some of it was two years old!)

You name it, the government buys it (probably)

The wind-energy branch of what is now the Department of Energy (then the Energy Research and Development Administration) paid me $6,000 to answer its mail. Staff members couldn't keep up with it themselves, since the chief of the branch insisted that every letter merited a personal response rather than a form letter. I was hired to help them catch up with a two-year backlog of about 200 letters. The letters I answered came from all kinds of correspondents: college professors, scientists, engineers, ordinary citizens, inventors, and would-be inventors. (Many citizens sent in their ideas in the form of rough sketches on yellow paper, which the chief referred to caustically as "one-page inventions.") In any case, I was forced to exercise my imagination and think up plausible reasons for having taken two years to respond to some of the mail.

I was paid $1,800 by the General Services Administration to critique a training program (which I attended for one week); the Civil Service Commission (now the Office of Personnel Management) paid me $100 each for a series of 80-minute lectures on procurement for federal employees; and I received $600 for an expense-paid two days in Vermont as an EPA consultant.

None of these examples are particularly unusual—I've won both larger and smaller jobs. I've worked as a small, independent government contractor from a suite of offices in downtown Washington, D.C., but I've also won and handled contracts using my own home as an office. And so have many other people.

Government contracts have been let to round up wild horses, rent mules and handlers, referee sports events, supply go-go dancers, bag groceries, produce theatricals, print bumper stickers, make rubber stamps, repair typewriters, fell trees, manage warehouses, run office copiers, rent cabins in national parks, guard buildings, manage subscriptions to government periodicals, scatter sterilized screwworm flies from the air, answer government telephones, operate travel bureaus, organize seminars and conferences, operate government computers, run a bus service, make sandwiches, and perform thousands of other jobs, most of them more mundane than these.

A few of the myths

Perhaps the most common myth about contracting with the government is that you have to be a big corporation. As a single individual, I have personally had many thousands of dollars worth of contracts, many of which were worth more than $25,000. Another fable is that you need influence or "pull" to win government contracts. I have no special influence and my "contracts" in government are the ones I made by working with the agencies. I started cold and built my list of acquaintances. Even now, I have no high-level contacts.

Like all myths, these fables have a tiny speck of truth which has been thoroughly distorted. Certainly little guys aren't going to win the multimillion-dollar contracts awarded for some jobs, and certainly influence has been used occasionally to help bring in the really big contracts. But even in those special cases the effect of "influence" is not nearly as great as the myths would have it, and all the influence in the world is not going to win contracts for those who do not compete well. The use of influence has severe limitations in our system.

Do it better than the government does and sell it to them

If you can do something the government is doing or is supposed to do, and you can do it better than the Great Bureaucracy does, you can sell it back to the government! One enterprising gentleman who became aware of the shortcomings of the official telephone directories each agency publishes compiled his own *Federal Telephone Directory.*

It lists 18,000 executives in all the Washington-area federal offices, and is kept up to date by annual revision. He sold subscriptions, which cost more than $100 per year, to private organizations doing business with federal agencies. But to his delight and surprise, the agencies themselves became his best customers!

Another man publishes a biweekly listing of federal job openings in Washington and elsewhere, for job seekers. Lo and behold, federal personnel offices subscribed in great numbers to the service.

When the Consumer Product Safety Commission began, its offices were frequented by a young man who was launching the *Product Safety Letter,* a weekly newsletter intended for industry. But Safety Commission offices have many subscriptions, since commission executives learned that they could keep abreast of commission affairs better through that newsletter than through any official means. (Almost every agency subscribes to a number of privately published newsletters about their own activities.)

Big government = Big business

No one knows just how much our government spends each year for goods and services. Estimates vary widely, even official ones, but it's safe to say that over $100 billion worth of contracts and purchase orders are issued yearly, and the figure is probably on the order of $170 billion. Government warehouses and supply depots bulge with an inventory of more than 6 million items. Each year, the Federal Supply Service alone buys about $3 billion worth of "common use" items (ordinary commodities). Some contracts have been in excess of $1 billion each, and multimillion-dollar contracts are commonplace. In fact, anything under $10,000 is a "small purchase" in government circles and doesn't even require a formal contract, but may be authorized by a simple purchase order.

Startling Statistics

To many, the U.S. government is a maze of bulky monolithic buildings frowning over busy streets just east of downtown Washington. The fact is that the U.S. government is something more than that. It includes:

- Approximately 2,800,000 employees, with more of them in California than in Washington, D.C.
- More than 34,000 facilities or activities.

- 405,000 buildings owned by the government, 54,000 rented buildings, plus rented office space in many more high-rise buildings.
- About 760 million acres—one-third of the U.S. land area—owned by the government.

That's only the beginning:

- The U.S. Army has the largest fleet of wheeled vehicles in the world, but the U.S. Postal Service is second in size, with well over 100,000 vehicles and more than 300 repair shops (vehicle maintenance facilities).
- To pay for all this, the U.S. Treasury must issue some 800 million checks every year.
- And since all this buying requires a great deal of work, there are about 15,000 purchasing offices.

In addition to a great deal of buying every day of the year, our Uncle must maintain several centralized procurement and supply organizations:

The Federal Supply Service (General Services Administration)
The Postal Service supply organization
The Veterans Administration supply organization
The Defense Supply Agency

The structure of the bureaucracy

There are 12 departments in the government—Treasury, Labor, Commerce, Transportation, Interior, Energy, State, Army, Navy, Air Force, Housing and Urban Development, and Health, Education and Welfare.* (There's a bit of an anomaly here because the Department of Defense is listed as a department, but so are the three major military arms; yet, only the Secretary of Defense is a cabinet officer.)

There are more than 60 "independent agencies"—NASA, EPA, GSA, and others—and quasi-official agencies, such as the American Red Cross. Gaining department status is not based on size. Some of the independent agencies are larger than some of the departments. Within agencies, which we'll use as a generic term for all federal organizations, are many large subdivisions, some of them better known than the agency itself. For example, the well-known and large Forest Service is part of the Department of Agriculture, although everyone admits its missions are better suited to the Interior Department.

*At this writing, the Department of Health, Education and Welfare is being reorganized into two new departments, tentatively known as the Department of Education and the Department of Health and Human Services.

This adds up to hundreds of agencies—the best estimate is 1,800—but even that doesn't tell the whole story. Most of these agencies have a number of offices throughout the United States, so we wind up with a complex set of markets, rather than a single market, that includes thousands of customers who can pay with U.S. Treasury checks.

The government divides the United States into ten federal regions, and most major agencies have a regional office in each region. However, some have many offices. Commerce and the Small Business Administration have about 80 each, for example (see Appendix 1 for a listing), and there are even more for some agencies. In addition, all of the many military bases in the United States and overseas do some independent buying.

Programs and Missions

Some of the agencies, particularly the older and better-established ones, have straightforward missions, indicated by their names. The Government Printing Office, for example, does printing, typesetting, and a few related tasks. The Treasury handles fiscal matters and disbursements. The Postal Service delivers the mail (most of the time). But it's a different story with the newer agencies. As the government and the society it governs become more complex, so do the organization and missions of the many bureaucracies within the Great Bureaucracy.

The Department of Labor is concerned with working people, and has been assigned missions relating to training unemployables, through Job Corps, for example, to administration of labor laws and standards, and to occupational safety and health.

The Economic Development Administration of the Department of Commerce is also concerned with jobs—with *creating* them. They are usually assigned the chore of administering such things as public works grants. But the Department of Labor has the job-creating Comprehensive Employment and Training Administration (CETA).

The Bureau of Indian Affairs is in the Department of Interior, to which it was transferred years ago from the War Department (which no longer exists).

Change Is Inevitable

If death and taxes are inevitable, so is change, especially in government. Each new administration will work some changes, creating new departments, shifting agencies and missions around. Among the more recent creations have been the Department of Energy and the Pension Benefit Guaranty Corporation, but other agencies (for example, Department of Transportation and the U.S. Postal Service) are creations of recent years. And the Office of Economic Opportunity (OEO) dwindled from a large operation to a small office, handing off its major programs to other agencies.

Some agencies are highly visible and well-known because they touch on matters of great concern or of interest to almost everyone, while others are relatively obscure because their work is so highly specialized. For example, who hasn't heard of the Social Security Administration? But how many citizens know that there is something called the Community Services Administration? That very fact has an effect on contracting: Because the National Cancer Institute is highly visible the Institute finds it necessary to pay out over $1 million per year to a contractor to answer its telephones and mail and send out information to the concerned citizens who call and write.

Redundancy in the Agencies

Many people, including presidential candidates, decry the redundancy and duplication of effort among federal agencies and call for reform to eliminate such duplication. However, there is often a clear distinction among the missions of agencies which appear to duplicate each others' functions.

For example, a small business may apply to the Small Business Administration for a loan guarantee. Or it may apply to the Economic Development Administration, within the Department of Commerce. But each would require a different type of justification. For SBA assistance, the business must qualify as a small business according to the standards established by SBA. For EDA, the business must demonstrate that the loan will either create new jobs or save jobs which are threatened. And it would also have to demonstrate that the jobs would be created in a "labor surplus" area (as designated by the Labor Department).

In short, it is important to understand such distinctions if you are to do business with the agencies.

Perhaps an even finer distinction is that between the Occupational Safety and Health Administration (OSHA), in the Labor Department, and the Environmental Protection Agency (EPA), an "independent." OSHA is concerned with the health and safety of workers in their workplaces; EPA is concerned with the health of the general public—

that is, with health hazards arising out of pollution. Suppose you have some device to reduce the pollution arising from some industrial process. Do you offer it to OSHA or EPA? You do either or both, but in one case you must address the protection of the worker, and in the other you must address the protection of the atmosphere and the general public.

If you have a device to make some consumer product less hazardous, you might want to talk to the Consumer Product Safety Commission, although it might have application to other agencies' missions as well. For example, if it has to do with automotive safety, it might interest the Highway Traffic Safety Administration in the Department of Transportation; if it would affect boating safety, take it to the Coast Guard, also in Transportation.

Overnight experts

You've probably heard that "Man proposes and God disposes." In Washington, Congress legislates and the bureaucrat procrastinates. But not without some justification. Frequently, what Congress legislates is a hot potato for the administration and its bureaucracy.

Let's take the case of the Pension Benefit Guaranty Corporation (PBGC), formed under new legislation several years ago to protect workers who are denied their pensions because of circumstances such as a union pension fund going into bankruptcy. Suddenly, an organization exists, largely on paper, and the administration must begin a frantic search for people who can implement the new program. /

When an agency is an entirely new entity, people who appear to have at least some of the right qualifications are borrowed from various other agencies and assigned to form a temporary cadre for the new organization. In the case of PBGC (a new government agency quickly becomes identified by its initials), it took the temporary staff two years before they had begun to assemble a staff of actuaries and other specialists. And then, woefully short on all but professional bureaucrats and new hires, they began to seek contractors to write training programs to train the new staff in all the special fields they needed to know.

When the Energy Research and Development Administration (ERDA) was formed, initial staff was drawn from technical agencies such as the National Science Foundation and the National Bureau of Standards. But even when the staff is reasonably well qualified, there are never enough people available right away, when enthusiasm and funding are high and when Congress wants to see immediate action. The answer is, of course, to call on industry and issue contracts.

Prior to ERDA, there were few "energy" experts, and no one had, in fact, used that term before. But once ERDA announced that it wanted help, and in a hurry, there were numerous applicants who assured ERDA that they were indeed experts. Those who got in on the ground floor and won some of the first contracts established their reputations quickly, although they may never have worked in that field before. It was not long before we had many energy experts—whole companies of them!

One of the most dynamic situations revolving around new agencies and new programs sprang up almost overnight when Lyndon Johnson took office and announced the advent of his Great Society and his War on Poverty. The effort centered immediately around the new Office of Economic Opportunity (OEO) at 19th and M Streets, NW, in Washington, D.C.

Shortly after OEO opened its doors and staffed its building on 19th Street with a few government bureaucrats and many recruits from the nation's universities, the building began to swarm with people from companies large and small. Most of them had been affected by the recent slowdown in defense spending and were attracted to what they thought was going to become a multibillion-dollar market in training, education, and social welfare programs. The erudite contracting officer of OEO, Milton Fogelman, summed it up laconically this way: "Look at them. They're like dogs around the butcher shop: They smell the meat, but they don't know how to get at it." Nevertheless, OEO (and the Office of Education (OE), which soon followed) transformed downtown Washington. The neighborhood buzzed with psychologists, sociologists, and educators of many kinds.

It was literally true that one could wander through the offices of OEO and emerge with a contract, not quite sure how it all happened. On one occasion, while strolling past an office, I was summoned by a harried OEO program manager and challenged. "Look at that requirement," he said, handing me a typed statement of need, "and tell me if you could do that job in 30 days and for how much." (We settled, ultimately, on 45 days and just under $50,000 for the project.)

Dozens of small companies sprang up, fueled initially by contracts from OEO, and some of the larger companies—General Electric, Westinghouse, IBM, and Xerox, for example—organized or bought education and training companies and went after OEO contracts.

Those days and that frenzied atmosphere are gone, as is the Embers, the ground-floor watering place for OEO and its habitués. Some of the consultants and small companies in demand by the program are gone, too. But many have survived, and are today carrying out projects to aid other agencies in their many "social intervention" programs, which work to provide child care, help for the elderly, education, aid for the handicapped, minority enterprises, jobs programs, alcohol and drug abuse programs, mental health programs, and so on.

Trends and projections

For years, the trend has been to more and more programs to aid those in need and distress, and that trend shows no signs of abating, despite inflation and a ground swell of taxpayer protest. But not all new programs and trends are "social" in the sense of succoring the unfortunate and the underprivileged. Safety and environment are prominent programs, as is energy, of course. And despite the lower profile of NASA since the Apollo program was completed, NASA's budget is still quite large.

There will be work, then, for psychologists, sociologists, educators, scientists, engineers, and specialists of many kinds. The government, despite nearly 3 million employees, has not nearly enough hands and feet to carry out all the programs. In fact, many agencies are hard-pressed to find people to manage the contracts let to private industry. Without the contracted help of private industry, almost all the programs would falter and fail from sheer lack of nourishment.

Some of the markets are vertical ones. Engineers and scientists in the physical sciences will find their projects among technical agencies: NASA, the military departments, EPA, the Department of Energy, and, to some extent, the Department of Transportation. Educators, sociologists, psychologists, therapists, and others in related fields will find their chief markets such agencies as HEW (with its many bureaus), the Department of Labor, and, to some extent, the military.

On the other hand, there are horizontal markets, too—markets which are totally unrelated to the mission of the agencies. All agencies use computers and data processing, for example, and the computer specialists may find projects almost anywhere in government. The same considerations apply to writers and certain other kinds of specialists.

The architect-engineer may find good prospects at HUD, as may real estate specialists, but a daily scan of the *Commerce Business Daily*

(CBD) will reveal that few agencies turn their new-construction needs over to the General Services Administration's Public Buildings Service, so almost any agency may have architectural and engineering requirements to bid for.

Printers will find the Government Printing Office the source for virtually all government printing contracts, of which there are many every day, although there are a few exceptions to this general rule.

What the government buys, typically

By now you should be starting to appreciate that the U.S. government is necessarily a customer for virtually *everything*, both goods and services. The military forces must be fed, clothed, housed, armed, and equipped. The thousands of buildings and other facilities must be repaired, maintained, cleaned, serviced. New construction must be carried out. The programs require studies, surveys, analyses, reports, execution, and evaluation. The computers need to be fed their thousands of programs and must be operated by humans, who are frequently under contract.

The needs of the agencies for outside help are of several types. Some represent simply the need for more hands and feet than the in-house staff can provide. Some needs are for skills and abilities which do not exist in-house. Some are for physical facilities which the government does not have.

Specific arrangements vary depending on the circumstances and the agency's regulations. Contractors may work "on site" (at the government's own facilities) or "off site" (at the contractor's facility). Some jobs may be performed anywhere the contractor chooses, while others must be performed within some prescribed proximity to the government's issuing facility. The government will let one-time contracts to meet specific, discrete needs, but it will also issue annual contracts year after year to satisfy permanent, on-going needs. Among this great diversity of needs, many contracts are for standard commodities, in both goods and services, while many contracts are for custom-designed goods and services. And in many cases, the government's requirements are somewhat unusual. In fact, the U.S. government is not only the biggest and best customer, for many things it is the *only* customer! (Who else would pay you to run a travel bureau or sell prophylactics on the streets?)

Small wonder, then, that many suppliers to the government have tailored their operations to satisfying unique needs. For example, "management consultants" are individuals and companies, usually, who will respond to a wide variety of government solicitations with proposals to design unique products and services. To give you an appreciation of the diversity of goods and services bought frequently and routinely, here are *just a few* of the ones purchased almost daily by many agencies:

Services

Typewriter repair
Automotive repair and service
Advertising
Shoe and clothing repair
Striping parking lots
Construction
Trash removal
Architecture, engineering
Architectural design
Food services, catering
Printing and duplicating
Making rubber stamps
Mailing
Lecturing and training
Maintaining subscription lists
Managing conventions
Drafting and illustrating
Photography (still and aerial)
Movie making
Studies and surveys
Parking cars
Rug cleaning
Administering correspondence
   courses
Title searches
Painting, plumbing, and electrical
   work

Writing, editing, and proofing
Laundry and dry cleaning
Road building
Air-conditioning repair
Moving and hauling
Janitorial work
Electronics maintenance
Making sandwiches for immigrants
Typesetting
Typing
Answering mail and telephones
Computer programming
Hiring consultants
Providing temporary office help
Renting cars, trucks, and buses
Mapping
Photo finishing
Providing subscriptions, books
Bagging groceries
Managing government facilities
Repairing machinery
Research and development
Auditing and accounting
Civil engineering
Medical and dental services
Laboratory services

Goods

Foods, raw and processed
Valves, machinery
Office supplies and equipment

Lumber and mill work
Computers and computer supplies
Construction materials

Goods (continued)

Cameras and photography equipment

Rope, cable, and marine supplies

Clothing and insignias

Aircraft and aircraft parts

Missiles, weapons, and ammunition

Textiles and findings

Paper goods (all kinds)

Bags and wrapping supplies

Lubricants

Waxes

Tractors and agricultural machines

Bearings

Ores and minerals

Metal bars, sheets, and forms

Abrasives

Hardware

Pumps and compressors

Medical and dental supplies

Alarm and signal systems

Electrical supplies

Electronic parts and supplies

Crude materials (metallic and non-metallic)

Fuels

Household furnishings

Hospital supplies and equipment

Paints, solvents, and brushes

Furniture (home and office)

Photo lab equipment

Automotive parts and accessories

Tires and inner tubes

Vehicles (all types)

Shoes, leather goods, and findings

Air conditioners

Dinnerware and flatware

Laboratory and scientific equipment

Books, subscriptions, and maps

Ships and boats

Cranes and hoists

Training aids and devices

Handtools

Measuring tools

Fire-fighting and safety equipment

Pipe, tubing, and hoses

Lighting fixtures and lamps

Communications equipment

Toiletries

Chemicals and chemical products

Nursery supplies

First-aid equipment, supplies

Earth-moving vehicles

Cleaning materials and supplies

That's just the beginning. See Appendix 4, which lists Federal Supply Schedules, for an indication of the range of goods and services bought by the government. The government buys goods and services in over 100 general categories; each category has many subcategories, and each subcategory has many individual kinds of items. And there are "miscellaneous" categories, too!

It's almost literally true that the government buys *everything*. And if the budgets and purchases of the CIA and other federal intelligence services (for example, the National Security Agency and the many military intelligence services) were not secret, we could probably eliminate the word "almost" from the first sentence of this paragraph. (We have learned through recent revelations, for example, that the CIA has paid members of the oldest profession to help carry out CIA missions.)

Among the thousands of contracts announced regularly by the government are many large ones to large companies, but there are also many small ones to small companies and to individuals. Contracts under $25,000, however, are not usually announced because the law does not require it. But here are a few small contracts let to individuals and small companies, just to illustrate that it is not only manufacturers and wholesalers who can and do sell to the U.S. government:

CANDY MILES, *Alexandria, Virginia*
$11,600 to revise the FCC *Broadcast Procedures Manual.*
JAMES E. BONE, *Columbus, Georgia*
$41,187 for "repairs to garages."
MARVIN MARKOWITZ, *Miami, Florida*
$139,680 worth of kitchen cabinets sold to the Air Force.
LEM'S COUNTRY KITCHEN, *Nashville, Tennessee*
$285,900 worth of cakes and pies.
MIKE BASS, *Potomac, Maryland*
$5,000 to write test questions for an OSHA home-study course.
EDDIE'S CONSTRUCTION COMPANY, *Honolulu, Hawaii*
$92,285 to reroof seven buildings.
BYWATER SALES AND SERVICE, *Louisiana*
$31,900 worth of paints, sold to GSA.
PACKTICS, *Baltimore, Maryland*
$40,000 for bumper stickers.
SUGARMAN BROTHERS, *Massachusetts*
$104,915 for paper bags, sold to GSA.
VINCELLI'S TIRE SERVICE, *Redding, California*
$25,000 for tires, sold to GSA.
JAMES KENDRICK, *Washington, D.C.*
$5,200 to revise a draft manual for OSHA.
TATE SPARGUS, *Washington, D.C.*
$63,000 for photo services.
CHUCK GOODMAN, *Reston, Virginia*
$1,400 for writing services for Department of Labor.

Note that these small companies and individuals are scattered around the United States. None of them are large companies; in fact, many who sell merchandise are retail dealers.

Although my own office is near Washington, D.C., I have done work for agencies in Missoula, Montana; Topeka, Kansas; Norman, Oklahoma; Orlando, Florida; and other places. I have had jobs as small as $75, although many have run into thousands of dollars too. (And government agencies have bought my books and reports on how the federal procurement system works!)

Anyone can do business with the government.

2

Understanding the system

It's actually several systems

The basis is competition

The government is a complex structure of 1,800 departments, bureaus, administrations, offices, and other agencies, located throughout approximately 34,000 installations, with about 15,000 procurement offices. The procurement offices are guided by four sets of procurement regulations, in which contracting officials can find the basis for doing almost anything they want to do. However, in the vast welter of policies, procedures, and practices a few unifying features can be found.

The basis for all government procurement is *competition*. That word, as you will learn, has more than one meaning in federal procurement, and there are some exceptions to the rule of competition. The basic intent of all federal procurement practice and law is to utilize competition and procure that which is "in the best interests of the government."

At the basic level there are only two kinds of procurement/purchasing: through price competition, which the contracting community refers to as *formally advertised* procurement, and through technical/quality competition, which is referred to officially as *negotiated* procurement. There are but two basic types of contract: *fixed-price* and *cost-reimbursement.* The complexities arise from the exceptions and from the variants or hybrids of these basic types.

It's a simple matter when the U.S. Army wants to buy a quantity of 105mm howitzers. The Army issues a specification, to advise the bidders as to exactly what they must manufacture and deliver, and accepts bids, to be delivered sealed and then opened publicly at a set time, place, and date. Given no unusual technicalities, the low bidder will win the contract.

It's quite another matter when the Army wants a special howitzer, to be mounted on a vehicle, equipped to fire special ammunition, or with other departures from the usual specifications and standards. In such a case, the Army cannot furnish detailed specifications because the item has yet to be designed. It's an R&D (research and development) job. No one knows with any certainty how long it will take to get the new weapon out of the laboratory and ready to be manufactured, much less what it will cost or just what the final hardware specifications will be. The Army can furnish some performance specifications—what it would like the new weapon to be capable of doing—and perhaps some hardware specifications, such as "not to exceed 3 tons weight." But that's about it.

Such a contract usually calls for a cost-reimbursement arrangement or the famous "cost-plus" contract. The government will reimburse the contractor his costs plus a fixed fee or profit, within some estimated amount. But how does the Army select a contractor for such a job *and* keep the basic procurement a competitive one?

In a procurement of this type, price is only one consideration, and not necessarily the most important one. The government is also concerned that the contractor be fully qualified in all respects to do a satisfactory job: Low price is not going to mean anything if the contractor cannot deliver. Therefore, using the case of the new howitzer as a continuing example, the Army wants to somehow be assured that the contractor to whom it awards a contract meets certain qualifications:

1. Fully understands what the Army wants.
2. Has the necessary know-how, people, and other resources to do the job.
3. Has a track record of experience and demonstrated competence in such work.

This, then, becomes a "negotiated" procurement, which means that the army is not bound to award the contract to the low bidder, but may use its judgment as to which bid is "in the best interests of the government, price and other factors considered." (This is standard language, to explain the conditions under which the successful bidder will be established.)

To establish competition, proposals are requested. Each bidder writes a proposal that demonstrates an understanding of the requirement and describes the plans for carrying out the program and the bidder's qualifications. The government takes all this into account, along with the cost estimates, and decides to whom the contract will be awarded. But that decision is not entirely arbitrary or subjective. An "objective rating scheme" is used to help ensure that each bidder gets fair consideration in what is primarily a *technical* competition and only partially a price competition.

Types of solicitations

Because there are only two basic types of contract, there are only two basic types of solicitation. For formally advertised procurement, in which the bids are sealed and opened publicly, the government issues an information for bid (IFB). The fact that it is an IFB trumpets the announcement that it is formally advertised. When the government wants proposals and a negotiated procurement, it issues an RFP—request for proposal.

In most cases, the same form, Standard Form 33, is used. The first page of this four-page form is shown in Figure 1. As you can see, item 2 on that form ("solicitation no.") has two boxes, where the contracting official who issues it may check off IFB or RFP to advise the reader immediately what type of solicitation and procurement is contemplated. The form also advises the reader when the bid or proposal is due, where it is to be delivered or where the public opening will be held, and has a space for the bidder to sign.

There is a third type of solicitation, which is really not a solicitation at all, technically, but is often used as one: the RFQ, or request for quotation (Standard Form 18). (See Figure 2.) This form is supposed to be used simply to give the government an idea of how much an item or service will cost; the quotation furnished is not binding on either party, as the small print stipulates. However, many agencies use this form to solicit proposals, particularly for small jobs, and it is also often used to decide who is lowest in price and then issue a purchase order. The RFQ itself is not a contractual document, as Form 33 is, and cannot be used as such. Therefore, if the contracting official wishes to issue a contract on the basis of quotations furnished via the

RFQ, he must issue a formal negotiated contract or a purchase order (if the award is less than $10,000).

If you look closely at Form 33 (Figure 1), you'll see that when the bidder signs, he or she has actually signed a contract. Should the contracting official sign in the place provided for his signature, the contract exists immediately.

In practice, this is rarely done. Usually, if the contract is sizable, and sometimes even if it is small, there is a negotiating session in which the contracting official tries to whittle the price down a bit. Even for a small job in which the official is quite satisfied with the price, the contracting officer usually calls and has the bidder verify willingness to contract before the document is signed and copies are sent to the bidder.

The purchase order (see Figure 3) is even simpler. The contractor's signature is not required at all. The purchase order simply authorizes him to proceed with the work at the price stipulated.

Rules of small purchases

Under the Small Purchases Act, as amended most recently, no competitive bids are required for purchases up to $2,500. For purchases above $2,500 but not above $5,000, the government official is supposed to get three bids, but they may be oral bids. For purchases above $5,000 but not above $10,000, the bids should be written, but may be quite informal. In practice, in most agencies, a purchase order for work not exceeding $10,000 may be awarded rapidly and without formality to anyone the agency wishes to award it to.

Note the "in most agencies." There is always the matter of agency policy. While the law *permits* certain practices, it does not mandate them. An agency chief may restrict small purchases to some figure less than $10,000, or be firm about getting written bids on everything, no matter the size, or restrict the use of whatever the law permits in any way he or she sees fit. Therefore, what you can do in one agency you may not be able to do in another!

You may find in one agency that price is highly important, even in a negotiated procurement, while it is of little importance in negotiated procurements in another agency.

You must therefore know what the procurement regulations permit, but you must also know what policies exist in the agencies you want to do business with, and how they choose to interpret certain of the procurement regulations.

Figure 1. Standard Form 33.

SOLICITATION, OFFER AND AWARD

1. CONTRACT (Proc. Inst. Ident.) NO.	2. SOLICITATION NO.	3. CERTIFIED FOR NATIONAL DEFENSE UNDER BDSA REG. 2 AND/OR DMS REG. 1 RATING.		4. PAGE	OF 1

☐ ADVERTISED (IFB)   ☐ NEGOTIATED (RFB)

5. DATE ISSUED	6. REQUISITION/PURCHASE REQUEST NO.

7. ISSUED BY

CODE

8. ADDRESS OFFER TO (If other than block 7)

In advertised procurement "offer" and "offeror" shall be construed to mean "bid" and "bidder".

SOLICITATION

9. Sealed offers in original and _____ copies for furnishing the supplies or services in the Schedule will be received at the place specified in block 8, or if handcarried, in the depository located in _____ until _____ local time _____ .

(Hour)   (Date)

If this is an advertised solicitation, offers will be publicly opened at that time.

CAUTION — LATE OFFERS: See pars. 7 and 8 of Solicitation Instructions and Conditions.

All offers are subject to the following:

1. The Solicitation Instructions and Conditions, SF 33-A, _____ edition which is attached or incorporated herein by reference.

2. The General Provisions, SF 32, _____ edition, which is attached or incorporated herein by reference.

3. The Schedule included herein and/or attached hereto.

4. Such other provisions, representations, certifications, and specifications as are attached or incorporated herein by reference.

(Attachments are listed in schedule.)

FOR INFORMATION CALL (Name & telephone no.) (No collect calls) ▶

SCHEDULE

10. ITEM NO.	11. SUPPLIES/SERVICES	12. QUANTITY	13. UNIT	14. UNIT PRICE	15. AMOUNT

See continuation of schedule on page 4

OFFER *(pages 2 and 3 must also be fully completed by offeror)*

In compliance with the above, the undersigned agrees, if this offer is accepted within _____ calendar days *(60 calendar days unless a different period is inserted by the offeror)* from the date for receipt of offers specified above, to furnish any or all items upon which prices are offered at the price set opposite each item, delivered at the designated point(s), within the time specified in the schedule.

16. DISCOUNT FOR PROMPT PAYMENT *(See par. 9. SF 33-A)*

| % 10 CALENDAR DAYS. | % 20 CALENDAR DAYS. | % 30 CALENDAR DAYS. | % _____ CALENDAR DAYS |

17. OFFEROR

CODE _____   FACILITY CODE _____

NAME AND ADDRESS *(Street, city, county, State and ZIP code)*

☐ Check if remittance address is different from above — enter such address in Schedule

AREA CODE AND TELEPHONE NO. ▶

18. NAME AND TITLE OF PERSON AUTHORIZED TO SIGN OFFER *(Type or print)*

19. SIGNATURE

20. OFFER DATE

AWARD *(To be completed by Government)*

| 21. ACCEPTED AS TO ITEMS NUMBERED | 22. AMOUNT | 23. ACCOUNTING AND APPROPRIATION DATA |

| 24. SUBMIT INVOICES *(4 copies unless otherwise specified)* TO ADDRESS SHOWN IN BLOCK _____ CODE | 25. NEGOTIATED PURSUANT TO ☐ 10 U.S.C. 2304(a) ( ) ☐ 41 U.S.C. 252(c) ( ) |

26. ADMINISTERED BY *(If other than block 7)*   CODE

27. PAYMENT WILL BE MADE BY   CODE

28. NAME OF CONTRACTING OFFICER *(Type or print)*

29. UNITED STATES OF AMERICA

BY _____ *(Signature of contracting officer)*

30. AWARD DATE

Award will be made on this form, or on Standard Form 26, or by other official written notice

33-130

Standard Form 33 Page 1 (REV. 3-77)
Prescribed by GSA, FPR (41 CFR) 1-16.101

Figure 2. Request for quotation.

STANDARD FORM 18, MARCH 1971
GENERAL SERVICES ADMINISTRATION
FED. PROC. REG. (41 CFR) 1-16.201

REQUEST FOR QUOTATION
(THIS IS NOT AN ORDER)

OMB Approval No: 0P9-0188

PAGE	OF
	1

1. REQUEST NO.

2. DATE ISSUED

3. REQUISITION/PURCHASE REQUEST NO.

4. CERTIFIED FOR NATIONAL DEFENSE UNDER DPS REG. 1 AND/OR DMS REG. 1 RATING:

5. ISSUED BY

6. DELIVER BY (Date)

7. DELIVERY

☐ FOB DESTINATION ☐ OTHER (See Schedule)

FOR INFORMATION CALL (Name, area code and tel. no.) (No collect calls)

8. TO NAME AND ADDRESS (Street, city, state, and ZIP code)

9. DESTINATION (Consignee and address including ZIP code)

10. Please furnish quotations to the issuing office on or before close of business (date) _____. Supplies are of domestic origin unless otherwise indicated by quoter. This is a request for information, and quotations furnished are not offers. If you are unable to quote, please so indicate on this form and return it. This request does not commit the government to pay any costs incurred in the preparation or the submission of this quotation, or to procure or contract for supplies or services.

SCHEDULE

11. ITEM NO.	12. SUPPLIES/SERVICES	13. QUANTITY	14. UNIT	15. UNIT PRICE	16. AMOUNT

17. PRICES QUOTED INCLUDE APPLICABLE FEDERAL, STATE, AND LOCAL TAXES.

DISCOUNT FOR PROMPT PAYMENT _____ %10 CALENDAR DAYS; _____ % 20 CALENDAR DAYS; _____ % 30 CALENDAR DAYS; _____ % _____ CALENDAR DAYS.

NOTE: Reverse must also be completed by the quoter.

18. NAME AND ADDRESS OF QUOTER (Street, city, county, State, including ZIP Code)	19. SIGNATURE OF PERSON AUTHORIZED TO SIGN QUOTATION	20. DATE OF QUOTATION
	21. SIGNER'S NAME AND TITLE (Type or print)	22. TELEPHONE NO. (Include area code)

18-112

Figure 3. The purchase order.

STANDARD FORM 147, JUNE 1964—FED. PROC. REG. (41 CFR) 1-3.605

ORDER FOR SUPPLIES OR SERVICES

PAGE 1

OF _ _ _ _

ISSUING OFFICE	General Services Administration 18th & F Streets, NW Washington, DC 20405	MARK ALL PACKAGES AND PAPERS WITH ORDER AND/OR CONTRACT NUMBERS ▼	

| | DATE OF ORDER
2/25/77 | CONTRACT NO. (If any)
03023709(A) | ORDER NO |

ACCOUNTING AND APPROPRIATION DATA

192X75.71.P0010001.901.25.516

REQUISITIONING OFFICE

CO-Office of Value Management - PWV

REQUISITION NO./PURCHASE AUTHORITY

CONTRACTOR (Name and address, including ZIP code)

TO→ Mr. Herman Holtz
1001 Connecticut Avenue, NW
Washington, DC 20036

SHIP TO (Consignee and address, including ZIP code)

Mr. R. Glenn Woodward
GSA-PBS-PWV-Room 6316
18th & F Streets, NW
Washington, DC 20405

VIA

TYPE OF ORDER	PURCHASE ☒	REFERENCE YOUR Written Proposal of 5/22/75 as revised by letter of 6/11/75. PLEASE FURNISH THE FOLLOWING ON THE TERMS SPECIFIED ON BOTH SIDES OF THIS ORDER AND ON THE ATTACHED SHEETS, IF ANY, INCLUDING DELIVERY AS INDICATED. THIS PURCHASE IS NEGOTIATED UNDER AUTHORITY OF FPR Tempo Req. 33 dated 8/6/74
	DELIVERY ☐	EXCEPT FOR THE BILLING INSTRUCTIONS ON THE REVERSE, THIS DELIVERY ORDER IS SUBJECT TO INSTRUCTIONS CONTAINED ON THIS SIDE ONLY OF THIS FORM AND IS ISSUED SUBJECT TO THE TERMS AND CONDITIONS OF THE ABOVE-NUMBERED CONTRACT.

F O B POINT	GOVERNMENT B/L. NO.	DELIVERY TO F O B POINT ON OR BEFORE	DISCOUNT TERMS

SCHEDULE

ITEM NO.	SUPPLIES OR SERVICES	QUANTITY ORDERED	UNIT	UNIT PRICE	AMOUNT	QUANTITY ACCEPTED
	Amendment No. 1 Delete all present wording and replace as follows:					
1.	Develop and produce a 15-minute storyboard for audiovisual presentation of "Overview of Value Management." Revise, per Government review comments, and deliver final draft version as deliverable end-item.				$1,875.00	
2.	Prepare a brochure version of storyboard, including artwork, through one revision, per Government review and comments. Deliver final version in typed camera-ready copy, with all illustrations also camera-ready. No change in costs is requested.				625.00	—
	Items required to be delivered by May 13/977. PW _____					

SIZE CLASSIFICATION   (Check one)   [X] SMALL BUSINESS   [ ] OTHER THAN SMALL BUSINESS

SEE BILLING INSTRUCTIONS ON REVERSE

SHIPPING POINT	GROSS SHIPPING WEIGHT	INVOICE NO.

TOTAL FROM CONTINUATION PAGES

GRAND TOTAL $2,500.00

MAIL INVOICES TO*

Office of Finance, BCFF, 19th & F Sts., NW
Washington, DC 20405

*Include ZIP code

UNITED STATES OF AMERICA

BY _____ (Signature)

NAME (Typed) A. IUDICELLO

TITLE CONTRACTING/ORDERING OFFICER

(See reverse for rejections)

STANDARD FORM 147, JUNE 1964

147-105

Where the Regulations Came From

Strange as it may seem, the United States government, in all its majesty, had no organized set of procurement regulations until World War II. In fact, except for earlier wars, the United States government hadn't been much of a customer and didn't perceive a need for an elaborate set of procurement regulations.

World War II changed that. The government was forced to buy on a scale never seen before. This came on the heels of a number of years during which the Great Bureaucracy had grown sensibly, to a far larger size than ever before, as the President and the solons on Capitol Hill combatted depression and unemployment with federal bureaus. Obviously, some sort of control over all this spending had to be established, so the ASPR (Armed Services Procurement Regulations) was created. And in time, Son of ASPR was born: the Federal Procurement Regulations (FPR), patterned closely on the ASPR, but tailored to civilian-agency procurement. A few years later, the National Aeronautics and Space Administration mushroomed from a small bureau into a multibillion-dollar operation that marshaled its administrative forces and modified ASPR into NASPR—NASA Procurement Regulations. In addition, the Postal Service, which had been spending $10 billion a year even before inflation became serious, had and has its own procurement regulations.

Today there is, within the Office of Management and Budget (OMB), an OFPP or Office of Federal Procurement Policy. That entity's Federal Acquisition Regulations (FAR) project has been busily combining ASPR, FPR, and DAR (Defense Acquisition Regulations) and making them a uniform set to be known as FAR. Despite all the labors of the FAR project team, the changes will not be of great substance, because the various sets of regulations do not have a great deal of substantive difference among them. Some forms are different—where military organizations use Form DD 633 for estimating costs, civilian agencies use Form 59 or 60 (60 most often), which is quite similar to the 633. The chief difference among them is that the military operations have many provisions in ASPR for which there is no parallel application or need in FPR.

The alphabet soup gets thicker

Until now, we've kept things on a rather simple level: There are two basic kinds of procurement, formally advertised and negotiated; two types of solicitation, information for bid (IFB) and request for proposal (RFP); and two types of contract, fixed-price and cost-reimbursement. The exception is the small purchase, for which purchase orders are issued. There may or may not be a solicitation formally announced for small purchases, but they may be arranged informally and spontaneously between buyer and seller.

But there are variants, hybrids, and combinations which defy definition in the above terms. An RFP may result in either a fixed-price or a cost-reimbursement contract. Both fixed-price and cost-reimbursement contracts have several versions or mutated offspring.

The term "cost-reimbursement," for example, includes all of these:

CPFF (cost plus fixed fee)
CPAF (cost plus award fee)
CPFF/AF (cost plus fixed fee and award fee)
BOA (basic ordering agreement)
T&M (time and material)

Even these may have variants such as below-the-line provisions (where certain cost items are billed at actual cost, with no profit) or provisions for a labor-hour contract (which is suspiciously close to a T&M). Fixed-price contracts may be for definite fixed quantity or for indefinite quantity—in which case it is unit priced! There is also the two-step procurement, which is a hybrid of the negotiated and formally advertised procedures.

Now that your head is reeling, let's back up and look at these one at a time.

Cost Plus Fixed Fee

I once won and operated a contract to support the NASA/Goddard Space Flight Center with technical publications and some related engineering services. Our contract was a CPFF/AF. The reason for this was that NASA did not know just how much work we would be asked to do through the three years of the contract. In fact, as requirements arose, we were asked in to estimate each job and quote a price, based on our contract. That made our contract also a BOA or T&M (which are really the same thing, in this case, and the contract could have been called a labor-hour or a task-type or even a call contract). All this will soon become much clearer, I promise you.

Since NASA could not predict just how much work we would be

asked to do (although they could and did provide a fair estimate), we were required, in bidding, to provide a billing rate (hourly) for each category of labor called for—writers, editors, engineers, illustrators, draftsmen, typists, and so on. Once the contract was in force, we would use these rates in estimating each job—for example, so many hours of writing, so many of editing, and so on.

The contract was a basic ordering agreement that established the conditions under which we would bid each task and since the primary cost was labor, with supplies a minor item, it was principally a time-and-material or labor-hour contract.

When I say we "bid," I do not mean that we bid against other contractors: We had the contract, and only we could bid. But if the customer did not agree with our estimate, we had to negotiate that task. So we did not have a license to steal.

We had a combination fixed-fee and award-fee arrangement. Our fixed fee was 1 percent of the total costs we had originally estimated the whole contract at (which was, in this case, about $1.6 million). No matter what happened to costs—whether the contract ultimately proved to cost more than $1.6 million or less than that—we would get, not 1 percent of the ultimate cost, but 1 percent of $1.6 million. (That could change, under certain circumstances, but usually does not in cost-plus contracts.)

One percent is rather small for a fixed fee. More usual is 6−9 percent. However, NASA is fond of "incentive" contracts, and wanted a small fixed fee and a larger award fee. Each quarter, a NASA board would sit and judge the amount of award fee we had earned by our diligence, dependability, cost-reduction suggestions, and so on.

In billing each task, we billed our actual costs. If we had a ceiling rate of $8.00 an hour for a senior writer, we could not bill more than that. If we paid the writer who worked on that task less than $8.00, we billed less—we billed what we actually paid the writer, plus overhead.

Variants

Not everyone contracts cost-plus jobs in that exact manner. In some cases, an *average* hourly rate is established for each labor category, and that is what is billed, regardless of which individual worked on the job or what his actual salary was. In still another variation, once the government accepts the contractor's estimate of the costs of a given task, that becomes his *fixed price* for that task, and that is what he bills, regardless of what it actually costs him.

These are the major variants, although different agencies use different terms to characterize such a contract, and each may add their own small flourishes.

Indefinite Quantity

Similar considerations may apply to contracts for goods. One contract may be for a given amount of something or other, at a fixed price. Another may state "indefinite quantity" and ask for unit prices, stipulating only that the total order will be not less than _____ or more than _____. Again, orders will be issued throughout the year if it is a term contract rather than a one-shot procurement, and each billed at the established rates.

Where such a contract is for more than one year, whether for services or supplies, the bidder is asked to estimate his price increases, recognizing that costs are almost inevitably going to go up. And usually, in contracts for more than one year, the government has options each year, so that it may drop an unsatisfactory contractor should it choose to do so. (There is a strong tendency to keep the contractor, however: Bureaucrats are usually reluctant to admit that they made a bad choice originally.)

Annual Supply Contracts

What we have discussed so far are primarily those single contracts for custom goods or services and for needs of the moment. But there are thousands of standard commodities—what the government refers to as "common use" items, which most, or at least many, agencies use regularly: cleaning compounds, office supplies, furniture, typewriters, calculators, pipe, cameras, clothing, and many other items. There is a variant of this too: There are many items which many agencies use frequently, but not regularly or predictably. This makes for two different situations:

In the first situation, where most agencies will want typewriters, stamp pads, and ball-point pens on a predictable, regular basis, the government stocks these items and disburses them as necessary from distribution points. (The Federal Supply Service, for example, maintains 10 warehouses and 75 stores, stocks nearly 5 million items, and spends about $3 billion annually.)

But there is the second case, in which many agencies will want photographic supplies, let's say, or dry cleaning services. The need may not be predictable and the requirement may vary widely from year to year. Therefore, the Federal Supply Service may not want to actually stock the item. Yet the item must be readily available to any agency which has a sudden need. In this case, the item may be placed on one of the 300 Federal Supply Schedules or 200 similar purchasing arrangements, to be supplied as needed, at prices agreed upon for the year.

When, as in the case of such services as laundry and dry cleaning, it is not possible to supply the services except on a local basis, the government prefers to enter into annual contracts to ensure a dependable service at negotiated prices. Hence, these too are usually procured as annual supply agreements.

A Few Examples

Each military base must necessarily do some local buying—of milk, bakery products, cleaning services, laundry services, and other such supplies and services. Many federal installations use cleaning rags, and these are generally contracted locally on an annual basis. Moving and hauling, crating household goods, carpets, draperies, valves, and literally thousands of other items are on regular annual supply schedules. However, this does not prevent agencies from buying such items and services independently, if they choose, with a few exceptions.

Here, again, the matter of agency policy is paramount. There are schedules for graphic arts services in many areas of the country, including Washington, D.C. When an item or service is on a schedule, and a contractor for the item is listed as one of the suppliers on that schedule, he has agreed to a scale of prices for the year. (The schedules are agreements for one year; they are, in fact, basic ordering agreements with each listed supplier.) Any federal agency (and many local governments) may order from that supplier by writing a purchase order. (Here, the $10,000 limitation does not apply, but is governed by the terms of the schedule, which may be more or less than $10,000.) Some contracting officers pooh-pooh the schedules, which are supposed to be more convenient for them. They believe that they can write their own purchase order as easily as they can write one under the schedule, and can see no extra convenience in using the schedule. Other contracting officers have a policy of buying only from suppliers listed on the schedule, where there exists a schedule for the item or service in question.

As a small, independent government contractor, I have operated under both situations: some contracting officers did not care if I was on the schedule or not, and others would not give me the contract unless I were on the schedule.

Some ground rules and case histories

Ground rules for formally advertised procurements are much more stringent and severe than they are for negotiated procurements. In the case of formally advertised procurements, there are extremely few exceptions to the rule of award to the low bidder, for that's the entire objective of the procedure—to find the lowest bidder. But because cost is only one of several considerations in negotiated procurements, the law allows the agency a great deal of latitude in selecting a winner.

For example, a formally advertised bid must be opened at the exact time and place advertised, unless formally changed by a modification to the solicitation. A bidder may withdraw and/or modify his bid any time up to the time of opening, but not one minute later. A contracting official will usually allow you to withdraw your bid after that time, but the law does not require him to: He *can* hold you firmly to that bid. For that reason, such solicitations are usually accompanied by a warning sheet urging you to check and double-check your figures, to be sure to sign your bid, and so on.

Your bid will be rejected and disqualified if you have failed to sign it properly. This happened to one of my own bids. I was the low bidder, but my secretary had typed the bid and mailed it without bringing it to me to sign. I had not given it another thought until the contracting official called me with a tremor in his voice to advise me that he had to most regretfully reject the low bid.

There are a few other causes for rejecting bids: failure to respond and provide the information requested; failure to tell the truth in your representations; being on a blacklist. Wrongdoing as a contractor may put you on such a blacklist, as a punishment, either permanently or, as in most cases, for some defined length of time.

On the other hand, being the low bidder with all your paperwork in order assures you of the contract. If you are so low that the customer believes you have made a mistake and can't possibly deliver at the price quoted, he may so caution you and offer you the opportunity to withdraw your bid voluntarily. But should you insist on having the contract, he cannot compel you to withdraw your bid nor withhold the contract from you.

Theoretically, he can disqualify your bid on the grounds that you do not demonstrate technical capability to deliver. In practice, that is so difficult to prove that a contracting official will rarely try to proceed with that. Even if he should proceed, you may have other recourse, especially if yours is a small business. (We'll take this matter up again, in Chapter 3.)

In some cases, bidders make mistakes in their arithmetic, and there are some ground rules for this, too. For example, let us suppose that your price quotation looks something like this:

Item	Price per Unit	Number of Units Required	Total Price
No. 2 pencils	$0.02	2,750	$550.00

The mistake is obvious: .02 × 2,750 = 55, *not* 550. What will prevail here will be the unit price quoted: $0.02, or 2¢ per unit. The contracting official will correct the extension to $55.00, but neither he nor you can change the unit price. If you meant to quote $0.20, rather than $0.02, that is unfortunate. You are stuck with $0.02 for this bid. If the mistake is a disastrous one, you may be allowed to withdraw the bid— and you may not!

If it is your practice to attend bid openings and record figures quoted, be watchful for possible errors in other people's bids, for the same things apply to all bids. In one case, I found myself the low bidder, as I expected to be, down to the opening of the last bid in the stack. To my dismay, that bid was a bit lower than mine. But in checking the figures, I discovered that the bidder had made a mistake in his extensions, and I was, in fact, the low bidder. I pointed this out to the contracting official, but it wasn't necessary. He routinely audits all the figures in the bids before deciding who is the low bidder, for this very reason.

In Chapters 5 and 6 we will discuss bids in somewhat greater detail and will explore the cost strategies you may use, so we'll talk about pricing your bid again.

Negotiated procurements have entirely different and less stringent rules by the very nature of the procedure. While you cannot arbitrarily elect to change your proposal after the opening date and time, the contracting official is empowered to convey such a right to you, if he deems such action to be "in the best interests of the government." And he can do so by inviting you to submit additional or changed information, or he can do it during the course of actual negotiations. If you have failed to provide something or to sign something, he has the power to reject and disqualify your proposal as "non-responsive," but he is not required to do so. He can permit you to make necessary changes, again if he thinks such is "in the best interests of the govern-ment."

This does not mean that there are no rules, or that he may arbi-trarily do anything he likes; you still have certain rights as a bidder (or "proposer," as requests for proposal solicitations often refer to bid-ders). Here are the basic ground rules:

1. The proposal must be submitted, in a sealed condition, before the time and date noted, at or to the place indicated.
2. Technical proposals must not reveal costs. Costs are in a separate docu-ment, which may be in the same package, but must be separately bound. Some solicitations call for costs to be sealed in their own separate envelope within the package. Almost all RFP solicitations call specifically for *two* proposals: a technical proposal and a cost proposal.
3. Proposals must be individually evaluated by prescribed criteria, with at least some revelation or indication of those criteria made known to the bidders.
4. Those reviewing and evaluating technical propoposals must not see or know the costs before making their evaluation, but must evaluate the proposal on technical merit alone.
5. The proposals are delivered to the contracting or procurement office. The contracting official will separate technical proposals from cost pro-posals and deliver technical proposals to the evaluation team (often called the "source selection board" or panel).
6. Bidders who do not win have the right to a debriefing, which consists of a review of their proposals, after the award has been made, and an ex-planation of where and how their proposals fell short or were judged less meritorious than the one that won.
7. Bidders who do not win have a right to appeal, called a protest, which can be made directly to the contracting official or to the General Ac-counting Office. Such protests are often made by losers who believe that the evaluation and decision were unfair to them.

These are the basic rules and the safeguards built into the system. When the system fails to deliver what it is designed to deliver, or when a bidder receives unfair treatment or wins through influence and par-tiality, the true fault generally lies in the failure of bidders to pursue the prescribed remedies. The machinery is there to keep the system com-pletely honest and above suspicion. But it is foolish to expect the sys-tem to police itself, as foolish as assigning a cat to guard a canary. Only the bidders themselves can police the system properly.

There are a number of other considerations, many of which require detailed explanations, which will be presented a little later on. However, before leaving this chapter, here's a little tale to illustrate the truth of the preceding paragraph.

Several years ago, NASA held a proposal contest for design and construction of its "ATS" satellite, a $65 million project. The chief contestants, it turned out eventually, were General Electric and Fairchild.

The award was made to GE, which had done quite a bit of work for NASA. Fairchild immediately launched its own investigation, and discovered that GE had delivered its proposal *after the deadline*, and *NASA had accepted it after the deadline.* This was a clear violation of the procedures prescribed. (NASA could have granted an extension of time, but would have had to offer that extension to everyone.)

I happened to bear witness to the fact that Fairchild had delivered on time (barely) because I had personally bound up its proposal (I had been hired to provide certain assistance) and had sent it out to NASA by special messenger. It was delivered with only minutes to spare.

Fairchild proved its case in protesting the award. The GE contract was voided, and a contract was awarded Fairchild instead. But without Fairchild's vigilance and protest, an illegal award would have been perpetuated.

3

Get help
from the government
to sell to the government

They call it "socioeconomics"

Why the U.S. government wants to help you sell to it

There are two reasons for the government's interest in helping you sell your goods and services to the federal agencies:

1. The intent of all procurement policy (in theory, at least) is to maximize competition, which is presumed to result in getting lower bids and better offers from suppliers and contractors.
2. There are numerous laws on the books which require federal agencies to provide ample business opportunity (and, frequently, preferential treatment) for small business generally, for minority- and women-owned businesses especially, and for other special classes and cases, such as those handicapped physically and those located in economically depressed areas, where federal contracts would presumably create a few jobs.

A third reason, never openly admitted, is the knowledge that many who ought to be offering their goods and services to the government are hampered in doing so, or even prevented from doing so, by the lack of information on how to proceed to learn about business opportunities.

There is also the consideration that ours is supposed to be a democratic government and the public is *entitled* to know all about the what, where, when, why, and how of government procurement. It's public information by its very nature.

Every federal agency has responsibilities in this respect. Some have comprehensive, well-organized programs of aid, some exist solely to provide such aid, and others give little more than lip service to their obligations to aid businesses in winning government sales. First, let us consider some of the things all federal agencies are supposed to do.

Small business setasides

All agencies are supposed to identify those purchases or procurements they plan to make which could be satisfied amply by small businesses. That is, the agency is supposed to determine whether there is an ample number of small businesses that could respond to a given solicitation, to assure the agency that satisfactory bids or proposals would result and that there would be ample competition.

For example, suppose the Air Force wants to design an entirely new missile system. It is fairly obvious that no small business can handle such a program. The companies that could and would bid for such a contract would be companies such as Fairchild, General Dynamics, Boeing, North American, Lockheed, GE, McDonnell-Douglas, and other major aerospace/defense firms.

On the other hand, suppose the requirement is to prepare a set of technical manuals or drawings. There are a large number of small firms that do such work, and there is no doubt that a number of them would respond to an invitation to bid or write proposals for such a contract. Under the law, the agency should have determined this and have "set aside" the procurement, which means that the procurement is restricted to small business firms; large firms are barred from bidding.

What Is a Small Business?

The Small Business Administration sets the standards by which an agency can determine how small a business must be to qualify as a "small business." They call this, in SBA parlance, a *size standard.*

Size standards are not the same in all industries, but must be established for each one. In many cases, there are several size standards, and the contracting officials must identify the size standard that applies in each case, if the procurement is to be set aside for small business. In the case of technical writing and related services, there are three such size standards:

1. Not more than $2 million per year in sales, averaged over the last three years.
2. Not more than $5 million per year in sales, averaged over the last three years.
3. Not more than 500 employees.

In general, the law says that a firm must be "not dominant" in its industry to qualify as a small business, and the size standards presumably define the yardstick for determining whether a business is dominant in its industry. That is, "size" is never absolute, but is relative to the typical firms in the industry, and is established in terms of the industry.

In the refining industry, to illustrate that last statement, size is determined by number-of-barrels-per-day capacity of the firm.

The responsibility for setting such procurements aside, for restricting the bidding to firms qualifying as small businesses under the SBA standards, belongs to the contracting official. Here again, internal policy has a decided effect on how well the program works in a given agency. In some cases, a firm policy will dictate that all procurements of a given type (technical writing and drafting, in certain agencies) are automatically set aside.

Such is the policy in the contracting office at Fort Belvoir, where the Army Corps of Engineers conduct a great deal of research and development. A few years ago (during the Viet Nam conflict) the Night Vision Laboratory wanted to procure certain engineering support services. The contracting office's policy dictated that the procurement be set aside, but the "program" managers did not believe that the work could be handled satisfactorily by a small business. To solve their dilemma, they arranged to have the procurement handled through the Army Material Command, which is at another site and did not have a policy preventing the program managers from opening the solicitation to all comers. The contract was awarded to a firm which did not qualify as a small business.

Small business subcontracts

Every large contract results in a number of subcontracts. When the U.S. Air Force awards that large, prime contract to General Dynamics or GE, the awardee invariably must look to many suppliers and subcontractors for help; no one does *everything*. Moreover, if the firm is already quite busy, it often does not have the staff or physical capacity to do the whole job itself. When RCA was awarded over $1 billion for the BMEWS (Ballistic Missile Early Warning System) project, which was the largest single contract ever awarded up to that time, RCA did approximately one-third of the work in-house, and awarded more than 300 subcontracts to handle the remaining two-thirds.

Prime contractors are constantly urged, encouraged, and pressed to award at least some subcontracts to small businesses, minority enterprises, women-owned enterprises, and so on. And lately, legislation has mandated some of this activity. The Department of Defense, because it is such a large purchaser, has an organized system to follow up on these goals, with many employees functioning both in the department and in major defense plants to implement such policies and regulations.

The pressure is increasing today. When Congress had the Economic Development Administration of the Department of Commerce disburse $6 billion in public works grants to state and local governments (to stimulate employment in construction industries) grantees were advised that at least 10 percent of the funds must be used to subcontract with minority-owned enterprises. In addition, NASA decrees that all bids for large NASA projects must be accompanied by at least a general plan for subcontracting with minorities, and a detailed plan must be submitted and approved before a contract will be finally let.

Many of the larger agencies have their own special publications to advise business people on their general needs, procedures, and special arrangements, if any, for winning some of their business. And many agencies have a special program for contracting with minorities, and have issued publications to explain their programs. The Treasury and Interior Departments are two such agencies.

All agencies are supposed to have small business representatives or other people whose principal duties are to aid small business people in finding their way around the agency and learning of business opportunities within the agency. But there are also agencies whose sole purpose is to provide assistance of various kinds to small businesses, minority-owned businesses, and others the law says are entitled to special aid and preference of some kind in winning government contracts. Perhaps the best known of these, but not the only one, is the Small Business Administration (SBA).

The Small Business Administration

The Small Business Administration was created by the Small Business Act of 1953, and derives its authority from that and other statutes. It is not a large agency in terms of total number of employees or total budget, yet it maintains well over 80 regional and district offices throughout the United States.

It was originally created to further the interests of small business generally, through a variety of programs offering publications, training, counseling, and aid in winning government contracts, in addition to several plans for assisting businesses in getting financial aid. Many of its publications and services are entirely free; others are made available at a small charge.

In recent years, SBA programs have been widened to include aid to minority-owned enterprises, under its "8(a)" program. The term derives from clause 8(a) of the Small Business Act, which is interpreted to provide the authority for the activities designated as part of that program. In that program a firm may be certified as an 8(a) firm and thereby be entitled to be awarded federal contracts without the usual competition. Briefly, the program works as follows.

A federal agency identifies an anticipated procurement as one for which there are minority-owned firms qualified to do the work (or asks SBA to help it make such a determination). Having thus decided, the agency negotiates a contract for the work with SBA (which thus becomes the prime contractor). SBA then negotiates a *sub*contract with a chosen 8(a) firm, without competition. Since the 8(a) firm cannot compete successfully with established firms (at least, theoretically), SBA may award the *sub*contract for a larger price than it negotiated for the *prime* contract. SBA has money (Business Development Funds) which it may use to make up the difference.

That's how the system is supposed to work. In practice, it does not always happen that way. For one thing, most agencies do not exercise a great deal of initiative in studying procurement needs and identifying those which may be set aside for 8(a) awards. Many of the 8(a) awards result from aggressive marketing efforts on the part of the 8(a) firms and the SBA.

Further, while the SBA in theory may arbitrarily decide what 8(a) firm gets the subcontract, in practice the awarding agency makes a "recommendation" to SBA, after reviewing several 8(a) firms and their capabilities. The awarding agencies often request technical proposals from the 8(a) firms (but not cost proposals; 8(a) firms must not discuss costs with anyone but SBA). SBA almost always accepts the agency's "recommendation," although this is the reverse of how the system is supposed to operate.

There are approximately 1,565 8(a) firms certified in the United

States at the time of this writing. More than 60 percent of them are black-owned firms, others are owned by Hispanics, American Indians, and Orientals, although 8(a) certification is not confined to these ethnic minorities alone. In fact, no one automatically qualifies by virtue of belonging to an ethnic minority. The law requires that each case be judged on its individual merits—a black or Hispanic citizen who is not "culturally and socially disadvantaged" should not qualify, under the law. However, many do "qualify," despite being relatively prosperous, well educated, and so on. However, the law was designed for blacks, American Indians, Aleuts, Eskimos, Spanish-speaking Americans, and Orientals, and they are the chief beneficiaries of the law. But to illustrate the law in practice, there is the case of the woman who owned an R&D firm in Bethesda, Maryland. She is white, and her company had been certified as an 8(a) firm. However, SBA later decided that she did not belong to a minority which was "socially and culturally disadvantaged," and revoked the 8(a) certification. She sued, arguing that as a woman, white or not, she was in a field historically dominated by males and therefore she *was* a minority in that field, and suitably disadvantaged. Her 8(a) certification was restored.

Today it has become increasingly difficult to win 8(a) certification, especially if the applicant is in one of the fields already crowded with 8(a) firms. These tend to be service fields, because service fields usually require far less capital investment than do manufacturing or wholesaling/retailing. And among the more popular service fields, for those seeking to establish a business base with government contracts, are computer data processing and that broad sweep of activities which are marketed as "management consulting" and "management support." The attitude of SBA recently has been that it will not certify a new firm as 8(a) unless the firm is in a field for which the SBA perceives distinct contracting opportunity, the field is relatively uncrowded, and/or the firm can show evidence that it has federal contracts lined up and merely needs certification to get going. On the other hand, SBA vows that if a minority-owned firm does do its marketing and finds an agency willing to issue an 8(a) contract to the firm, SBA will process the 8(a) certifications swiftly and aid the firm in taking advantage of the offer of a contract.

The Newest SBA 8(a) Program

Under legislation enacted by the 95th Congress (Public Law 95–507), SBA has been given some heavier weaponry in its battle to aid minority firms in winning government contracts. Under the new law, SBA is to be given authority to arbitrarily select projects for 8(a) contracting. The U.S. Army has been designated by the President as the first agency to be involved in this program, to test out the new law. SBA will review the Army's planned procurements and select those which SBA believes ought to be 8(a) contracts. Should the Army disagree, an appeals and decision-making process is prescribed by the law.

New legislation has also broadened SBA's programs for supporting women in business, an objective which has received little but oratory as a program until now.

SBA's "PASS" Program

Federal agencies have long complained that they are hampered in their efforts to make awards to small businesses or to set aside programs for small businesses by their own difficulties in determining whether small business capability exists for procurements they plan. To combat that problem, SBA contracted for the development of the Procurement Automated Source System (PASS).

This is a computerized file of small businesses, suitably coded and updated each year, with access terminals in 11 federal agencies, including SBA. The purpose of the system is to provide a library of small businesses, so that any agency may swiftly search the files and determine what small business capability exists. SBA has solicited all small businesses to apply for listing, and will gladly send application forms to any who ask.

Other SBA Programs

SBA has a variety of other assistance programs for small business, including many free publications, other publications available at a nominal cost, seminars, counseling, financial support (loans and loan guarantees), and advocacy.

The latter has some interesting facets. In Chapter 2, I pointed out that in theory, at least, a contracting official may disqualify your bid on the grounds that you do not exhibit the technical capability to deliver what is called for. If this happens, you may take your case to the SBA. SBA administrators will take action to hold up award of the contract while they check out your capability. If they are satisfied that you can handle the job (remember they are working in your behalf) they can issue you a "Certificate of Competency," which legally cancels the contracting official's action of disqualifying you.

In a counseling program, SBA utilizes the services of retired executives, and some who are not yet retired, who volunteer their time to aid small business people with advice and guidance. That program is called SCORE (Service Corps of Retired Executives).

SBA also provides some training programs, including seminars, through an SBA training division. At the time of this writing, SBA is planning to expand its training functions. (For example, see *Management Assistance*, SBA Office of Public Information.)

Department of Commerce

The U.S. Department of Commerce has a number of divisions, as do most agencies. However, since the Department of Commerce is concerned entirely with American business and industry, many of their activities are relevant to this book and its objectives.

Economic Development Administration (EDA)

The overall mission of EDA is to create new jobs and to save jobs which are threatened, and it focuses especially on geographic areas where unemployment is high; that is, above the national average. Its programs are carried out through grants, loans, and loan guarantees.

For example, Congress voted in two bills in 1977 to provide a total of $6 billion in grants to state and local governments (local governments, primarily) for local public works. The program was assigned to EDA for administration, and EDA awarded grants for approximately 8,000 local public works projects, under which were built roads, schools, water systems, industrial parks, libraries, fire stations, airports, and other such projects. The main objective was to stimulate employment in the various construction trades, which were suffering relatively high unemployment. However, the projects also created many other jobs.

Throughout the year, EDA continually awards grants, under other legislation, to stimulate economies in various communities and so create jobs. Ordinarily, grants are made to nonprofit organizations, usually local governments, but sometimes to institutions of learning, for such projects as vocational training, counseling small businesses, studying local economic problems to seek solutions, and so on.

Loans and loan guarantees are generally resorted to when privately owned enterprises require assistance. Again, the rationale is to create new jobs or save threatened ones. The applicant for such assistance must demonstrate that jobs will be created or saved by the financial assistance. In a recent program, EDA furnished approximately $20 million to about 20 small organizations in economically depressed areas to establish revolving funds for small business loans. Small businesses can thereby borrow money at relatively low interest rates. The program is experimental and will probably be expanded if it's successful.

A business suffering "foreign import damage" (losing business because of imported goods) may get EDA financial assistance. First, the Labor Department must certify that the company is suffering such damage. However, it is not the company which applies for such certification, but the employees whose jobs are threatened, usually through their unions. Once the certification is granted by Labor, the employer may take the application and the plan for using the money to EDA.

EDA has a large number of programs, each with its own enabling legislation. Among them are the following:

EDA Planning Grants for Economic Development
EDA Grants for Public Works and Development Facilities
Business Development Assistance
Technical Assistance
Economic Development Districts
Trade Adjustment Assistance
The Indian Industrial Development Program

Office of Minority Business Enterprise (OMBE)

As its name suggests, OMBE is a special Office in Commerce, devoted solely to aiding minorities start and succeed in business. Next to SBA, it is the most comprehensive and active program of its kind, although it has been heavily criticized in Congress for an alleged lack of effectiveness. Funded at approximately $50 million a year, OMBE devotes virtually its entire budget to training and technical assistance efforts. Translated into action, this means that OMBE supports approximately 300 organizations throughout the United States, which have agreed to furnish certain assistance functions to minority entrepreneurs. The organizations funded fall into 12 categories:

Business Development Centers
Business Management Development (organizations)
Business Resource Centers
City OMBEs
Construction Contractor Assistance Centers
Contracted Support Services
Experiment and Demonstration (projects)
Local Business Development Organizations
Minority Business and Trade Associations

National Business Development Organizations
Private Resource Programs
State OMBEs

Many of these organizations receive all their funds from the federal (Commerce Department) OMBE, while others are also supported by SBA, Labor Department, and other funding organizations, both public and private.

The programs vary widely. Some provide direct technical, training, and counseling assistance to the individual entrepreneur, while others pursue larger companies to provide business opportunities for minority firms. Some of the programs are organized solely to apply for OMBE and SBA funding and carry out the programs contracted for, while others are existing organizations which have expanded their activities to handle OMBE and SBA assistance programs, for example, trade associations, local chambers of commerce, and so on.

As a whole, OMBE officials take most pride in their track record in aiding minority enterprises in getting funding (bank loans) and they appear to measure their success primarily by this yardstick.

Overall, OMBE activities are administered by six regional and 12 field offices in the United States. Unlike the SBA program, minority enterpreneurs do not have to be certified in any way to participate in and be eligible for OMBE assistance, but merely need to be qualified as owners, with at least 51 percent, of a business enterprise. And minorities are defined as including, "but not exclusively, blacks, Puerto Ricans, Spanish-speaking Americans, American Indians, Eskimos, and Aleuts." What "not exclusively" refers to is not made clear, but Orientals are generally included in minority programs and, presumably, other minorities could qualify without undue difficulty.

Commerce also offers assistance in importing and exporting, much of it entirely free of charge, some at a special low cost. American business people may, for example, participate in trade shows held by the Department of Commerce in other countries. Commerce also provides a great deal of information about foreign buyers' needs, and functions in several ways to bring American suppliers and foreign buyers together. For example, Commerce prints notices almost daily in the *Commerce Business Daily* (explained in Chapter 4). A few examples are given in Figure 4.

The U.S. State Department operates AID (the Agency for International Development) under which it provides aid of many kinds to other nations, especially to the Third World or developing nations. The

Department of Commerce also publicizes these, when they provide opportunities to American business, in its *Commerce Business Daily*. Figure 5(a) is an example of one such notice.

Also published in the *Commerce Business Daily*, as a service to American business and individuals (although private individuals would rarely see the *Commerce Business Daily*), are notices of government surplus property for sale. For an example, see Figure 5(b).

The government-owned surplus property for sale varies widely, in both types of property and condition. Some of the property is quite old and worn, having only salvage value in many cases. Some of it is quite serviceable. And some of it is brand-new, still in its original packing.

The property may be raw materials, timber, real estate, equipment, furniture, or almost anything else, including strategic materials no longer needed. In most cases, surplus property is disposed of by the Defense Department or the General Services Administration. (Instructions for getting on mailing lists to bid for surplus are supplied in Appendix 6.)

Usually, such bids are sealed, and where it is appropriate, notice is given of where and when the property offered may be inspected.

Other types of aid

There are other ways in which the U.S. government helps business generally, especially in winning federal contracts. One of these is a provision which authorizes government agencies to lend government-owned property to contractors.

It is expected, of course, that the loan of government-owned property to a contractor will result in some lowering of the contractor's price (although it does not appear always to have that result). In the free-swinging days of huge cost-plus contracts for military goods, it was the practice of military agencies to buy property especially for the purpose of then lending it to contractors! However, it is not uncommon to furnish a facility with government-owned desks, typewriters, and so on, especially for cost-plus contracts.

Another variation of this, again usually for cost-plus contracts, is to authorize the contractor to buy from GSA stores, which usually means a somewhat lower price for supplies. In some cases, the saving is considerable. In one case which comes to memory, toner for duplicating machines that cost $40 on the open market was available from GSA for $8.

Figure 4. Samples of foreign trade opportunities,

FOREIGN TRADE OPPORTUNITIES
DEPARTMENT OF COMMERCE

Many trade opportunities received from U.S. Embassies are not included in the Commerce Business Daily. For information on how you can receive all such Trade Opportunities, contact your local U.S. Department of Commerce District Office, or the Trade Opportunites Program, Room 2014, U.S. Department of Commerce, Washington, D.C. 20230. (202) 377-2091.

The Commodity codes shown are based on the Standard Industrial Classification Manual, 1972, listing.

U.S. firms should be aware that the listing in "Commerce Business Daily" of opportunities to trade in specific commodities and technical data does not necessarily imply approval of their export by the Department of Commerce pursuant to the Department's Export Administration Regulations. Applicable export licensing regulations must be followed.

Every effort is made to include only firms or individuals with good reputations. However, the Department cannot be responsible for any trade relations.

DIRECT SALES

Foreign private firms and government agencies are interested in direct purchases of these products.

38720—WATCHCASES—INDIA - - Rajendra Singh, Managing Director, Western Maharashtra Development Corp. Ltd., Red Cross House, 3rd Fl., Mahatma Gandhi Rd., Poona 411 001, India, Cable: Westdev; Tel. 28146/25710, wishes to locate U.S. firms interested in supplying a reconditioned plant with a capacity to produce one million watch cases annually. WMDC is a government of Maharashtra undertaking, est. in 1970 with the objective of promoting industries in the western Maharashtra region. WMDC in collaboration with Hindustan Machine Tools, Bangalore, have started a watch assembly unit in the Shiroli Industrial Area at Kolhapur and propose to expand the assembly operation into a watch manufacturing complex. The proposed watch case manufacturing plant will be located adjacent to the watch assembly unit. The project initially envisages manufacturing 500,000 cases, and progressively increase production to one million cases/yr. The watch cases are to be manufactured from stainless steel and brass to international specs. Est. total project cost Rs.20 million ($1 - Rs. 8.20 approx.) of which fixed assets would be Rs.15.6 million. Plant and machinery including measuring and inspection equip. has been est. at Rs.8.0 million. WMDC's proposal envisages the importation of a reconditioned watch case plant to manufacture 1.0 million watch cases. The plant will be operated in conjunction with the watch assembly unit which requires 300,000 cases/yr. The remaining cases would be marketed locally as well as abroad. WMDC would be interested in a buy back arrangement for 500,000 unity. It is proposed that the watch case unit will be wholly owned by the corp. Mr. Singh stated that he is willing to negotiate ASAP with interested U.S. firms. (127)

as reported in *Commerce Business Daily.*

22810—YARN MILLS—ISRAEL -- Mr. Danon from Tel Aviv will visit New York City 15-25 May 79 to purchase combed cotton yarns, carded cotton yarns, and blended polyester/cotton yarns for the textile industry. Mr. Danon also wants to negotiate an agreement to represent U.S. yarn suppliers as exclusive agent and distributor in Israel. Mr. Danon estimates that he can handle an annual sales potential of 3,000 tons for cotton yarns and 2,000 tons for blended yarns. Est. in 1943, this family owned company employs 5 and reportedly imported $5 million in yarns from Italy and Spain last year. Interested U.S. suppliers may call or write Mr. Corfitzen, USDOC, Washington D.C. 20230; Tel 202/377-3265. (110)

35590—SPECIAL INDUSTRY MACHINERY—EGYPT -- Mr. Reda Elias Khalil from Cairo will visit U.S. 30 Apr. He wishes to purchase complete line of equip. for making shoe soles and related articles out of therm-plastic materials. Mr. Khalil is especially interested in 3 injection-molding machines with appropriate attachments each capable of producing 40 pairs of soles per hour. He estimates the value of the required machinery at approx. $200,000, and is ready to immediately open a letter of credit. For additional info. contact Jane Puse, Foreign Buyer Program, Rm. 2015-B USDOC, Washington DC 20230, 202/377-3265, ref. Cairo 7287/Khalil. (110)

33160—STEEL SHEETS—PAKISTAN -- Mr. Ghauri from Lahore will visit New York City, Cleveland, Baltimore, and San Francisco in Jul to purchase ferrous and non-ferrous scrap. Specifically, buyer wants to purchase: A) iron and steel items of secondary quality such as galvanized plain steel sheets, soft commercial quality, bright spangled, thickness 20 gauge to 30 gauge; B) CRCA sheets, soft commercial quality, thickness 16 gauge to 28 gauge; C) Hot rolled mild steel sheets coils. soft, thickness 9 gauge to 16 gauge; D) Stainless steel sheets Type 384/392, 2B/2D/PA finish, thickness 20 gauge to 26 gauge; E) Non-ferrous scrap such as aluminum scraps, brass scrap and copper scrap of any description; and F) Ferrous scrap such as Isis Code No. 200 Hms 1 and Isis Code No. 210/211 shredded scrap. U.S. suppliers interested in contacting Mr. Ghauri may call or write Bill Corfitzen, Rm. 2015-B, U.S.D.C, Washington DC 20230; Tel 202/377-3265. (127)

11110—ANTHRACITE—UNITED KINGDOM -- High grade Anthracite sizes 1½ to 2" & 2 to 3" for domestic use. Smokeless mfrd. solid fuels especially hard ovoids approx. 2" long. Firm is recently formed small buying agency with 2 employees. Owner is also involved in solid fuel retail firm. E.A. March & Sons, Andover, Est. 1868. Claimed local production insufficient to meet current demand for above fuels which are now being imported from various overseas sources. Quotations Requested. REF-MIDLAND Bank Ltd., Andover, Hampshire. This is a free notice. Your account is not charged. Reply to: D. March, Derrick

Figure 5. Trade and purchasing opportunities,

DEPARTMENT OF STATE
AID FINANCED

Suppliers of goods and services are advised that the Agency for International Development has a policy of obtaining maximum possible competiton for projects that it finances. All qualified contractors are encouraged to participate. A.I.D. will not finance any procurement in which boycott or other restrictive trade practices are applied.

EGYPT: PLANNING AND PRE-FEASIBILITY STUDIES FOR DEVELOPMENT OF THE SINAI. Phase I of the studies will consist of the identification of technically, financially and economically attractive projects in the western section of the penninsula to which access will soon be available. Potential projects to be identified in course of study may include, but not be limited to, agricultural, industrial, mining, (exclusive of petroleum), energy and transportation infrastructure and new settlements. The consultant will establish the overall regional context for such projects by development of a preliminary planning strategy for the entire peninsula. Selected projects will be developed to pre-feasibility levels, for subsequent feasibility study by specialized consultants. The purpose of phase I work is to provide the initial impetus to sound development of the Sinai within a rational, long range strategy. It is anticipated that phase I studies will require twelve months for completion. For information, phase II studies, not a part of this proposed contract, will, tentatively, consist of expansion of pahse I studies into other areas of the Sinai Peninsula as access becomes available, and the development of a 25-year economic and regional plan for the Sinai and detailed master plans for selected areas of the Sinai. It is estimated that phase II studies will require approximately three years to complete. Dollar costs for these professional services will be financed by aid. Local costs will be paid in Egyptian pounds by the Ministry. A cost-plus-fixed-fee contract for the above services is contemplated. Pre-qualification information must indicate the firm's or joint venture's experience and expertise in studies of similar nature. Submittals must include completed standard forms 254 and 255 (Architect-engineer questionnaires) which can be obtained by calling the near east office of project development (202)632-9815. Data indicating firm's financial status must also be submitted. Interested firm's brochures and annual reports may also be of value in presenting qualifications. Joint ventures seeking pre-qualification must supply full information on all firms in venture. Prequalifying data must be received by Dr. Hassan Marie, chairman, Advisory Committee for Reconstructin, Ministry of Development and New Communities, 1 Ismail Abaza Street, Cairo, A.R.E., by May 31, 1979. One information copy each should also be sent to: (1) NE/PD,, Room 4716, Attn: T.A. Sterner, AID, Washington, D.C. 20523, and (2) USAID, Attn: P.S. Lewis, American Embassy, Box 10, FPO New York, 09527. After evaluation of qualifying information, the ministry will establish a short-list of prequalified firms to whom request for technical proposals will be issued. Firms thus selected who wish to submit technical proposals will be required to attend a pre-proposal conference in Egypt. The firm finally selected may, upon satisfactory completion of the phase I study, and at the option of the ministry, be requested to provide, under a contract amendment or new contract, subsequent services relative to performance of phase II of the study. (120)

(a)

as reported in *Commerce Business Daily.*

SURPLUS PROPERTY SALES

FORMER U.S. ARMY RESERVE CENTER Short Cut Rd., Cottrellville Township, MI; 18.89 acres of land, improved with 11 misc. structures, located approx 4 miles southwest of Marine City.—Sealed Bid sale, D-MICH-697, will be opened 25 May 79. (113)
  GSA, Region 5, Business Service Center, Rm 3670, Fed. Bldg., 230 S. Dearborn St., Chicago, IL 60604, Tel: 312/353-5383

VACANT U.S. POSTAL SITE at Fifth St. and Banning Ave., White Bear Lake, MN: 0.57 acre of vacant land, ideal commercial or office site.—Minimum acceptable bid price is $60,000.—IFB P-MINN-524.—Sealed Bid opening 23 May 79.—(113)
  GSA, Region 5, Business Service Center, Rm 3670, Fed. Bldg., 230 S. Dearborn St., Chicago IL 60604

ELECTRONIC MEASURING/TESTING EQUIP Air Purification Equip, Analog Control System, Misc Electronic Components, Misc Hardware, Special Test and Hydraulic Equip, and Project Tooling, condition ranges from Unused Excellent to Poor, Repairs Required. U.S. Navy-owned Research and Development Material of Commercial and Specialized type; 19 lots——Acq Cost $447,391.86—Sealed Bid Sales Case S-4014—Bid Opening 15 May 79— Property Location: 227 Curtis Ave., Milpitas, CA. (113)
  Lockheed Missiles & Space Co., Inc., PO Box 504, Sunnyvale CA 94086, Attn: John Vincent, Org. 41-50, Bldg. 514, Tel: 408/743-0226

VEHICLES: AMC, Ford, Plymouth, Oldsmobile, Cadillac, Buick, Pontiac sedans, station wagons, sedan deliveries, panel trucks, and eight four-wheel drive vehicles: used, 114 lots—Auction Sale, 5DPS-79-46—to be conducted at the GSA Personal Property Center, 4100 W. 76th St., Chicago, IL 60652—3 May 79.—Inspect between 8:30 a.m. and 4 p.m., 1-2 May; and 8:30 until 10 a.m. 3 May. (113)
  GSA, Sales Branch, Personal Property Div, 230 S. Dearborn St., Chicago IL 60604. Tel: 312/353-6061

(b)

Other Types of Financial Aid for Small Business

Any contractor may specify a need for financial assistance, when undertaking a contract. Usually, this is specified as "progress payments," although other types of financial aid are possible, including advance payments. The latter, however, are the exception, rather than the rule. For example, the Department of Defense may authorize an advance payment, under 10 USC 2700, if the need satisfies the conditions under which advance payments may be made. But advance payments are a last resort, to be used when no other means of financing is feasible and when the agency believes it to be "in the best interest of the government" to consummate a contract with the organization bidding. (Ordinarily, the ability to finance a contract is a required qualification for being awarded a contract.)

However, a contractor is always justified in requesting progress payments, as a contract performance goes forward, and a small business is legally *entitled* to progress payments; that is, the agency cannot deny them that right.

Usually, a long-term contract carries with it a provision for progress payments, often in the form of monthly billings for work accomplished or tasks completed. However, my own experience has been that most contracting officials are willing, especially for small businesses, to accept billings as frequently as every two weeks, although monthly billings are more common.

Assistance in Winning Subcontracts

All the military organizations have small business representatives at major military procurement centers and/or industrial plants engaged in major contracts with the military. It is their main function to see to it that a fair percentage of subcontracts let are awarded to small business firms.

However, there is an organization known as the Defense Contract Administrative Services, which performs several functions for the military agencies. For one, DCAS (as it is generally referred to) is responsible for "facility clearance." That is the function of awarding security clearances to establishments doing secret work, and policing those facilities by inspections. Another function is to represent the agency in inspecting products in cases where it is not expedient for agency officials to do this themselves. A third function is to support small business programs in military procurement. DCAS offices, of which there are a number throughout the United States, have small business representatives.

All of these resources may be used by small businesses in seeking subcontracts in military procurements.

To report in detail on all the programs referred to in this chapter would be all but impossible, unless we are to produce an encyclopedia-size book. However, each agency produces its own literature—brochures, manuals, news releases, memoranda, and even newsletters, most of them free to the public. (And even those publications for which the Government Printing Office charges may often be gotten free, as explained later in this book.) Requests to the various agencies for information on any of the programs referred to here will bring back armloads of literature on each subject. (Some of the specific titles of relevant government publications appear in Chapter 9 and in Appendix 5.)

4

Finding out about government needs

It takes legwork

The *Commerce Business Daily*

The *Commerce Business Daily* ("CBD") is published five days a week by the Department of Commerce and printed by the Government Printing Office in Chicago. Its main purpose is to advise everyone interested in government requirements where and how to order a copy of the solicitation package (or "bid set," as many bidders refer to it). However, the publication is utilized to make other information and announcements known to readers:

- Contract awards made: Nature and size of contract, agency, awardee.
- Trade leads: Notices of opportunities for foreign sales, such as shown in Chapter 3, Figures 4 and 5(a).
- Notices of government surplus for sale (see Figure 5(b)).
- Research and development sources sought: Advance notices of anticipated procurements, with invitation to apply for inclusion on bidders list.
- Business news: Notices of government-sponsored seminars on federal procurement, trade shows, conferences, conventions, and other such activities of interest to government contractors.

A typical issue lists hundreds of solicitations and other notices. (See Figure 6.) Solicitations and awards are divided into two broad groups: services and supplies, equipment and material. Each of these is subdivided into a number of subcategories, amounting to over 100 in all.

Figure 6. Front page of *Commerce Business Daily.*

See the boxes shown on these pages for the goods and services under which solicitation notices are listed in the CBD. In spite of the length of this list, there is a "miscellaneous" category for both goods and services, for those items which do not appear to fit into any of the categories. However, each category is sufficiently broad to accommodate a wide range of goods and/or services which appear to fit

---

Goods and Services Listed in the Commerce Business Daily

Services

A   Experimental, developmental, test, and research work

H   Expert and consultant services

J   Maintenance and repair of equipment

K   Modification, alteration, and rebuilding of equipment

L   Technical representative services

M   Operation and maintenance of government-owned facility

N   Installation of equipment

O   Funeral and chaplain services

P   Salvage services

Q   Medical services

R   Architect-engineer service

S   Housekeeping services

T   Photographic, mapping, printing, and publication services

U   Training services

V   Transportation services

W   Lease or rental, except transportation equipment

X   Miscellaneous (services)

Y   Construction (various)

Z   Maintenance, repair, and alteration of real property

Supplies, Equipment, and Materiel

10   Weapons

11   Nuclear ordnance

12   Fire control equipment

13   Ammunition and explosives

14   Guided missiles

15   Aircraft and airframe structural components

16   Aircraft components and accessories

17   Aircraft launching, landing, and ground-handling equipment

18   Space vehicles

19   Ships, small craft, pontoons, and floating docks

20   Ship and marine equipment

22   Railway equipment

23   Motor vehicles, trailers, and cycles

24   Tractors

25   Vehicular equipment components

26   Tires and tubes

28   Engines, turbines, and components

29   Engine accessories

30   Mechanical power transmission equipment

31   Bearings

32   Woodworking machinery and equipment

34   Metalworking machinery

35   Service and trade equipment

36   Special industry machinery

37   Agricultural machinery and equipment

38   Construction, mining, excavating, and highway maintenance equipment

39   Materials handling equipment

under the heading. "Maintenance and Repair of Equipment," for example, may fit *any* kind of equipment, from ships to typewriters, and "maintenance" may range from minor service work to major overhaul.

The CBD is virtually a "bible" for government contractors, especially those seeking custom service work. At the same time, it should

40	Rope, cable, chain, and fittings	67	Photographic equipment
41	Refrigeration and air-conditioning equipment	68	Chemicals and chemical products
42	Fire-fighting, rescue, and safety equipment	69	Training aids and devices
43	Pumps and compressors	70	General purpose ADP equipment, software, supplies, and support equipment
44	Furnace, steam plant, and drying equipment; nuclear reactors	71	Furniture
45	Plumbing, heating, and sanitation equipment	72	Household and commercial furnishings and appliances
46	Water purification and sewage treatment equipment	73	Food preparation and serving equipment
47	Pipe, tubing, hose, and fittings	74	Office machines, visible record equipment, and data processing equipment
48	Valves	75	Office supplies and devices
49	Maintenance and repair shop equipment	76	Books, maps, and other publications
51	Hand tools	78	Recreational and athletic equipment
52	Measuring tools	79	Cleaning equipment and supplies
53	Hardware and abrasives	80	Brushes, paints, sealers, and supplies
54	Prefabricated structures and scaffolding	81	Containers, packaging, and packing supplies
55	Lumber, millwork, plywood, and veneer	83	Textiles, leather, furs, apparel and shoe findings; tents and flags
56	Construction and building materials	84	Clothing, individual equipment, and insignia
58	Communications equipment	85	Toiletries
59	Electrical and electronic equipment components	87	Agricultural supplies
61	Electric wire; power and distribution equipment	89	Subsistence
62	Lighting fixtures and lamps	91	Fuels, lubricants, oils, and waxes
63	Alarm and signal systems	93	Nonmetallic fabricated materials
65	Medical, dental, and veterinary equipment and supplies	94	Nonmetallic crude materials
66	Instruments and laboratory equipment	95	Metal bars, sheets, and shapes
		96	Ores, minerals, and their primary products
		99	Miscellaneous

not be presumed that daily reading of the CBD will keep you posted on all or even most of the current requirements. Far from it; the CBD listings probably reflect not more than about 10 percent of the requirements, at best.

Why is this? There are a number of factors explaining why the CBD reflects probably not more than $10 billion in federal procurement, whereas the total procurement is almost certainly well in excess of $100 billion. One reason is that a large percentage of federal buying is done under special arrangements, such as by using the Federal Supply Schedules. Another is that under the law, agencies are required to list in the CBD only those procurements expected to be in excess of $5,000. Still another reason is that the agencies are habitually remiss in their obligations to list procurements, and often do not list even rather large procurements.

In any case, valuable though the CBD is (and, used properly, it is quite valuable to the marketer), other means must also be used to stay on top of the market. Fortunately, there are other ways to learn of government requirements and buying intentions, and alert marketers utilize all of them.

Reading the CBD

The CBD is an "in" kind of publication. Anyone reading it for the first time is almost inevitably thoroughly confused, partially by the trade jargon used in it, and partially by the abundance of categories. Here, for example, are a few of the commonly used phrases and abbreviations:

Term	Means
RFP	Request for proposal (Proposal required; contract will be negotiated)
IFB	Information for bid (Sealed bids, with public opening; sometimes called "formally advertised" procurement. Low bid will win)
Indef qty	Indefinite quantity (Will call for unit prices, to be ordered as needed, possibly for entire year)
FOB	Free on board (Contractor will include shipping costs in price)
B/L	Bill of lading (Usually used when government will pay for shipping by providing a B/L shipping document)
RFQ	Request for quotation (Not binding on either party, but may be the basis for issuing a government purchase order)

IAW	In accordance with (Usually followed by a part number or specification number)
P/N	Part number
o/a	On or about (Followed by date)
COB	Close of business (Followed by date)
Multiple award	More than one contract will be issued (Several suppliers desired)
NSN	National stock number
FSC	Federal stock code
IG	Industrial group

These are by no means all the abbreviations and designators used, but are a sampling. (See Glossary (Appendix 8) for a more complete list.)

Despite the many categories in the CBD, or perhaps because of them, many items are misfiled. Category 69 is for training aids and devices, for example, meaning training equipment of various sorts. Yet, requirements for training manuals may often be found here, although they ought properly to appear under T or U. And sometimes such a requirement may be found under category H, or even "Miscellaneous." It is wise, therefore, to read every possible category every day, or you are almost certain to miss an occasional opportunity. And those often turn out to be the best opportunities, because many other people have missed them, and the competition may be rather light!

Using the CBD

Using the CBD is not the same thing as reading the CBD. In some ways, it's even more important than reading the CBD. A great deal of market research may be done every morning by using the CBD as one information source.

First of all, there is that special category which is in the CBD almost every day: "Research and Development Sources Sought." These are advance notices from various federal agencies of anticipated procurements. The purpose of the notice is to develop a list of qualified bidders. The notice describes the kind of technical and professional capabilities sought, and requests that anyone interested in becoming a bidder furnish a "statement of capabilities."

The capabilities statement may be a regular, printed brochure, but usually it is something developed especially for the purpose. Only those whose capabilities statements satisfy the agency that the organization is technically qualified will be invited to submit a proposal later, when the solicitation package is ready for distribution.

Periodically, the CBD also carries advance notices of military procurements anticipated for the future. And occasionally a notice will advise readers that they can write to an agency, for example, the U.S. Navy, and get a complete brochure on some procurement plans of the agency.

The front page of the CBD is used to announce conferences, seminars, symposia, and other events which should interest contractors, under the general heading "Business News." Such conferences are held regularly at various places throughout the United States, frequently under the sponsorship of your own congressional representative. At these meetings, you often get the opportunity to listen to procurement specialists from various government agencies who counsel listeners on future procurements, methods of selling to federal agencies, and related matters. In other cases, the meeting is a professional conference, at which you may be able to gain useful information about trends, both business and technical.

And finally, daily reading of the CBD will eventually reveal certain patterns of procurement to you. You'll begin to perceive which agencies are buying these days, and what they are buying. That is, you'll see some agencies buying certain classes of supplies or services on a regular basis, rather than intermittently, and that should set off an "alert signal" and cause you to visit the agency and investigate the reasons behind the surge of buying. It will help you identify which agency or program represents a long-term source for a flow of business, as distinct from the target-of-opportunity source. Such a prospect merits placing that agency on a must-call-on list, just as you would a commercial prospect for business. And reading the awards section of the CBD every day will help you analyze your competition even more readily than you can in the commercial markets, because you can learn exactly what they sold, to whom, and for how much!

Bidders lists

Agencies that buy with any regularity maintain bidders lists. And it is "lists," rather than "a list," for two reasons:

1. In many cases, the agency buys with such diversity that different *kinds* of suppliers are required; hence, many different bidders lists must be maintained.

2. In some cases, so many bidders apply for inclusion on the lists that several lists are maintained and the bidders are "rotated"; that is, any given list may be used only for every third or every fourth procurement.

On the other hand, many agencies have difficulty establishing and maintaining bidders lists because their requirements are always custom requirements and are almost always unique needs, so that they are never certain which of those listed are right for the procurement. In such cases, it is often necessary for the agency to go to the effort of establishing a bidders list for each procurement. That's one function of the CBD—to help agencies find bidders for their needs.

How Solicitations Originate

People who initiate requests for procurements, often referred to as "program people," are not the same people as "procurement people" or "contracts people." Their interests and their desires are different, and it is helpful to bidders to understand and appreciate those differences.

Program managers often do not have all the help they need on their own staff to carry out their programs. They must therefore look to outside, contracted services to help them get their jobs done. Let's take a typical case, to show how the mechanism works generally, and what the various roles are in the process.

Branch Chief Jones has been charged with developing a training program in occupational safety and health. He studies the project, develops a generalized outline of what should be contained in such a program, and searches around his branch for someone to write and produce the program.

He soon discovers that he either does not have enough help available to do the job or that he does not have a staff with the right knowledge and skills to produce the program. He is now forced to consider alternatives, which usually means "contracting out"—seeking contract assistance. First, he must be sure that he has the money and can get an okay to spend it (or has the authority himself to spend it). But before he can do that, he must get a pretty good idea of what the job will cost.

There are several ways he can get a fix on probable price. He might call in some suppliers he knows or who have been calling on him and leaving their cards. A little discussion, and they will "ballpark" the price for him. He could go out with an RFQ (request for quotation) and solicit prices. Or he could make inquiry within government circles—call offices in other agencies who have bought similar products and services—and ask them to provide estimates.

In any case, he will eventually come up with an in-house estimate or projected budget for the job. He is now ready to ask for the money, to make a purchase request or sit down with the boss. Or he may be able to earmark the money, if it is his to spend on his own authority. He will have to decide whether this is to be a formally advertised procurement or a negotiated one. In the case cited here, it is almost certainly going to be negotiated, however.

To actually announce the requirement and invite proposals, he has to turn the package over to the contracting officer who is going to handle the procurement. But before he can do that, he will have to write an "SOW," or Statement of Work, in which he describes to bidders (proposers) what he wants and what they are to propose. Once he has that prepared, he will probably consult with the contracting officer about related matters: Who will evaluate the proposals, how long he will allow for preparation of proposals, who is to be invited to bid (he can suggest bidders to the contracting officer, and may even be invited to do so), and many other details. But at this point, the contracting people take over.

The program people are interested in getting a good contractor, one who will turn out a fine job for them, meet all deadlines, and be easy to get along with. Writing a statement of work, reading and evaluating proposals, negotiating, and all the other tasks connected with awarding a contract competitively is extra work that the program people would rather not have to do. On the other hand, it is just that kind of work that the contracting people are responsible for; that's the reason their jobs exist. The program people are interested only in getting the help they need to get the job done, while the contracting people are interested in doing things by the book, so the interests of the two groups do not always coincide.

It's no accident that most contracting officials are either lawyers or accountants, and are frequently both. The two areas of their greatest concern are the law (procurement regulations) and the "numbers" (costs, accounts, and so on). To look at this another way, the contracting official's goal is to get the best job done or best product delivered, in the shortest possible time, at the lowest possible price. That should be the program manager's objective too, but procurement is not his occupation, it's just a necessary evil, and as far as he's concerned the time he devotes to that is lost time. Therefore, he is often less concerned with getting the lowest price than he is with other matters, such as speeding up and simplifying the procurement procedures. Given his "druthers," he might very well elect to avoid a competitive procurement entirely and simply select a contractor with whom to conduct negotiations. In fact, many do exactly that whenever they can.

One way to get the best possible price, and perhaps the best possible job done in the shortest possible time, is to maximize the competition—to get as many bids or proposals as possible. Contracting officers therefore usually welcome your bids and are happy to have as many names as possible on bidders lists.

Keep this attitude of the contracting officer in mind. It will help you to understand contracting procedures. At the same time, remember that contracting officers are human beings too, and as variable as is the rest of the race: jovial, dour, easygoing, hard-driving, and so on. The contracting officer's personal characteristics are often a factor in selecting awardees for contracts.

How to Get on a Bidders List

Getting on bidders lists simply requires filling out Standard Form 129. (See Figure 7.) It's a simple form, and all agencies use this form or one closely resembling it. However, agencies which do a great deal of procurement, such as NASA, often have their bidders lists entered into their computers, and they ask you to submit another form, which lists a great many services and products.

A Standard Form 129 must be filed with each contracting office in which you are interested and with which you hope to do business. Agencies rarely utilize the bidders lists of other agencies. There are thousands of "buying activities" scattered throughout the United States. Therefore, once you make up your Standard Form 129, you'll want to duplicate it in enough quantity to distribute to all contracting offices which interest you.

Notice that you must file with all *contracting offices,* not all *agencies,* of interest. The reason is that many agencies have more than one contracting office; for example, a multi-division agency may have a contracting office in each division, and may even have a contracting office in each of its locations in the United States. That accounts for the reported 15,000 contracting offices. (It takes a lot of people, offices, and organizations to spend over $100 billion a year!)

What Being on a Bidders List Means to You

Reading the CBD every day does not bring all procurement solicitations to your attention, and neither does filing Form 129, even if you file 15,000 of them. There are at least two reasons for this:

Figure 7. Standard Form 129.

STANDARD FORM 129 JANUARY 1966 EDITION FPR (41 CFR) 1-16.802	BIDDER'S MAILING LIST APPLICATION	INITIAL APPLICATION REVISION

Fill in all spaces. Insert "NA" in blocks not applicable. Type or print all entries. See reverse for instructions.

TO *(Enter name and address of Federal agency to which form is submitted. Include ZIP code)* DATE

1. APPLICANT'S NAME AND ADDRESS *(Include county and ZIP code)* | 2. ADDRESS *(Include county and ZIP code)* TO WHICH SOLICITATIONS ARE TO BE MAILED *(If different from item 1)*

3. TYPE OF ORGANIZATION *(Check one)* | 4. HOW LONG IN PRESENT BUSINESS

INDIVIDUAL   PARTNERSHIP   NON-PROFIT ORGANIZATION

CORPORATION, INCORPORATED UNDER THE LAWS OF THE STATE OF

5. NAMES OF OFFICERS, OWNERS, OR PARTNERS

PRESIDENT   VICE PRESIDENT   SECRETARY

TREASURER   OWNERS OR PARTNERS

6. AFFILIATES OF APPLICANT *(Names, locations, and nature of affiliation. See definition on reverse)*

7. PERSONS AUTHORIZED TO SIGN BIDS, OFFERS, AND CONTRACTS IN YOUR NAME *(Indicate if agent)*

NAME	OFFICIAL CAPACITY	TEL. NO. *(Incl. area code)*

8. IDENTIFY EQUIPMENT, SUPPLIES, MATERIALS, AND/OR SERVICES ON WHICH YOU DESIRE TO BID *(See attached Federal agency's supplemental listing and instructions, if any)*

9. TYPE OF BUSINESS *(See definitions on reverse)*

MANUFACTURER OR PRODUCER   REGULAR DEALER *(Type 1)*   REGULAR DEALER *(Type 2)*

SERVICE ESTABLISHMENT   CONSTRUCTION CONCERN   RESEARCH AND DEVELOPMENT FIRM

SURPLUS DEALER *(Check this box if you are also a dealer in surplus goods)*

10. SIZE OF BUSINESS *(See definitions on reverse)*

SMALL BUSINESS CONCERN *   OTHER THAN SMALL BUSINESS CONCERN

If you are a small business concern, fill in (a) and (b): | (a) AVERAGE NUMBER OF EMPLOYEES *(Including affiliates)* FOR FOUR PRECEDING CALENDAR QUARTERS | (b) AVERAGE ANNUAL SALES OR RECEIPTS FOR PRECEDING THREE FISCAL YEARS

11. FLOOR SPACE *(Square feet)* | 12. NET WORTH

MANUFACTURING   WAREHOUSE   DATE   AMOUNT

13. SECURITY CLEARANCE *(If applicable, check highest clearance authorized)*

FOR	TOP SECRET	SECRET	CONFIDENTIAL	NAMES OF AGENCIES WHICH GRANTED SECURITY CLEARANCES *(Include dates)*
KEY PERSONNEL				
PLANT ONLY				

THIS SPACE FOR USE BY THE GOVERNMENT | **CERTIFICATION**

I CERTIFY THAT INFORMATION SUPPLIED HEREIN *(Including all pages attached)* IS CORRECT AND THAT NEITHER THE APPLICANT NOR ANY PERSON *(Or concern)* IN ANY CONNECTION WITH THE APPLICANT AS A PRINCIPAL OR OFFICER, SO FAR AS IS KNOWN, IS NOW DEBARRED OR OTHERWISE DECLARED INELIGIBLE BY ANY AGENCY OF THE FEDERAL GOVERNMENT FROM BIDDING FOR FURNISHING MATERIALS, SUPPLIES, OR SERVICES TO THE GOVERNMENT OR ANY AGENCY THEREOF.

SIGNATURE

NAME AND TITLE OF PERSON AUTHORIZED TO SIGN *(Type or print)*

129-104

Figure 7. *(continued)*

INFORMATION AND INSTRUCTIONS

Persons or concerns wishing to be added to a particular agency's bidder's mailing list for supplies or services shall file this properly completed and certified Bidder's Mailing List Application, together with such other lists as may be attached to the application form, with each procurement office of the Federal agency with which they desire to do business. If a Federal agency has attached a supplemental Commodity List with instructions, complete the application as instructed. Otherwise, identify in Item 8 the equipment, supplies, and/or services on which you desire to bid. *The application shall be submitted and signed by the principal as distinguished from an agent, however constituted.*

After placement on the bidder's mailing list of an agency, a supplier's failure to respond *(submission of bid, or notice in writing, that you are unable to bid on that particular transaction but wish to remain on the active bidder's mailing list for that particular item)* to Invitations for Bids will be understood by the agency to indicate lack of interest and concurrence in the removal of the supplier's name from the purchasing activity's bidder's mailing list for the items concerned.

TYPE OF BUSINESS DEFINITIONS
(See Item No. 9)

A. MANUFACTURER OR PRODUCER means a person (or concern) owning, operating, or maintaining a factory or establishment that produces, on the premises, the materials, supplies, articles, or equipment of the general character of those listed in Item No. 8, or in the Federal Agency's supplemental Commodity List, if attached.

B. REGULAR DEALER (Type l) means a person (or concern) who owns, operates, or maintains a store, warehouse, or other establishment in which the materials, supplies, articles, or equipment of the general character listed in Item No. 8 or in the Federal Agency's supplemental Commodity List, if attached, are bought, kept in stock, and sold to the public in the usual course of business.

C. REGULAR DEALER (Type 2) in the case of supplies of particular kinds *(at present, petroleum, lumber and timber products, machine tools, raw cotton, green coffee, hay, grain, feed, or straw, agricultural liming materials, tea, raw or unmanufactured cotton linters).* "REGULAR DEALER" means a person (or concern) satisfying the requirements of the regulations (Code of Federal Regulations, Title 41, 50–201.101(b)) as amended from time to time, prescribed by the Secretary of Labor under the Walsh-Healey Public Contracts Act (Title 41 U.S. Code 35–45). For coal dealers, see Code of Federal Regulations, Title 41, 50–201.604(a).

D. SERVICE ESTABLISHMENT means a concern (or person) which owns, operates, or maintains any type of business which is principally-engaged in the furnishing of nonpersonal services, such as *(but not limited to)* repairing, cleaning, redecorating, or rental of personal property, including the furnishing of necessary repair parts or other supplies as part of the services performed.

E. CONSTRUCTION CONCERN means a concern (or person) engaged in construction, alteration or repair (including dredging, excavating, and painting) of buildings, structures or other real property.

DEFINITIONS RELATING TO SIZE OF BUSINESS

A. SMALL BUSINESS CONCERN. A small business concern for the purpose of Government procurement is a concern, including its affiliates, which is independently owned and operated, is not dominant in the field of operation in which it is bidding on Government contracts and can further qualify under the criteria concerning number of employees, average annual receipts, or other criteria, as prescribed by the Small Business Administration. (See Code of Federal Regulations, Title 13, Part 121, as amended, which contains detailed industry definitions and related procedures.)

B. AFFILIATES. Business concerns are affiliates of each other when either directly or indirectly (i) one concern controls or has the power to control the other, or (ii) a third party controls or has the power to control both. In determining whether concerns are independently owned and operated and whether or not affiliation exists, consideration is given to all appropriate factors including common ownership, common management, and contractual relationship. (See Items Nos. 6 and 10.)

C. NUMBER OF EMPLOYEES. In connection with the determination of small business status, "number of employees" means the average employment of any concern, including the employees of its domestic and foreign affiliates, based on the number of persons employed on a full-time, part-time, temporary, or any other basis during the pay period ending nearest the last day of the third month in each calendar quarter for the preceding four quarters. If a concern has not been in existence for four full calendar quarters, "number of employees" means the average employment of such concern and its affiliates during the period such concern has been in existence based on the number of persons employed during the pay period ending nearest the last day of each month. (See Item No. 10.)

COMMERCE BUSINESS DAILY

The Commerce Business Daily, published by the Department of Commerce, contains information concerning proposed procurements, sales, and contract awards. For further information concerning this publication, contact your local Commerce Field Office.

GPO : 1975 O - 591-035

1. Where there are a large number of names on the bidders list, the names are "rotated," as you've already been informed. If a bidders list contains 300 names, let us say, and the contracting officer believes that 50 solicitations are enough (he is most unlikely to send out as many as 300), he will select the next 50, then rotate to the following 50 for the next solicitation, and so on. So you will be sent only one out of every six solicitations, and you will miss the other five, if you simply file Form 129 and then wait for bid sets to arrive automatically in the morning mail.

2. When custom services are required, the contracting people are trying to *interpret* your 129 to see whether you are likely to be interested in or qualified for the solicitation in question. Suppose, for example, that you have listed in block 8 (goods and/or services you wish to bid for) your interest in writing training manuals, and a solicitation comes up for an audiovisual training program. You might very well wish to bid that contract, but the contracting officer may not (and probably will not) make the connection. He is likely to sigh, decide that this one is not for you, and pass you over.

I was once editorial director of a firm manufacturing a "teaching machine," whose materials were recorded on 35mm film and projected onto a screen of normal page size. Learning too late that we had not been invited to bid for a "paper program" (printed text) by a good customer, we asked why. To our horror, the customer was surprised to learn that we did not confine ourselves exclusively to 35mm film.

Therefore, filing copies of your Form 129 and getting on bidders lists is one of your marketing tools, just as reading the CBD is one such tool. Both are important, but neither is sufficient of itself to cover the market adequately. Nor are the two together enough, if you want to be made aware of most bid opportunities.

One thing I did learn is that actually responding to a solicitation by submitting a bid or proposal was far more effective at getting me on a bidders list than filing Form 129 was. For some reason, even after filing the 129, you may not be getting bid sets from the agency. However, once you have submitted a bid or proposal, you are likely to see many bid sets from them.

But in the meanwhile, it is wise to try to learn of requirements by any and all means possible, and request all solicitations you believe will be of interest, whether or not you have filed a 129 with the agency.

Bid Rooms and Bid Boards

Every contracting office must keep a file or display of outstanding requirements (solicitations) available for public inspection. A busy contracting office (one that buys almost continuously) usually maintains a bid room and bid board. On the wall of that room you will find a large bulletin board, on which are pinned many bid sets. In some cases, they are even arranged in categories such as equipment, services, and so on.

The public is welcome to drop into the bid room at any time, during normal office hours, and inspect the bid sets posted. And if you do so and find one which interests you, you are welcome to request a set for yourself. Since many contracting offices require that requests for bid sets be in writing, it's a good idea to carry some noteheads or letterheads with you, so that you can submit a written request there and then!

In smaller purchasing offices, there may not be a special bid room. But the outstanding solicitations are still available for your examination, although they may be simply bound in a folder. You are entitled, however, to inquire and to see them.

How often you should visit contracting offices and bid rooms depends on the amount of purchasing they do. In some cases it may be advisable to drop by every week, while in others it may not be necessary to visit more often than once a month.

It's a good idea to get to know the contracting official and his staff in any agency where you believe you will be able to do business. This helps him remember you when he has solicitations to send out, and it also often results in friendly tips which may mean business for you. (In many respects, doing business with the government is not much different from doing business anywhere else. You need to establish and maintain productive contacts to stay in business.)

In agencies where I did business fairly often, I found the contracting officer and others tipping me off in advance of new requirements coming up. And I made it my business to keep in touch with the program people as well as with the contracts people.

Making "cold" calls

As in doing business in the private sector, business can sometimes be generated by standard marketing tactics: "making the calls." Here's an example:

An acquaintance gave me the name of an individual in charge of writing standards for OSHA, and I made it my business to drop in and look the gentleman up at the first opportunity. We had a friendly chat, after I introduced myself, but it turned out that he had nothing to offer me at the time. However, I asked him if he could suggest another prospect in the office to me. He took me to meet someone else in another office. The result was the same, but I again asked for a suggestion.

In this manner, I was introduced to five people in the course of about two hours. But Number 5 was pay dirt! He had a need, and I looked like the right guy to handle it. It turned into a $2,400 job, which was followed by a $2,500 job, which was followed by a $23,000 job. He also recommended me to another agency, where I did quite a bit of business, and it in turn recommended me to still another agency.

Those two hours were responsible for some $65,000 worth of business over the next two years! Of course, I had the slight advantage of a name and a mutual acquaintance. But the advantage was only slight. Anyone can walk into a federal agency and seek business. There are many ways to go about it, and several places where one can start.

• If you are a small business (the Small Business Administration can tell you whether or not you are, if you are in doubt), try finding the agency's Small Business Representative. Most agencies have one, and that person can help you find your way around and meet the right people.

• You can call on the contracting officer to discuss your business needs. Many contracting officers I've known are sincere and sometimes even jovial people who will try to help you.

• You can visit the agency's library and have a look at the organization charts, to see who's who. The agency's librarian can often be very helpful.

• Most agencies also have a public information office of some sort (not necessarily called that, however), and the staff there may be able to offer some guidance. That's part of their function.

Most agencies have their own personnel office or personnel function, a publications function, and a training or education function. I say "function" because in one case an agency will have an office set up for each of these, while in another the functions may be combined. So you may or may not find a "training office," but the training function will exist (possibly under the personnel office).

In any case, among the things you should want to know are (1) how the agency is organized, (2) who's who, in terms of what you may wish to offer, and (3) what the agency normally buys or what it happens to be in the market for at the moment.

Market research

A large corporation for which I worked some years ago had an automation division housed in the same building as the division for which I was editorial director. They built automation systems to order, and one of their orders was for an automatic candy-packing machine, for a large candy company in Canada. After many months of intensive labor, they developed the machine, which cost on the order of one-half million dollars. While the machine was being developed, an inspired salesman on the staff sold a second one to another candy company, and still another one to a third candy company. Galvanized by this promising new business, the marketing vice-president ordered two extra units made up for stock and mounted a brisk marketing attack on the automatic candy-packing market.

Months later, the two spare machines gathering dust in the warehouse, the vice-president of marketing began to grow uneasy at the lack of success in selling these two machines, and began to research the candy market. To his horror, he discovered that there were only six candy companies in the entire world who were large enough to even consider a capital investment of $500,000 for packing candy. And the company had already captured one-half of that market. It was a bitter lesson in the need for market research *before* investing time and money. (The two machines, worth $1 million, were eventually sold off for their salvage value.)

Many make the same mistake in pursuing government business. When the Department of Transportation was organized some years ago, a firm engaged in technical support, primarily technical writing and related services, invested heavily in marketing to the new agency. The basis for this decision was the large operating budget of the new DOT, which inspired the belief that there would be lots of "contracting out."

The company was mistaken in its belief. There was relatively little contract work suitable for that company. Most of the contracts at that time were for demonstration "people-mover" systems, such as high-speed electric cars, and for studies of transportation problems, such as those of the railroads. The company, ignoring the advice of its marketing director (who knew better), succeeded finally in winning one subcontract to assist another contractor who had won a people-mover contract. They never did succeed in winning a direct contract with DOT.

The mistake they made was to see only the new department's overall budget, without regard to their programs and missions—*how they would spend the money*. In fact, a great deal of the agency's money was earmarked for subsidies to state and local governments, and relatively little was spent for contracted services or goods. Market research into government markets must consider more than the overall budget: It must consider the agencies' missions and programs, their buying history, any new enabling legislation, and any other factors that indicate *how* each agency will spend its budget and *what* it will buy.

There are many ways to do this. Information is abundant, although much of it is not organized. Today, the Office of Federal Procurement Policy (OFPP), which is a temporary ("sunset") office in the Office of Management and Budget (OMB), has begun operation of its new Federal Procurement Data System. It has not yet been decided firmly what information will be available for public use, but the system is supposed to produce detailed information on what, how, where, and when the various federal agencies buy—and from whom, as well.

However, it is not necessary to resort to even this system to get a fair idea of the government market for any given commodity or service. There are other sources and methods that can help you arrive at reasonable estimates. One of the most readily available sources is the *Commerce Business Daily,* which lists contract awards, as well as requirements, as Figure 8 shows. It's a relatively simple matter to review several months' issues and arrive at a reasonable estimate of total purchasing in any given category.

For example, asked to estimate the amount of furniture (in dollars) that the government buys, I resorted to this method. After only about two hours' work with my filed copies of the CBD and a small calculator, I estimated that federal agencies were buying at least $170 million a year in furniture. That was in 1977. About a year later, the new Commissioner of the Federal Supply Service mentioned, in a public statement, that the government was buying about $225 million worth of furniture a year. Obviously, my "ball park" estimate was close enough for market-research purposes. (Allowing for inflationary ef-

Figure 8. Contract awards listed in *Commerce Business Daily.*

CONTRACT AWARDS

It is the Government's policy to publish information on unclassified contract awards exceeding $25,000 in value for civil agencies and $50,000 for military agencies.

The letter or number preceding each item is the service or supplies classification code.

Supplies Equipment and Material

61 Electric Wire, and Power Distribution Equipment.

61 -- AMPLIFIER, ELECTRONIC CONTROL, P/O Antenna, Type #AS-2199 and P/O Receiver-Transmitter, Radar, Type #RT-899/APS-94D, NSN: 6110-00-449-5112 and6110-00-239-5990. Contract DAAB07-79-C-0821, 31 May 79 $91,997 (No RFP) Canadian Commercial Corp, Ottawa, Ontario, Canada.

61 -- POWER SUPPLY, PP6224, 220 Each, NSN: 6130-00-133-5879 (DAAB07-79-R-1909). Contract DAAB07-77-C-2664, P00012 31 May 79 #689,436, Saratoga Industries P.O. Box 422, Saratoga Springs, NY.

61 -- POWER SUPPLY (18A1A), 240 Each, NSN: 6130-00-466-0158 (DAAB07-79-B-1922). Contract DAAB07-79-C-1952, 31 May 79 $80,320 Wire-Pro, Inc., P.O. Box 211, Bridgeport, NJ.

61 -- BATTERY, DRY BA-4386/PRC-25, NSN: 6135-00-926-8322, 92,016. Contract DAAB07-78-D-6344, D.O. 0004, 31 May 79 $778,842 (No RFP) ESB, Inc., 101 E. Washington Ave., Madison, WI.

61 -- BA-1568/U BATTERY, Dry, NSN: 6135-00-838-0706, 13,770 ea. Contract DAAB07-79-D-6714 25 May .79 $90,606 D.O. 0001 (No RFP) PR Mallory & Co., Inc., South Broadway, Tarrytown, NY.

61 -- BATTERY, STORAGE CELL, Type BB-600 A/A, NSN: 6140-00-881-6887. Contract DAAB07-78-D-6325 D.O. 0008, 25 May 79 $579,576 (No RFP) PR Mallory & Co., Inc, South Broadway, Tarrytown, NY.

61 -- BATTERY, STORAGE CELL, Type BB-600 A/A, NSN: 6140-00-881-6887. Contract DAAB07-78-D-6325 D.O. 0008, 25 May 79 $579,576 (No RFP) Marathon Battery Co., 8301 Imperial Dr., Waco, TX.

U.S. Army Communications and Electronics Material Readiness Command, Fort Monmouth NJ 07703

61 -- CIRCUIT ASSEMBLY, NSC 6110-NONE, Contract DLA400-79-C-2174, 31 May 79 (RFP DLA400-78-R-2105) 241 ea $127,741 Leland Electrosystems Inc., 740 E. National Rd., Vandalia, OH 45377.

Defense General Supply Center, Richmond, VA 23297, Tel: 804/275-3350

61 -- SILVERCEL BATTERIES—$79,993—Yardney Electric Division, Pawcatuck, CT. Contr NAS5-24611, 7 May 79.

NASA/GSFC, Greenbelt, MD, Code 242.1

62 Lighting Fixtures and Lamps.

62 -- FIXTURE, LIGHTING, NSN 6210-00-548-0222, Contract DLA400-79-C-2175, 31 May 79 (RFP DLA400-79-R-1177) 8677 ea $309,254 The L. C. Doane Co., 10 New City St., Essex, CT 06426.

Defense General Supply Center, Richmond, VA 23297, Tel: 804/275-3350

65 Medical, Dental, and Veterinary Equipment and Supplies.

65 -- APPLICATORS, DISPOSABLE (M1-94-79) contract V797P-1070g $66,960 Hardwood Products Co., School St., Guilford ME 04443.

66 -- CELL, SALINITY INDIC. P/N ICCN853, CEL-261, NSN 1H6630-00-983-2577, Contract N00104-79-C-3345 (RFP-N00104-78-R-6085) dtd 21 May 79, 554 ea. $65,649. McNab, Inc., 20 North MacQuesten Parkway, Mount Vernon, New York 10550.

Navy Ships Parts Control Center, Mechanicsburg, PA 17055

67 Photographic Equipment.

67 -- PRINTER, Projection Photographic (2RH6740-00-069-5462), Contract F42600-79-C-0498 dated 24 May 79 (RFP F42600-79-R-0170) 45 each. $97,785 Berkey Photo Inc, 25-15 50th St., Woodside NY 11377.

67 -- RECEIVER (6720-01-039-3324), Power Supply (6760-01-039-0504), Infrared Performance Analyzer (6720-01-038-4972), Handling Plate Assembly (6760-01-043-6140), Card Assembly for Anti-Hump Clamp and Air Timing Generator (6720-01-046-3630), Card Assembly for Anti-Hump Clamp and AGC Waveform Generator, Appl AN/AAD-5, Contract F42600-79-C-0396 29 May 79, 12 line items. $304,296. Honeywell Inc, 2 Forbes Rd., Lexington MA 02173.

Directorate of Procurement & Production (PPE-1), Ogden ALC, Hill AFB, UT 84406, Tel 801/777-4759

67 -- SPARE PARTS FOR KG-29A CAMERA and LG-15B Magazine, Contract F42600-79-C-0584, 4 Jun 79 (RFP F42600-79-R-0695) 1 SE $84,654 Recon/Optical Inc, 550 West Northwest Hwy, Barrington IL 60010.

Directorate of Procurement & Production (PPE-1), Ogden ALC, Hill AFB, UT 84406, Tel 801/777-4759

67 -- MEDIUM STREAK AND FRAMING CAMERA Imacon 790/S20—Contr. N00173-79-C-0176, 31 May 79—$85,501—Marco Scientific Inc, 1031-H E. Duane Ave., Sunnyvale, CA 94086.

Naval Research Laboratory, Washington DC 20375

69 Training Aids and Devices.

69 -- COUPLER UNIT PANEL (6920-01-003-7805), and Drawer (6920-00-107-0685), appl AN/GSP-T34, Contract F04606-76-A-0072-QPU3 21 May 79 $164,000 Rockwell International Corp, 3370 Miraloma Ave., Anaheim CA 92803.

69 -- DESIGN, FABRICATE AND INSTALL A PROTOTYPE MODIFICATION KIT for A/F37A-T33 (A-7D; F1t Sim (6930K4309315A; and follow-on production kits, installation, technical and engineering data, initial spare parts provisioning and technical manuals, Contract F34601-76-A-2175-QP54 dated 24 May 79. $360,000 McDonnell Douglas Corp, PO Box 426, St Charles MO 63301.

Directorate of Procurement & Production (PPE-1), Ogden ALC, Hill AFB, UT 84406, Tel 801/777-4759

70 General Purpose ADP Equipment Software, Supplies and Support Equipment.

70 -- REFURBISH AND INSTALL FIELD CHANGES on two Model CP642B Computers originally manufactured by Sperry Univac. N00024-77-A-7150, Order WQ3J—$70,400, Sperry Univac, PO Box 3525, St. Paul MN 55165.

70 -- REFURBISH AND INSTALL FIELD CHANGES on two each Model CP642B Computers; one originally manufactured by Sperry Univac and one by Sylvania. N00024-77-A-7150, Order WQ3N, $75,700, Sperry Univac, Univac Park, PO Box 3525, St. Paul, MN 55165.

DCASMA Twin Cities, Federal Building, Fort Snelling Twin Cities MN 55111 fects, my brief study came up with a figure within 10 percent of the government's figures.) This is a fairly reliable method for estimating the government's annual buy of commodities, since virtually all such procurements are listed in the CBD. However, it is also important to note that the CBD does not list everything bought by federal agencies, especially in custom services.

Another way to reach an estimate of annual volume in an item of supply is to query the Federal Supply Service, which is part of the General Services Administration. That organization can usually give you a good idea of the volume in any given category.

The Small Business Administration can help, too, in many cases, with at least estimates of the market among federal agencies for given items of goods and services.

In some cases, the Department of Commerce is an even better source of information along these lines than is the Small Business Administration, since Commerce takes an interest in business between the federal agencies and the private sector.

If you are interested in a particular agency, queries to the contracting office of that agency will often produce good estimates of what the agency buys, or at least what it has bought in the year previous.

Even Government Markets Change

All markets change, and the federal government markets are not an exception. In fact, in many respects the government markets are even more subject to change, including sudden and abrupt change, than are markets in the commercial and industrial community. There are various causes for such change.

About 10 years ago, the Post Office Department was abolished and the U.S. Postal Service, a government corporation, was established to replace the old Department. This also wiped out the formerly close congressional control and political influence exercised over the Post Office, and conferred a semi-autonomy on the new managers of postal service. Many things happened as a result.

First, the new department announced a plan to establish 10 training centers at university sites, primarily to train postal employees in technical trades and automation, which the new Postal Service planned to install to modernize the establishment and its handling of mail. Second, the Postal Management Institute was established in Bethesda, Maryland, a Washington suburb. At the same time, a Postal Service Technical Institute was established on the University of Oklahoma campus, at Norman, Oklahoma. (The remaining training centers were never established.) Simultaneously, the Postal Service began buying a great deal of automation equipment, vehicles, and real estate to house 21 new bulk-mail centers.

With a $10 billion annual gross, the Postal Service invested a great deal of its money in these new activities, and let a great many contracts for equipment, much of it custom-designed, and for training programs and services. At one time, many contractors (yours truly included) were doing business regularly with the Postal Service.

Postal Service contracts for these new activities began to slow down by the mid-1970s and, as postal deficits mounted, they came to an almost complete halt by 1977. The Postal Service came under heavy criticism from Congress, which threatened to take over the Postal Service and once again make it an integral element in the bureaucracy, where it would be under closer control. Today, the Postal Service still lets many contracts for real estate, transportation services, and supplies, but little for training and custom-designed equipment. Many small companies for whom the Postal Service had been almost the sole support were suddenly in straits, and not all survived.

During 1964 to 1965, the Office of Economic Opportunity, Job Corps, was a similar bonanza for many, and other elements of the OEO, such as Head Start and VISTA, soon added their own requirements for millions of dollars' worth of services. That, too, dried up eventually, as the OEO was all but disbanded and its programs dispersed to older agencies.

New legislation often creates new markets in government. Organization of the Federal Energy Administration and Energy Research and Development Administration (now the Department of Energy) created many contract opportunities. Likewise, the formation of the Environmental Protection Agency led to many new contract opportunities. But not every new agency becomes a major business opportunity. For example, the new Consumer Product Safety Commission and the new Pension Benefit Guaranty Corporation produced some new contract opportunities, after a year or more of their existence, but neither ever turned into major markets.

Sometimes legislation creates a new market within an existing agency, rather than a new agency. The Occupational Safety and Health Administration (OSHA), for example, was assigned to the Labor Department, and its related agency, the National Institute of Occupational Safety and Health (NIOSH), was assigned to HEW. Both have required some assistance from private industry, of course, and have been a source of contracts.

Those who prosper most from new organizations are usually those who get in on the ground floor by starting their marketing efforts early in the existence of a new agency. The energy field is a good example of this. Prior to 1974, no one thought of themselves as "energy" experts, although there were organizations expert in petroleum, natural gas, coal, etc. But the government's programs and needs soon created energy experts, many of them seizing the opportunity early, although they had never worked in the field before! Congress sometimes creates entire new professions, with its legislative mandates.

Some "Old, Reliable" Government Markets

The markets discussed in this chapter are largely transient markets, targets of opportunity. Most of them involve custom work in direct support of an agency's mission, and the RFPs and SOWs often cite specific legislation mandating the requirement. The Department of Housing and Urban Development (HUD) has a legal requirement to do certain surveys, and lets contracts to have these done. The Commerce Department is required to conduct a census every 10 years through its Bureau of Census. In many cases, however, such requirements are not for work needed on a regular basis, but must be done once only. To work these markets, therefore, it is necessary to market continuously and aggressively, always searching out new opportunities and rarely doing exactly the same job twice.

It is therefore decidedly hazardous to your (business) health to ever sit back and rest on your merits, in these markets, or to permit your business to become dependent on one or two federal agencies or programs. A single budget cut cr congressional change of mind can wipe out your business almost overnight. It is wise to spread your contracts over as many agencies as possible, and to always be working on new markets.

On the other hand, there are certain government requirements, such as for furniture, which are fairly steady, year after year. These exist in services, as well as in supplies. There is a rather consistent demand for moving family goods, general hauling, janitorial services, food services, and a number of other such housekeeping and maintenance functions. In fact, for most of these kinds of supplies and services, the government often issues annual contracts to a number of suppliers, calling on the suppliers regularly as needs arise. Some of these are known as Federal Supply Schedules, but there are many others too.

If you wish to offer anything falling into one of these categories, it is probably wise to seek one or more annual contracts, many of which are available through the General Services Administration, but many others of which are announced periodically in the CBD. (Additional sources of information on these are listed in the Appendix.)

5

How to make bids

Appearing to be the low bidder is as good as being the low bidder—
in fact, it's better

How can you tell who is the low bidder?

Theoretically, it's easy to identify the low bidder in a contract competition; the bid with the smallest number on the bottom line is the low bidder, to wit:

Bidder A		Bidder B	
3 gr widgets @ $7.40/gr = $22.20		3 gr widgets @ $7.39/gr = $22.17	
2 dz bobbles @ $2.10/dz = 4.20		2 dz bobbles @ $2.25/dz = 4.50	
Total	$26.40	Total	$26.67

The list may be, and often is, much longer than this. Individual prices for individual items are not the significant factors, although a contracting officer may question any which appear to be seriously out of line with the market. It's the bottom line—the total—which established who is the low bidder.

That works out all right as long as the bid is for specific quantities to be delivered under specified conditions. However, there are many considerations. For one thing, the bottom line may include prompt-payment discounts.

Figuring in Prompt-Payment Discounts

Let's see how such discounts affect the actual cost to the government, using the example here:

Bidder A offers 2% 10 days, 0.5% 20 days, net amount due after
Bidder B offers 3% 10 days, 2% 20 days, 1% 30 days

Applying these discounts to the bids, we come up with these final figures for the bottom line of each bid:

	Bidder A	Bidder B
Paid in 10 days	$25.87	$25.87
Paid in 20 days	26.27	26.14
Paid in 30 days	26.40	26.40
Paid after 30 days	26.40	26.67

Bidder B is the actual low bidder and the winner of the contract because he offered a greater prompt-payment discount. For 10-day payment, the two bidders are exactly the same in their quotation. However, this is not a deadlock because the government will not count a 10-day discount, on the assumption that it is all but impossible for the government to process a payment in 10 days. The government will, however, take a discount for 20-day payment or longer into account. So any discounts you offer for 10 days are meaningless, despite the fact that bid forms provide a blank space for you to record 10-day discounts!

The actual bottom line on these two bids, for evaluation and comparison purposes, is this:

Bidder A: $26.27
Bidder B: $26.14

In a close race, therefore, discounts may well make the difference in deciding who is the low bidder. However, this is not the only complicating factor. Many other factors can make it difficult to judge who is the low bidder.

Pricing Indefinite Quantities

For example, many requirements are for indefinite quantities. The government can give you only a rough estimate or range to aid you in arriving at unit prices. Usually, such contracts are for a long term, probably a year, and the government will order from time to time, as the needs arise, at the prices you have agreed to in your bid. In actuality, the government may order a great many of some items, and extremely few of others. The government doesn't know, nor does the bidder, what the year's requirements are going to be.

Frequently, the solicitation package will give you the range by stating that the government will order not less than _____ number of units nor more than _____ number of units. In these cases, at least you know the minimum and maximum size of the contract, although you've no idea of the probable size of individual orders under the contract. This complicates the evaluation of prices enormously, because there is no true bottom line. Here's an example of what such a bid might call for:

Item	Minimum–Maximum Quantities	Price per Unit
5 × 7 notepads	150–300 gr	$ _____
Carbon paper	500–1,000 dz sheets	$ _____
No. 2 lead pencils	5,000–10,000 dz	$ _____

Now both the bidder and the government have a problem. The bidder has no idea of how to "bid smart" on this, and the government has to devise some sort of irreproachable scheme for deciding who is the low bidder. The difficulty in deciding who will be the *lowest-cost* supplier, which is the purpose of the bids, arises because of the uncertainty of quantities. To make this clearer let's look at a few typical bids.

Bidder	Notepads	Carbon Paper	Pencils
A	$15.70/gr	$2.25/dz sheets	$0.72/dz
B	16.35/gr	2.19/dz sheets	0.71/dz
C	15.22/gr	2.29/dz sheets	0.99/dz

It's immediately obvious that none of the bidders is either low or high on everything. Were the contract to be for any single item, there would be no difficulty. But the contract is to be for as-needed supplies of all the items.

The usual method the government uses to determine the low bidder here is a "bench test." A hypothetical order is used to test each bid, to see who would be the lowest-cost supplier. Let's make up a bench test of our own and apply it:

We'll assume that these will be the quantities for a typical order:

> Notepads: 20 gr
> Carbon paper: 50 dz sheets
> Lead pencils: 100 dz

Now let's price this order for each bidder, and see what the order would cost, in each case:

Bidder	Notepads	Carbon Paper	Pencils	Total
A	$314.00	$112.50	$72.00	$498.50
B	327.00	109.50	71.00	507.50
C	304.40	114.50	99.00	517.90

Bidder A is the low bidder, using this bench test. With another bench test, it could turn out differently. If the bench test were applied to the minimum or maximum figure, another bidder might appear to be the low bidder! Suppose maximum figures were given thus:

Notepads	5,000 gr
Carbon paper	1,000 dz sheets
Lead pencils	2,000 dz

Pricing by maximums would produce the following figures:

Bidder	Notepads	Carbon Paper	Pencils	Total
A	$78,500	$2,250	$1,440	$82,190
B	81,750	2,190	1,420	85,360
C	76,100	2,290	1,980	80,370

It is therefore the responsibility of the contracting officer to develop an evaluation method which provides a fair comparison.

In the actual case, such office commodities as carbon paper and lead pencils are generally bought by the Federal Supply Service in large quantity and stocked in the 10 warehouses and 75 stores of GSA. However, for many items, in both supplies and services, such bids as the above are common.

Example of a bid invitation

There are other complicating factors found among the many kinds of bid situations. Many items purchased are capital items of one sort or another, and some of these have repair and maintenance considerations, as well as other "cost of ownership" facts to take into account. Let's take an actual bid invitation as an example of this. Here is Solicitation No. 5-M-FSQS-79, an IFB issued on December 1, 1978 by the USDA in Minneapolis. It calls for bids on a "STAMP, Roller Dating," in accordance with specifications provided in the bid set. The public opening is to be held on January 4, 1979 at 2:30 P.M. at the USDA offices in Minneapolis. (See Figure 9.)

Figure 9. Sample of government solicitation.

SOLICITATION, OFFER AND AWARD	3. CERTIFIED FOR NATIONAL DEFENSE UNDER BDSA REG. 2 AND/OR DMS REG. 1 RATING	4. PAGE 1	OF

1. CONTRACT (Proc. Inst. Ident.) NO.	2. SOLICITATION NO. 5-M-FSQS-79 [X] ADVERTISED (IFB) [ ] NEGOTIATED (RFB)	5. DATE ISSUED 12-1-78	6. REQUISITION/PURCHASE REQUEST NO. 0457 0564 FAY 4190 FV-6-P

7. ISSUED BY CODE	8. ADDRESS OFFER TO (If other than block 7)
U.S.Department of Agriculture, FSQS ASD, Program Services Branch 123 East Grant Street Minneapolis, MN 55403	SAME AS BLOCK 7

In advertised procurement "offer" and "offeror" shall be construed to mean "bid" and "bidder"

SOLICITATION

9. Sealed offers in original and ___0___ copies for furnishing the supplies or services in the Schedule will be received at the place specified in block 8, or

if handcarried, in the depository located in ___See Block 7___ until ___1/4//9___ local time ___2:30 P.M.___
                                                                            (Hour)   *(Date)*

If this is an advertised solicitation, offers will be publicly opened at that time.   local time at

CAUTION — LATE OFFERS: See pars. 7 and 8 of Solicitation Instructions and Conditions.   Minneapolis, MN

All offers are subject to the following:

1. The Solicitation Instructions and Conditions, SF 33-A, _____   3. The Schedule included herein and/or attached hereto.

   edition which is attached or incorporated herein by reference.   4. Such other provisions, representations, certifications, and specifications

2. The General Provisions, XXXXXXXXXXXXXXXXXXX edition, which is   as are attached or incorporated herein by reference.

   attached or incorporated herein by reference.   *(Attachments are listed in schedule.)*

FOR INFORMATION CALL (Name & telephone no.) (No collect calls) ▶ Kent E. DesJardien 612-725-2136

SCHEDULE

10. ITEM NO.	11. SUPPLIES/SERVICES	12. QUANTITY	13. UNIT	14. UNIT PRICE	15. AMOUNT
	STAMP, Roller Dating, in accordance with the attached Bid Scehdule, Delivery Requirements, Service Requirements, Specifications and Special Conditions, for delivery F.O.B. origin for the period from date of award through September 30, 1979. The attached General Provisions, APHIS Form 326, Sections 1, 2 and 6 are made a part of this Solicitation and any resultant contract.				

See continuation of schedule on page

OFFER *(pages 2 and 3 must also be fully completed by offeror)*

In compliance with the above, the undersigned agrees, if this offer is accepted within _____ calendar days *(60 calendar days unless a different period is*

inserted by the offeror) from the date for receipt of offers specified above, to furnish any or all items upon which prices are offered at the price set opposite each

item, delivered at the designated point(s), within the time specified in the schedule.

16. DISCOUNT FOR PROMPT PAYMENT *(See par. 9. SF 33-A)*

% 10 CALENDAR DAYS.	% 20 CALENDAR DAYS.	% 30 CALENDAR DAYS.	% CALENDAR DAYS

17. OFFEROR CODE FACILITY CODE	18. NAME AND TITLE OF PERSON AUTHORIZED TO SIGN OFFER (Type or print)
NAME AND ADDRESS (Street, city, county, State and ZIP code) AREA CODE AND TELEPHONE NO. ▶ [ ] Check if remittance address is different from above — enter such address in Schedule	19. SIGNATURE	20. OFFER DATE

AWARD *(To be completed by Government)*

21. ACCEPTED AS TO ITEMS NUMBERED	22. AMOUNT	23. ACCOUNTING AND APPROPRIATION DATA

24. SUBMIT INVOICES (4 copies unless otherwise specified) TO ADDRESS SHOWN IN BLOCK _____	25. NEGOTIATED PURSUANT TO	10 U S C 2304(a) ( )
		41 U S C 252(c) ( )

26. ADMINISTERED BY (If other than block 7) CODE	27. PAYMENT WILL BE MADE BY CODE

28. NAME OF CONTRACTING OFFICER (Type or print)	29. UNITED STATES OF AMERICA BY *(Signature of contracting officer)*	30. AWARD DATE

Award will be made on this form, or on Standard Form 26, or by other official written notice

33-130

Standard Form 33 Page 1 (REV. 3-77)
Prescribed by GSA, FPR (41 CFR) 1-16.101

Figure 9. (continued)

STANDARD FORM 36, JULY 1966 GENERAL SERVICES ADMINISTRATION FED. PROC. REG. (41 CFR) 1-16.101	**CONTINUATION SHEET**	REF. NO. OF DOC. BEING CONT'D. 5-M-FSQS-79		PAGE 7	OF 8

NAME OF OFFEROR OR CONTRACTOR

ITEM NO.	SUPPLIES/SERVICES	QUANTITY	UNIT	UNIT PRICE	AMOUNT
	This Solicitation is being issued to establish a source of supply under contract for Roller dating stamps, as may be required by the U.S.Department of Agriculture, Food Safety and Quality Service, Fruit and Vegetable Quality Division, Processed Products Branch for the period from date of award through September 30, 1979.				
	Due to the nature of the program for which the stamps are required, it is impossible to accurately determine in advance or from past experience the number of stamps that will be required during the specified period. However, it is estimated that 120 roller stamps will be required during the period specified above. This estimate of needs is for information only and is not intended to imply that the estimate is an exact indication of the quantity that will be required.				
	It is agreed that the Fruit and Vegetable Quality Division will procure all of their needs during the stated contract period from the successful offeror at the price quoted and accepted by award of contract and that in consideration, therefore, the successful offeror guarantees by submission of his offer in response thereto, to furnish all of the requirements that may be required by the Fruit and Vegetable Quality Division.				
	BID SCHEDULE				
01.	STAMP, Roller Dating, in accordance with the following Delivery Requirements, Service Requirements, Specifications, Special Conditions and Drawings No. 1 and 2.			Price per Stamp	$_____
	DELIVERY REQUIREMENTS				
	Delivery of the stamps is required within thirty (30) calendar days after receipt of an order. Offerors offering later delivery will be considered nonresponsive.				
	OFFERORS are required to state below the percentage of the contract that will be performed in Labor Surplus Areas and the location of such area.				
	Percentage to be performed in Labor Surplus Area:_____.				
	Location of such area:_____.				
	OFFEROR to state number of Permanent Employees:_____.				
	SERVICE REQUIREMENTS				
	The U.S.Department of Agriculture, Food Quality and Safety Service, Fruit and Vegetable Quality Division requires the stamps for dating and identifying officially inspected products.				

36-108

Figure 9. (*continued*)

5-M-FSQS-79
Page 8 of 8

SPECIFICATIONS

Roller Date Stamp

The roller date stamp shall be a speed roller (pullman type) stamp constructed in accordance with Drawing No. 1 and shall be furnished with a double faced shield shaped die as illustrated in Drawing No. 2 and shall include two (2) date sets. Each date set shall consist of abbreviations for the 12 months, 2 sets of numbers from 1 through 0, and years (1978) starting with the current year and continuing for a minimum of 5 years. The date sets shall be in size 42, pica type.

Offeror shall state his net price for furnishing the following listed repair parts:

Compression Springs	$_____
Felt Ink Pads	$_____
Metal Drum	$_____
Date Set	$_____
Rubber Stamp Sheath with Dies	$_____
Wooden Drum	$_____
Retainer clips for Wood Drum	$_____

Repair parts shall be ordered at the above stated prices on an as needed basis by the various offices.

SPECIAL CONDITIONS

Orders:

Orders will be placed in writing by the Contracting Officer or his designee. The order shall show the destination(s) to which the stamps are to be shipped. The quantity, the city and state name(s) to appear on each stamp and any spare parts required.

Payment:

Payment will be made monthly for deliveries made during the month upon receipt of an invoice in duplicate by the ordering office.

Figure 9. (*continued*)

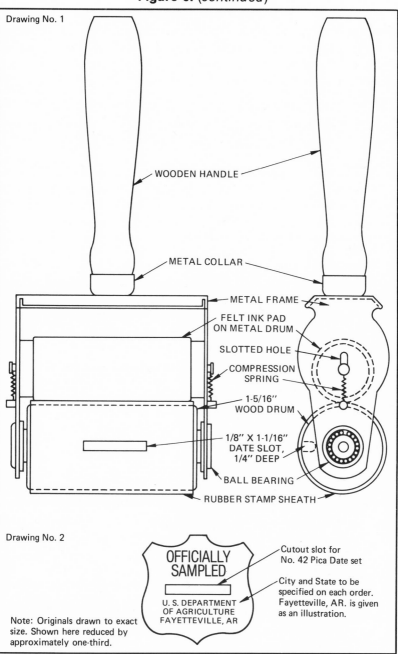

Drawing No. 1

WOODEN HANDLE

METAL COLLAR

METAL FRAME

FELT INK PAD
ON METAL DRUM

SLOTTED HOLE

COMPRESSION
SPRING

1-5/16"
WOOD DRUM

1/8" X 1-1/16"
DATE SLOT,
1/4" DEEP

BALL BEARING

RUBBER STAMP SHEATH

Drawing No. 2

OFFICIALLY
SAMPLED

U. S. DEPARTMENT
OF AGRICULTURE
FAYETTEVILLE, AR

Cutout slot for
No. 42 Pica Date set

City and State to be
specified on each order.
Fayetteville, AR. is given
as an illustration.

Note: Originals drawn to exact
size. Shown here reduced by
approximately one-third.

The specifications follow, and include two drawings to make the requirement absolutely clear. The "Special Conditions" section of the solicitation makes it clear that this is a requirements-type contract, to run from date of award (probably late January 1979) to the end of the government's fiscal year (September 30, 1979). This will be, therefore, an indefinite-quantity contract, with orders placed as needed.

The continuation sheet calls for pricing the stamps individually, with an estimate of 120 stamps to be ordered during the term of the contract. However, the bidder is asked also to supply prices for repair parts, and no estimate of probable orders for repair parts is provided. Each of the ordering activities—the various offices which will order stamps—will order repair parts as needed, but we do not know what that means. That is, we do not know whether each office will order repair parts when stamps need repair, or whether they will order a supply of spare parts to keep in stock. And that can make quite a difference in how to best bid the job.

Bidding for "Spares"

In military procurement, where spare parts and maintenance is a consideration, it is customary for the purchasing agency to make a determination of how many spare parts ("spares," as suppliers to the military often refer to parts) will be ordered and kept in stock. And in many cases, the spare-parts order is more important than the order for the original equipment. In fact, many equipment suppliers follow the example of the razor-blade manufacturer, who virtually gives the razors away, so that he can "lock in" customers for his blades. It is not at all uncommon for suppliers of equipment to bid the equipment contract at near the break-even point, when they believe that they can count on a large order for spare parts, which are usually much more profitable.

In the case of the dating stamp for the USDA, there is no apparent way for the bidder to judge what the spare-parts orders are likely to be. However, the government, the USDA contracting officer, is faced with the same dilemma: How will he determine who is the low bidder? Will he take the prices for repair parts into account, or will he consider only the original cost of the dating stamp? No clues are provided in this particular solicitation. The implication of this is that only the prices for the stamps themselves will be evaluated. But that is by no means certain. One rule the bidder for government contracts should observe scrupulously: *Take nothing for granted. Count only on what is specifi-*

cally stated or specifically provided for under the law and the procurement regulations.

In this case, you have three options:

1. Demand to know the basis for determination of the low bidder before you submit your bid.
2. Check on last year's bid to see how it was priced. For a standard commodity such as this, one should be available. Also ask how many repair parts were sold and how many stamps were sold, as a guide.
3. Make your best guess, submit your bid, and attend the opening. If you are dissatisfied with the final determination, lodge a protest, on the basis of inadequate information for bidding.

Choosing an option

If you were a bidder in this competition, and you chose option number 1, as described, here's what would probably happen:

The solicitation would be postponed; the date would be moved up by a week or two to allow the contracting officer to get you the answer you have demanded and have a right to get. But, having either gotten the information or worked out an evaluation plan, the contracting officer would feel obligated to write it up and distribute copies to everyone who had requested an invitation to bid. Your question would therefore have resulted in providing additional information to all prospective bidders, which may mean that you helped competitors more than you helped yourself.

You should adopt the second option, no matter what else you do, and as a first step. Under the Freedom of Information Act, you have a right to demand the information, and you should exercise that right. (This is one of the advantages of bidding to the government, as compared with bidding to a private company.)

The third option is always open to you, no matter what else you do, if you believe that the proceeding was less than completely fair or completely honest.

Usually, asking for information under the Freedom of Information Act does not result in distribution of information to other prospective bidders, because getting such information does not confer a special advantage on you, under the law. All the other bidders have equal access to the information (if they are smart enough to ask for it). They could not claim that you had information not available to them!

Most government documents are public documents and available for public scrutiny, on demand. The exceptions are those items of information which affect national security, information which is proprietary (trade secrets), and information which, if released, would be an invasion of privacy. You are therefore entitled to get a copy of any existing or prior contract, although proprietary information may be deleted from your copy. Usually, however, you are not really interested in the entire proposal and/or contract, but only in the "bottom line"—the prices the government is or has been paying.

Should the procurement officer refuse to state a method for identifying the low bid, however, your proper counter is not the Freedom of Information Act, but a protest. Filing a protest will probably force the agency to release such information. However, it will go out to all bidders.

Another Example to Illustrate the Case

The headquarters office of NASA used to issue a contract every three years for publications-support services (and perhaps still does). Typically, it was a basic ordering agreement, under which the contractor agreed to provide services at some specific prices, on an as-needed basis.

It was the typical "laundry list" of services, arranged somewhat as follows:

Function	Unit	Estimated Requirement	Price per Unit
Technical writing	hour	1,250 hours	$_____
Technical editing	hour	800 hours	$_____
Production editing	hour	300 hours	$_____
Drafting	hour	400 hours	$_____
Illustrating	hour	600 hours	$_____
Typing	page	1,400 pages	$_____
Proofreading	page	1,400 pages	$_____
Photography	hour	600 hours	$_____

This is the typical situation of indefinite quantity requirements. How does the government decide who is the low bidder? And, more important to the bidder, what strategies are possible in bidding this?

It's easy to visualize some sort of bench test being made to determine the relative ranking of the various bids. And, while government officials may explain the bench test in general (in fact, they must do so upon demand), they will not tell you exactly what the bench-test quantities are going to be, for obvious reasons.

One Kind of Cost Strategy

You can occasionally win government contracts through chance—the chance that few others have bid or that they have not been smart in their bidding—or you can win them consistently and frequently by using intelligent strategies. The Freedom of Information Act gives you an almost unparalleled opportunity to get the information you need to devise strategies.

Here is what we actually did to win the contract referred to here:

We checked on the history of the contract in past years, learning (1) who the previous years' contractors had been (they would be our competitors), (2) what quantities of each service or function had been ordered in past years, and (3) what the government (NASA Headquarters) was paying for each service.

We learned one very interesting fact: NASA Headquarters has ample in-house photographic capability, and had never ordered any photo services under this contract.

The implication is obvious. It is similar to that of the lady who visited her local grocery store to buy bananas. She was outraged to learn that bananas were 49¢ a pound, and she protested loudly. The proprietor apologized for the price, explaining that he had no choice in the matter: bananas were simply high at that time of year.

"But I can get them at Joe's Market for 29¢ a pound," she complained.

Gently, the grocer asked why she didn't get them there, since they were such a bargain.

"Joe's Market is out of bananas today," she wailed.

The grocer grinned. "Well, I sell them for 19¢ a pound when I'm out of them. But they're 49¢ a pound when I have them."

Moral: It's easy to give something away when you're out of it—or when there's no call for it.

By pricing photographic services at virtually nothing, our bid *appeared* to be the low bid.

Why does the solicitation include photographic services when none are needed? For one thing, there is always the possibility that they may be needed. But the real reason lies in the nature of the bureaucracy: No one has the initiative to change the bid set, so it remains the same, year after year.

Establishing prices this way is akin to the supermarkets' practice of offering "loss leaders"—items sold at or below actual cost to draw people into the store, where they will buy many other things, more than compensating for the loss on the leader.

A Variation on a Theme

There is another way this same idea can be used to *create* an item for which there will be no demand, enabling the bidder to bid it at a ridiculously low rate and come in the *apparent* low bidder. This plan requires a bit more explanation.

In many of these "laundry list" requirements contracts for general support services, various technical/professional specialities are called for at various levels of proficiency. For example, the customer may perceive a need for engineers of almost an apprentice level for some tasks, while other tasks, they believe, will require engineers with considerable experience. In such cases, the solicitation will describe the various levels, such as number of years of experience following graduation, graduate degrees, fields of specialization, and so on. The cost form might look somewhat as follows:

Category	Unit	Estimated Requirement	Cost per Unit
Engineer I	hour	1,500 hours	$_____
Engineer II	hour	2,200 hours	$_____
Engineer III	hour	850 hours	$_____
Draftsman I	hour	3,000 hours	$_____
Draftsman II	hour	2,400 hours	$_____

When the government has awarded a contract, both the government and the contractor are bound by the rates agreed upon. However, each time the government orders a task under the contract, the usual procedure is for an official to send a request and a task description to the contractor for an estimate. It is the contractor—not the customer—who decides what levels of personnel are required and for how many hours each. The contractor prepares the estimate, computing costs on the basis of hours for each specialist, and submits the estimate for approval. Once approved, the contractor is bound to do three things:

1. Perform the task and deliver a satisfactory result, as stipulated in the task description.
2. Charge for each person employed on the task those rates agreed upon. (Verifiable by audit.)

3. Stay within the total price quoted for the task (unless the task is modified by the customer).

The work is performed under contract, and by law the government may not tell the contractor how to "manage" the project. That means, in practice, that the government may not order the contractor to utilize such and such kinds of personnel nor order any specific person to be assigned the task.

Therefore—and mark this closely—the contractor is free to assign anyone he chooses to the task, as long as he meets the three conditions noted above.

If the contractor decides that one of the three levels of engineer, engineer II, perhaps, is really superfluous and need never be actually used on the job, it will cost nothing to bid Engineer II at a very low rate—and consequently come out low on the bench test!

As a variant of this, the contractor may bid Engineer II on a task estimate, but need never actually assign an Engineer II to the task. For example, suppose you (as the contractor) receive a request for an estimate on a task. You make a first cut which looks like this::

Engineer I	60 hours @ $18.00/hour =	$1,080
Engineer II	240 hours @ 6.00/hour =	1,440
Engineer III	110 hours @ 9.50/hour =	1,045
Total		$3,565

You will lose money if you use an Engineer II at $6.00 an hour because you actually pay him more than that. Still, the estimate involves 410 hours of engineering time, which is more than enough for the job, and you should be able to do it for $3,565. And you know that the customer will not consider $3,565 an exorbitant price for the job.

In fact, you can almost certainly do the job this way:

Engineer I	60 hours @ $18.00/hour =	$1,080
Engineer III	260 hours @ $ 9.50/hour =	2,470
Total		$3,550

You can estimate the job by the first set of figures, get the customer's approval (he's primarily concerned with the bottom line for the task), obtain a work order, and then go ahead and do the job per the second estimate. You will be able to bill your staff at the rates established for them—profitably—while staying within the total price originally quoted.

You have, in fact, created your own loss leader, but you need never actually suffer the loss! The objective was strictly to *appear* to be the low bidder, without really *being* low bidder!

The game of "changes"

Anyone who has built a house knows about "changes." Any change you make, even one that takes something out, costs you more money. That's a general fact of life in the construction business: Changes are almost inevitable, for any of a dozen reasons, and every change costs the owner more money than originally estimated. Rarely do changes result in a lowering of price.

Changes are not confined to construction work, however. Almost any long-term custom requirement is likely to involve changes; there are always circumstances and contingencies which no one could have foreseen at the onset or during the planning of the program.

Here are just a few of the reasons for changes:

- A material required is in short supply, and something else must be substituted for it.
- A new and superior material becomes available.
- The customer has a change of mind about something.
- An unforeseen problem arises during the course of early work, making a change mandatory.
- The customer does not keep all his commitments to the contractor, requiring the contractor to do more work than originally planned, or forcing an expensive slowdown on him, or causing extra costs in some way.

These changes are, of course, not the contractor's fault or the contractor's doing. Therefore, he has a legitimate claim on the customer for amendment of the contract. Changes are especially plentiful in long-term projects involving high technology, such as weapons systems, computers, radar, and the like, owing to the ultra-rapid growth of the technologies and the need to react to political and technological developments on the other side of the Iron Curtain. Rarely is a modern system of any size produced according to the original design configuration. As a system or new equipment is being developed, drawings are made. However, a new piece of equipment almost always needs "debugging," since prototypes rarely perform perfectly until they have been tinkered with at great length. As each change in design is finalized, that change is supposed to be made on the drawings. Therefore, an original drawing becomes "Revision A," to reflect the first change, "Revision B," to reflect the second change, and so on.

It's not at all uncommon to have revision letters well into the alphabet!

In practice, the designers and draftsmen rarely keep up with the actual changes, so that for a very large part of the life of a new system, none of the drawings extant are really up to date. The latest drawing available may be Revision G, even though 15 changes may have actually been made to the equipment!

Now comes the time to solicit bids for work involving the system—technical manuals, perhaps, or some related equipment, or even contracts for installation—and the bids submitted are based on the drawings, which are part of the solicitation package. That is, the bidders submit prices based on their analysis of the requirement as described in the drawings, of which there are often thousands.

But suppose the drawings are not up to date, suppose they do not reflect the system as it actually has been finalized. What if the bidders bid on the basis of Drawing Revision G and are handed Drawing Revision L when they are about to start work? What if they start working and discover that the actual equipment does not correspond with Drawing Revision G and that up-to-date drawings are not available?

The "what if?" is easy to answer. The contractor hollers, "Foul!" and claims a "change of scope," which the contracting officer can hardly refute. The contracting officer then invites the contractor to "document" the claimed changes and estimate the costs of the changes—that is, how much money should be added to the contract.

Ultimately, the amendment(s) to the contract is (are) negotiated, and the contract is amended, which means, usually, that money is added.

There are other situations which result in changes and amendments. A typical one is that in which a contractor has done the research and development work to develop a prototype, and has (probably deliberately) failed to indicate many key items of information in the drawings delivered with the prototype. An R&D contractor will frequently withhold information in this way if his contract does not have all the "teeth" in it to compel him to make a full disclosure of his work. The following example illustrates why this can be advantageous to a contractor.

It is common practice to issue an R&D contract on a cost-plus basis (because it is almost impossible to predict the costs of R&D) to a firm when a new, improved system is wanted. In the military, the arms race has created frequent need for this, as technology continues to explode. For every weapon we develop, the other side develops a counter-weapon, and we are compelled to develop a new weapon which is immune to their counter-weapon or to improve our original weapon so as to counter their counter-weapon! Military preparation is responsible for a great percentage of our technological development.

Now, suppose we develop a high-flying aircraft, such as the U-2, which can fly above the enemy's surface-to-air missiles (SAMs). If they catch up and shoot down our U-2, we seek another method, perhaps a satellite that flies even higher, or a low-level aircraft that flies *under* their radar. Or we might see a need for a more flexible or faster radar system. In any case, once our government decides that a new development is (1) needed and (2) possible, officials are likely to invite bids to do the R&D and produce a prototype.

Once the prototype is developed and delivered, and the government is satisfied that it works and should be added to the arsenal, a contractor is sought to produce the device in the numbers required. This is a *production contract,* whereas the original one was a *development contract.*

The development contract should have called for the developer to deliver a complete set of drawings that make full disclosure: show exactly how the device is built and assembled. There are overall drawings of the device, including views of the assembled end-item, detail drawings of each part (or other documentation of parts which may be bought off the shelf, if such is the case), parts lists, and assembly drawings, which show how the various parts are assembled into the final product. The drawings should also show how the various parts are made (whether stamped, pressed, rolled, punched, and so on) and of what materials. In short, if the drawing package is complete, as it should be, *any* competent firm should be able to build it exactly as it was prototyped.

However, the R&D contractor would like to win the contract to produce the item, too, and he is not going to provide any more information in his drawings than the law and his contract require him to. And unfortunately, sometimes the government fails to "cross all the t's and dot all the i's" in its contracts. So occasionally an R&D contractor delivers a set of drawings which do not permit another contractor to build the item! This virtually forces the government to give the production contract to the original R&D firm.

However, the government may not be aware that the drawings are deficient and do not make full disclosure, and therefore offer the drawings as specifications to back up a solicitation package. Later, having bid on the basis of the drawings, the production contractor discovers that the item can't be assembled in the procedure shown, or has other problems resulting from deficient information supplied by the government. He then has justification for a change in price.

This happens with such regularity in many fields that it is predictable. It therefore becomes the basis for a popular bidding strategy: If the bidder can be reasonably certain that he will have occasions for changes, during the course of the contract, he can afford to bid low, sometimes even below his anticipated costs, and get his profits out of the changes!

This is easily possible because, while he must bid competitively to win the contract, he has no competitive bids to meet in pricing changes. These are negotiated with the customer, and good negotiators can get the right prices when there are no competitive bids to worry about.

This kind of situation is not confined to construction and engineering, although it is almost invariably encountered there. Almost any long-term custom project will run into unexpected difficulties of one sort or another, or even meet other kinds of opportunities that will cause a change in scope and a consequent amendment.

Incidentally, for purposes of clarification, a change in a contract which does not affect the price is a "modification," whereas a change which does affect the price is an "amendment." Moreover, *only the authorized contracting official* may authorize an amendment, and not his "authorized technical representative," by whatever title he is known (for example, contracting officer's representative, contracting officer's technical representative, project manager, and so on).

Procedures for Changes

When a contract is going to be modified or amended, a certain protocol is usually observed. The talks may be initiated unofficially by either the government or the contractor; however, once the change is agreed upon, the usual procedure is to have the contractor write a formal request to the contracting official asking for the change. Here is a typical sequence of events, from an actual experience:

I was the manager of a three-year contract for technical support of a NASA center, under a cost-reimbursement contract. The contract listed, among other things, technical writers at three levels of proficiency, and established ceiling rates for each class for each year of the contract.

In the third year of the contract, circumstances made it almost impossible to recruit Level III writers at the rates contracted for. No one could have foreseen, two years earlier, that a combination of a seller's market and inflation would have led to this situation. Nevertheless, we were bound by a contract which could have forced us to lose money.

After studying the situation to find an escape, I was struck by an idea. I sought out the COTR (contracting officer's technical representative) and pointed out that there had been, in the past two years, an almost quantum leap in the sophistication of the systems we were writing manuals about, and because we had provided some very talented and capable people in the past, some of the work we were currently being asked to do was a bit beyond that originally envisioned for the project. I suggested that therefore we should "modify" the contract to establish a Writer IV category, at a slightly higher rate than that of Writer III.

I persuaded the COTR to agree with me, and he "suggested" that I write a request to the contracting officer, setting forth my arguments. The contracting officer, of course, passed the request to the COTR for comment, and when the COTR approved, the modification was made.

This was a modification, rather than an amendment, because it didn't change the government's commitment on total price for the contract or call for the "obligation" of additional funds, although it did authorize our billing at a higher rate for the new Writer IV level.

Ingenuity can also bring about changes, when circumstances do not compel them!

Rules and Exceptions on Changes

Every contract carries the clear warning that the contractor must not agree to changes calling for more money without the contracting official's approval and authorization. A COTR may request additional work and may promise that a contract amendment will be forthcoming, but it is most hazardous to proceed and incur additional expense on this assurance alone. The COTR does not have the legal authority to obligate the government for more money, and although he may be acting in good faith, he may very well find out that he cannot back up his promise. Also, COTRs are often replaced, during the course of a contract, and a new COTR is not likely to feel compelled to honor the pledge of his predecessor, especially when the pledge is not in writing and is not legally binding, in any case.

Even when a contracting official agrees to a change and amendment, it is hazardous to proceed before the amendment is formally in writing and legally binding. A contracting official may be replaced by another, too, before the contract is consummated.

There are exceptions, however. Here is one such case:

When the Air Pollution Control Office (APCO) of the Public Health Service was in existence (it's now the Environmental Protection Agency) the organization I managed was approached by that agency to help officials produce their four volumes of standards and specifications. The time pressure was great: The four volumes had to be completed, printed and bound, and in the mail, postmarked before January 1, 1970. Our aid was solicited in late November 1969!

Initially, the staff asked for minimal aid such as typing, proofreading, and perhaps some light editing and a few illustrations. When we looked the work over and advised them that we believed they would need more help than that, they assured us that they did not. Within a few days, the APCO staff was asking us for more support than we had contracted for. Knowing the hazards of proceeding without the contracting official's okay, we communicated this to the contracting officer. He asked us to draw up a list of changes required and submit them to him, with estimated costs.

While we were doing so, the APCO staff asked for still more support, as they began to perceive how far they really were from completing the job. We were compelled to call the contracting officer again.

He then authorized us—verbally—to provide whatever the staff asked for, and said that if we would keep track, he would settle with us at the end of the job. Under such exceptional circumstances, we agreed to proceed on his verbal assurances.

Ultimately, we amassed a bill of over $35,000 for what started out to be a job contracted for less than $5,000! And even though the customer had been almost supplicating us for help, we anticipated that we would have a tough negotiation at the end. (Gratitude vanishes quickly, when the crisis is over!) We weren't disappointed: We had to fight hard at the negotiating table to get everything that was coming to us.

In such a case as this, knowing the pressure to produce a job by a given date, and seeing how far the customer was from being ready to meet that date without massive help, it did not take a genius to foresee that there would be many changes before the job was over.

When all else fails, read the instructions!

We fallible humans have a great talent for overlooking the obvious. We seek complex answers to simple problems, when the simple is right in front us. Nowhere is this more apparent than when we read over solicitation packages.

The typical solicitation package includes a great deal of boilerplate material—standard instructions and forms. After a while the experienced bidder tends to skim by this familiar paper, and in so doing often misses information which would, or should, make the difference. He may make telephone calls and visits, and undertake a great deal of unnecessary research, when the information has been on his desk all the while.

In one such case, I had an invitation to bid the U.S. Forest Service for a basic ordering agreement to support their technical publications work. It was a typical laundry list of services that included writing, editing, drafting, illustrating, proofreading, typing, and so on. It was a formally advertised procurement, which meant, of course, that the contract would go to the low bidder.

As a matter of course, I invoked the Freedom of Information Act and obtained the prices being paid under the then-existing contract. I found them to be highly competitive, and was in something of a quandary for a strategy to be or appear to be the low bidder.

Almost in desperation, I leafed slowly through the rather voluminous bid set. But it was only after doing so several times that I made the discovery I should have made on first reading, which proved to be the key to being the low bidder—or apparent low bidder.

One of the items to be priced was, typically, double-spaced draft typing, by the page. The government then used $8 \times 10\frac{1}{2}$ inch paper (this was before the change to the commercial standard of $8\frac{1}{2} \times 11$ inch paper), on which a typical image area (typing area on a page) is approximately $6\frac{1}{2} \times 9$ inches. Typed on an elite (12-pitch) typewriter, a page would be about 27 lines long, and 75 characters wide. For a 10-pitch or pica machine, this would be 27 lines which are each 65 characters wide.

It occurred to me that I had not seen a definition of whether a "page" of typing was predicated on elite or pica typeface. I therefore began to read all the tiresome boilerplate specifications, to which I had paid little attention before.

I finally came to the specification for a page of typing. To my utter amazement a typed page was defined as 55 characters wide and 18 lines deep! If you get out your calculator, you'll find that this represents 990 typewriter strikes (or keystrokes, as many typesetting houses now refer to it), compared with 2,025 strikes for what I had presumed to be the "standard" page. Less than one-half!

That meant I could cut the per-page price considerably without running any risks, which enabled us to be the low bidder without cutting any other prices.

Different strategies for different situations

It might be thought that an incumbent, the present contractor on a project coming up for another year's contract, enjoys a decisive advantage over the outsider bidding for the contract. In many cases, this is entirely true, but not in all cases. There is one kind of procurement, in fact, where the incumbent is at a decided disadvantage: the "body" contract.

Under the law, the government may not "hire" people indirectly by contracting for labor to be done on-site (in or on the government's own premises), unless the work cannot be done off-site. If a contractor must manage or operate a government computer or R&D laboratory, he must obviously do so on the government's premises—on-site. If he is writing a manual for the government, he can usually do that on his own premises, and is required to do so.

Work that must be done on-site presents special problems and considerations in bidding for the contract. The pricing competition is quite close for such work because all employers must pay workers approximately the same hourly rates, so the difference among bids is usually rather small, sometimes only pennies per labor hour.

The staff of the incumbent contractor have been working on-site for at least one year, and often for several years. The contractor has tried to keep some continuity of staff by awarding merit increases each year, so that most workers are above the starting rate. When the time comes to bid for renewal of the contract, he is compelled to assume that his existing staff will remain in place (the customer would think him a poor contractor if he changed his staff every year) and will continue to get annual merit increases.

The other bidders are under no such restraints or obligations. They can, and do, bid the job at whatever they believe to be starting rates. They are prepared to replace the entire existing staff, if necessary. They cannot be criticized for so doing because they have no obligations to an existing staff and existing customer. In almost every case, such contracts represent a rough, tough game, with rough, tough competitors. Only by hardheaded, realistic bidding can one hope to win these contracts.

The strategies available in competing for formally advertised procurements (sealed-bid types of competition) are all variations on the theme of how to be or appear to be the low bidder. It is only the low bidder who wins, although the law does not say this explicitly. The law does, in fact, provide for a number of cases where the low bidder does not win. But, as you have already read, in practice it is rare for the low bidder to be denied the contract, unless he can be persuaded to withdraw his bid voluntarily.

The following case illustrates this clearly: When HUD (the Department of Housing and Urban Development) took over the old FHA mortgages, it inherited a warehouse packed with filing cabinets full of mortgage papers. The documents required a massive updating to reflect the changes occasioned by HUD assuming the mortgages. It was decided to hire a contractor with a crew of clerks to carry out the work.

Bids were invited by IFB (information for bid) and a public opening held. When the bids were opened, the contracting officer and the project manager were shocked by the low bid. It was, in their opinion, unrealistically low.

It is not in the interest of the government to have a contractor default on a project. The government gains nothing, and loses a great deal of time. Therefore, the contracting officer and the project manager took the low bidder aside and explained that he could not possibly do the job for the figure quoted without losing his shirt. The contracting officer offered to let the man withdraw his bid. The bidder flatly refused. He insisted that he knew what he was doing, and that he could and would do the job for the figure quoted.

The officials had no choice but to allow him to try, and they reluctantly awarded him the contract. Within two months, the contractor was in serious trouble, and, as predicted, was unable to perform. The officials were compelled to find him in default and cancel the contract. As soon as that was done, they scheduled another competition for the contract.

To their horror, history repeated itself. The same individual again submitted a low bid, again insisted that he now knew what he had done wrong, and again insisted on having the contract. History continued to repeat itself, and the contractor defaulted a second time, resulting in the contract being canceled a second time.

The contracting officer and the project manager anticipated the possibility that this individual might be bullheaded enough to try even a third time to do the impossible; they headed him off by a simple maneuver: This time they issued an RFP (request for proposal), which results in a negotiated procurement and does not obligate the government to award the contract to the lowest bidder.

This is one of the several reasons that the government often prefers to use negotiated procurement: The low bidder is not always the most desirable contractor, nor even a qualified contractor.

Negotiated procurement

In terms of total procurement dollars (not number of procurement contracts), about 85 percent of federal procurement is done through negotiation. The rules for negotiated procurements are different from those for formally advertised procurements in the following ways:

1. Openings are not public.
2. Price is not the only factor, and often is a negligible factor. (That is, the government is under no compulsion whatever to make an award to the low bidder.)
3. A technical proposal is required, and an evaluation made of the proposer's (bidder's) competence or capability, as well as of the general merits of his proposal.
4. Prices may be adjusted after the opening, and bidders may submit additional information and/or changes to their proposals after the opening, if the government wishes to grant them permission to do so.

There are a few points of similarity, too:

1. Everyone bidding (proposing) is entitled to have the same information and access to information. Proposals can be invalidated, if it is shown that one of the proposers had an unfair advantage over the others.
2. Price *may* be the deciding factor.
3. The announced "opening" date is actually the closing date. Proposals delivered after that date may be rejected, and usually are, unless the delay was caused by the postal service (the proposal having been mailed with such promptness so that it *should* have been delivered in time) or due to other excusable causes, as provided by law.
4. Proposers have the right to know, after award is made, what others bid, and may protest an award if they believe a protest is justified.
5. A proposal may lead to any type of contract, just as a sealed bid may. The form of the contract is not affected by the manner of the competition for it.

In general, the rules and procedures for negotiated procurement are much freer and more flexible than they are for formally advertised procurement simply because the contract is to be *negotiated,* and the selection of a winner depends on technical competition as well as on price competition. But to provide as fair and equable an atmosphere as possible, the agency must establish and use an objective rating scheme to evaluate all proposals. Further, to ensure that proposals are rated as objectively as possible on their technical merits, those who evaluate technical proposals are not permitted to know what costs each proposer has estimated.

Typical Evaluation Criteria

Unfortunately, there is no standard for evaluation schemes. Each agency, and this can mean an individual "office" or "administration" within an agency, sets its own criteria and schemes. Therefore, one solicitation package may describe a heavily detailed and highly sophisticated evaluation scheme, while another presents a rather cursory and general one. Or, one solicitation may state some specific number of evaluation points assigned to each criterion listed, while another will state merely the relative weight of one as compared with another.

In general, however, these are the factors weighed by these schemes:

- The proposer's understanding of the requirement, as shown by the proposal.
- The quality of the plan proposed for satisfying the requirement or solving the problems stated.
- The demonstrated ability to anticipate contingencies and cope successfully with them.
- The quality of the proposer's plan for managing the work.
- The qualifications of the staff proposed for the project, especially the key members of the staff, who will be responsible for the critical functions.
- The qualifications (experience, resources, and track record) of the proposing organization, as an organization.
- The commitment of the organization and/or its parent organization to the project.
- The qualifications of the proposer's proposed project manager.
- The proposer's financial resources for handling the project.
- The proposed schedule for deliveries and accomplishments of milestones.

The Source Selection Board

In most cases, proposals are evaluated by a team of three, five, or more members, who award each proposal a technical point score. In some cases, cost is itself a basis for points; in others, cost is considered more generally, with no points awarded specifically for it. No matter how detailed the criteria described in the solicitation are, the evaluation team is working with even more detailed guidance than that described. For example, the solicitation may state that a maximum of 20 points or 20 percent will be awarded for staff qualifications. Internally, in making the actual evaluation, the evaluators will have a breakdown of this, under which they will have perhaps 5 points maximum for the individual's formal education, 5 more points for general experience, and 10 points for directly related experience, to make up the 20 points total.

Although a team is usually used, except for the smallest contracts, the head of the team, who is quite often the individual who will be the government's project manager, is usually quite influential in making the final decision. The board also usually includes the contracting officer, either directly or indirectly. Although he is probably not a technical expert and can't contribute to technical evaluation, he is central to the process and can evaluate some of the factors.

Technical versus Cost Proposal

The solicitation calls for two proposals: technical and cost. That is, the cost presentation is to be bound separately from the technical information. When the proposal package is delivered to the contracting officer, he separates the two and retains the cost proposals under his security while the evaluation team reviews the technical proposals.

After technical review has been made and the proposals have been scored, the review of cost is made. This usually involves conferences between the technical evaluators and the contracting officer. They compare the merits of each proposal with the cost to the government. There are many variations of how the technical and cost considerations are finally reconciled to make a final award decision, but there are three general cases:

1. Cost is assigned specific point value, which is added to technical points awarded for a final score.
2. A complex scheme is used, wherein each proposal is given a rating based on cost per technical point awarded.
3. Cost is not evaluated on a point basis, but is part of a general and final evaluation, usually described as ". . . cost and other factors considered."

The Impact of Cost

As a result of this great variation in how cost affects award decisions, there are several basic situations, which can be summarized as follows:

1. The award goes to the lowest priced qualified proposer (that is, the lowest priced of those remaining after all technically unacceptable proposals have been rejected).
2. The award goes to that proposer whose final cost-per-technical-point score is lowest.
3. The award goes to that proposer whose proposal has received the highest technical-point score, if his price is (or can be brought) within an acceptable range (often referred to as the competitive range).

In the first situation, price becomes an important factor, particularly if a protest or award dispute arises, because it is not at all uncommon for two-thirds or more of the proposals submitted to be rejected on technical grounds. When the government commits itself to such an evaluation scheme, it lessens the importance of achieving the highest possible technical score, and places all proposers whose proposals are technically acceptable (within the competitive range) on an equal basis, with price now the determining factor. This places the competition on a basis somewhat similar to that of the two-step procurement (discussed later in this chapter). But it also lessens the effects of the evaluators' subjective judgments, and gives the protestor a "place to stand" if and when he chooses to dispute the award decision. It has become a matter of record which proposals are technically acceptable and which of those is lowest priced. It is by far the most objective rating scheme offered.

The second approach to evaluating costs is also reasonably objective, but is affected far more by technical scores, which are inevitably subjective. The usual approach is to select that proposal which has received the highest technical rating and use that proposer's costs as the baseline or reference standard by which to evaluate the others' cost-per-technical-point rating. Here is an example of how such a method usually works:

The highest scoring proposal receives 97 points (out of a possible 100). The price offered by this proposer (A) is $240,000.

$$\text{Baseline is } \frac{\$240,000}{97} = \$2,474.23 \text{ per technical point}$$

Proposer B is awarded 93 points, has offered a prize of $237,000.

$$\frac{\$237,000}{93} = \$2,548.39$$

Proposer C is awarded 90 points, offers a price of $278,000.

$$\frac{\$278,000}{90} = \$3,088.89$$

Proposer D is awarded 88 points, offers price of $216,000.

$$\frac{\$216,000}{88} = \$2,454.55$$

Therefore, comparative costs per technical point are

Proposer A: $2,474.23
Proposer B: $2,548.39
Proposer C: $3,088.89
Proposer D: $2,454.55

Although not the highest scoring proposer, D's price is lowest in terms of cost per technical point. This is interpreted as representing the best *value* to the government.

Variants of this basic approach are often used, some of them relatively complex, but all based on the same general idea.

The third approach is the least objective, since the customer evaluates prices subjectively to determine which represents the best value to the government. He will score all the technical proposals, rejecting those that do not meet his minimum requirements, and then decide which one he believes to be "in the best interests of the government," which may easily mean which contractor he likes best or feels most comfortable with.

Of course, there has been an in-house estimate made before the solicitation was issued; the requestor could not have gotten approval for the funds without some kind of estimate. Ordinarily, no proposal will be acceptable if the cost exceeds that estimate, which has now become the preliminary budget for the project. Presumably, the competitive range is established by identifying the limits of prices quoted by most acceptable proposals. However, in many cases, the customer may accept any quote which does not exceed the budget as being in the competitive range.

However, because this is a negotiated procurement, the price submitted by a proposer is not engraved in stone; it is still subject to negotiation. Therefore, the government may elect to negotiate with the highest scoring proposers to try to bring their prices down within the range established as acceptable. Typically, the solicitation package states that officials may select a proposal and proceed to make an award without further discussion. The government reserves that right, which is an inducement to the proposer to offer his best terms in the initial submittal. In the case of small contracts, especially when there is an urgency to consummate a contract before some deadline (such as the end of the fiscal year), awards are often made "without further discussion." However, large contracts are almost always negotiated before an award is made.

The Nature of Negotiations

Negotiations can take any of several forms, which may or may not resemble negotiations as practiced in private industry. The proposals have been evaluated, the prices for each have been noted, the contracting officer has discussed the evaluations and gotten the opinions of the evaluators and the program executive requesting the contract, and the proposals have been rank-ordered.

If an acceptable proposal has been priced so high as to preclude, in the contracting officer's opinion, the possibility of negotiating the price down to an acceptable range, no effort may be made to negotiate with that proposer, and usually is not. Barring that, any of the following approaches may be pursued:

1. Negotiations are opened with the top-ranking (preferred) proposer only. If successful, no other contracts will be negotiated. If not successful, the next-ranking proposer will be invited to negotiate.
2. The top three or more proposers are each invited to make a formal presentation, answer questions, conduct discussions, and submit any additional technical and cost estimates (or modify original ones).
3. All proposers whose original submittals were acceptable are invited to make presentations, and so on, and submit "best and final offers," as in (2) above.

The contracting officer and his influence

Much depends on the personality and policies of the contracting officer, who is the agent's authority on contract law and procurement regulations. (Most contracting officers are lawyers or accountants, and many are both.) Many contracting officers will fight hard for the lowest priced proposal, just as many program executives will fight hard for their own selection, irrespective of price. In some agencies, a contracting officer will demand that the source selection board submit a formal, written justification for the selection of any but the lowest priced qualified offeror. Because this is not always an easy thing to justify when much of the judgment has been subjective, it often has the effect of directing the award to the lowest priced qualified bidder, even though the evaluation system was not designed to achieve that result.

The goal of a dedicated contracting officer is to get, for the government, the best product (result) in the shortest possible time (shortest schedule) at the lowest possible cost. He is usually dependent on the program people, as technical specialists, to select the proposal which promises the best product or result, but he can see for himself who offers the best schedule and lowest price.

Policies versus regulations

Internal agency procurement policies are as important as the procurement regulations. The regulations are intended to stipulate what is permissible and what is taboo, under the laws, as enacted by Congress, and to lay down the basic procurement procedures. The regulations are, however, subject to interpretation by the agencies' contracting officials and executive heads. (In some cases, the chief executive of the agency is the designated contracting officer.) Policy may also be such as to restrict the application of the law.

For example, the law (Small Purchases Act) provides that small-purchase procedures may be used for procurements under $10,000. This means a limited and informal competition, using a purchase order as the contractual instrument, rather than a formal contract. However, there are agencies whose contracting officials permit small-purchase procedures for procurements under $2,500 only. In some agencies, best-and-final procedures are used for only large contracts, while in others they are used in all procurements over $10,000. And so on.

This applies even to profit figures. The National Cancer Institute, for example, permits a fee of up to 9 percent in a cost-reimbursement contract, while other agencies may restrict fees to lower percentages.

The hybrid "two-step" procurement

The two-step procurement referred to earlier in this chapter embodies the characteristics of both the formally advertised and negotiated procurement methods, and may well come into greater use, under present trends in government procurement and OFPP policies. Basically, it is a system in which technical proposals only (no cost information) are invited, as a first step. After evaluation, those proposers whose technical proposals are considered acceptable are solicited to submit cost proposals. Step 1 is accomplished by RFP, Step 2 by IFB.

This means that the second step is accomplished under the rules of formally advertised procurement, with sealed bids, and the award going to the low bidder. But the bidders are restricted to those who have submitted acceptable technical proposals, eliminating the hazard of awarding the contract to someone who cannot perform (*presumably* eliminating that hazard, that is). It is therefore a form of prequalifying bidders and screening out those who do not appear to be truly capable of carrying out the work satisfactorily. Ordinarily, this method is used only for large procurements, and is still not in widespread use.

What is "strategy"?

Given the enormous number of variants and possible permutations among those variants, it is obvious that what is decisive in one case is of little consequence in another. For example, it may be critically important to be the low bidder to win one contract, but totally unimportant for another; or, it may be necessary to win an extremely high technical-point score in one case, while in another case the effort to score above the acceptable threshold is wasted.

But there are other factors. In most cases, there is some single factor which is uppermost in the customer's mind, although that may not have been communicated in the statement of work and general information package. He may, for example, be definitely seeking something innovative, a totally new and different approach to his project. Or he may be totally opposed to innovation, and want what he considers to be the safe and sound, tried and true, classical approach. Here are some other considerations which are often critical:

The quality of the proposed staff. In many cases, the success of a proposal hinges almost entirely on the customer's reaction to the resumes in the proposal.

The technical plan for the project. The customer must be convinced that the plan is a sound one and has an excellent chance for being entirely successful.

The plan for management of the proposed project. In many cases, the customer considers the management of the project at least as important as the technical aspects of the program, and scrutinizes the proposed management plan especially closely.

Corporate commitment. Proposals are frequently submitted by a division or department of a larger organization. The customer may be especially watchful for evidence that the parent corporation is cognizant of and dedicated to success in the proposed project.

Organization experience. Even with well-qualified staff members proposed, the customer requires, usually, that the organization have relevant experience. The organization which has done related but not similar work in the past may not be credible enough to justify the risk of a large project.

Strategy is the *conceptual* approach for winning. In its simplest perspective, it involves two elements:

1. Identifying the factor(s) which is (are) most critically important in the customer's mind (*or can be made* most critically important), and which is (are) key to winning.
2. Structuring the proposal so as to persuade the customer that the proposer represents the best prospect for realizing or effecting the objective(s) represented by the critical factor(s).

That is, strategy consists of correctly identifying what the customer wants most and then persuading the customer that the proposer can and will deliver what is wanted.

An alternative to this is to help the customer identify the most important factor(s), and then sell the proposer's ability to deliver those things. That is, a successful proposal is often one in which the proposer has demonstrated that some factor(s) is (are) critical to overall program success, and then has gone on to present a plan and set of credentials specific to the factor(s) highlighted.

Beating the competition

Proposal writing is a competitive game, except for those specific cases of unsolicited proposals and sole-source or selected-source procurements, which we will take up in Chapter 7. It is not far different from competitive selling in the private sector, except for the fact that there are certain specific statutes governing federal purchasing, and the wise marketer becomes fully aware of these statutes and what they provide.

Earlier, we referred to some of the myths about government procurement. One was the myth that only large corporations can win government contracts, and another was that these large corporations usually make arrangements to "fix" the awards. What gives rise to such myths? Part of the reason is that too many contracts are won by large companies who have submitted mediocre proposals. However, they are being competed against by other proposals which are no better. That is, far too often a contract is awarded to a proposal which is the best of a poor lot.

Given an assortment of proposals, none of which are particularly meritorious, the customer often opts for the proposal submitted by the best-known or largest company. The reasoning is that since none of the proposals are very good, the best chance for a successful project is with the biggest or best-known company! Again and again, it has been demonstrated that a good proposal from a small and little-known organization will beat a mediocre proposal from even the largest and best-known company.

There is no use pretending that all contracts offered for competitive proposals and bids enjoy completely free competition. Indeed, many of them have been "wired" for a favored contractor. But experience proves that even these can often be un-wired by someone offering a truly superior proposal. Wiring offers one contractor great advantages over competitors, but it does not—cannot—*guarantee* the award. The entire process is open to public scrutiny and subject to appeals protests. In that environment, it is simply not possible to make the wiring process foolproof. In Chapter 2, you read of a case where an energetic and aggressive bidder forced an agency to award a contract to another bidder than the one for whom it had been intended. (In fact, the case involving the question about what constituted a typed page was one such.)

In general, beating the competition usually means being a bit smarter and working a bit harder. It is always a mistake to underestimate the competition. You should expect others to know their business and to prepare at least acceptable proposals. But it is equally mistaken to *overrate* the competition. The biggest and best-entrenched government contractors find themselves being beaten by small newcomers who have worked hard to gather reliable market information and design a *superior* proposal.

6

What about costs?

To train a dog, the trainer must be smarter than the dog

Understanding costs is the bidder's business

Every profession tends to shroud its workings in a protective cloak of mysterious jargon which is totally unintelligible to outsiders. Doctors and lawyers do it by using little-known Latin; insurance people say "premium" when they mean "payment"; psychologists build entire careers around the special meanings they ascribe to such words as "behavior" and "reinforcement."

Accountants are no different. They frighten others into total dependence on their wisdom by referring to "debits," "offsets," and the like, which other mortals are assured are beyond their comprehension. They draw up their own cabalistic arrangements in documents which only they can interpret, but which are supposed to report the health of the business and predict its future.

In many cases, the accountants are responsible for preparing and submitting a bid or proposal which is doomed to failure from the start. But in fairness to the accountants, it is not their fault that they are asked to do cost analyses and prepare cost estimates without adequate communication between the accountants and the technical/professional specialists who are responsible for preparing the bid or proposal. The true fault lies in the reluctance of the technical/professional specialist to make himself familiar with costs and their meaning. Yet, when the jargon is stripped away, costs are easier to comprehend than are the specialties called for in the bid or proposal.

In short, no bid or proposal can be prepared intelligently by two or more people who are not working together in every sense of the word: Communicating and establishing complete understanding between them. Nor can anyone design a program and prepare a proposal properly without understanding costs and what the various aspects of the design do to costs. It is essential that anyone preparing a bid or proposal understand costs at least to the extent of being able to discuss them readily with those who specialize in costs and accounting for them.

Have no fear: I'm not going to try to make an accountant of you (even if I were qualified to do so). But the subject is less complex than most people think it is, as you will soon see.

There are only two kinds of costs

In any business, there are two kinds of money flow: outgoing and incoming. Obviously, if the business is to survive, it must take in at least as much as it pays out. Bear that simple fact in mind, as we proceed; it's the rationale for almost everything we shall have to say about costs, no matter in what accounting column they appear or by what names they are called. As a result of all the necessary accounting manipulations and jargon of the profession, we may lose sight of this simple fact. (And losing sight of it, failing to fully grasp this simple relationship, has been the downfall of many businesses.)

Actually, a business must take in a bit more than it spends. The bit more is called profit, and profit is not a dirty word. It's essential to a healthy business enterprise.

One more essential fact, which is really another way of saying that the business must take in at least as much as it pays out: Any cost of doing business, by whatever name we call it, must be recovered before a profit can be realized. One of the problems in modern business, particularly in a complex business enterprise, is that many costs are hidden, which leads to severe problems, of course. For example, if an item costs you $3, you know that it represents a $3 cost immediately. But you also have some costs for handling it—rent, heat, light, advertising, sales commissions, and your own salary, at least. Your selling price must cover these, as well as the original $3 cost to you, plus some profit. One of the major functions of the accountants is to help us recognize and identify all the costs so that we know what we must do to recover them *and* show a bit of profit. It is this, classifying, categorizing, and identifying costs, which is complicated and can get us into trouble. In much government contracting, particularly for the larger, custom contracts, the government will not permit the contractor to simply charge some fixed price for his goods and services. The contractor must demonstrate that his cost estimates are valid, conform with standard accounting practices, and are fair and reasonable charges to the government.

The point of this discussion is that there are only two kinds of costs: direct and indirect. These are the two broad and basic categories, although each is subdivided into subcategories. It is necessary, for accounting purposes and sometimes for strategic purposes, to know which is which, just as it is necessary to *recover* both in the transaction.

In the example above of buying an item for $3 and reselling it at some profit, the $3 represents *direct* cost, and the other cost items listed (rent, heat, light, advertising, sales commissions, and your own salary) are usually *indirect* costs. (Sales commissions could be either direct or indirect costs, depending on how your accounting system is organized.)

This subdivision into direct and indirect is not absolute, but is somewhat arbitrary, and varies from one case to another. There are circumstances in which all your costs might be considered to be direct; for example, if you sold one item only, and that constituted your entire business. But if you sell a great many items, you will find it impossible to determine exactly what portion of your rent, heat, light, and so on is represented by the sale of that one $3 item. Yet, you must somehow recover all those costs in conducting your business. To solve this problem, your accountant organizes your books in such a way as to list both direct and indirect costs.

Types of Indirect Costs

The best-known name for indirect costs is overhead. Almost everyone has heard that term used, whether they fully understand it or not. For many small businesses, overhead is synonomous with indirect costs, which are those costs of doing business that must be allocated or spread among the sale of various goods or services because specific overhead dollars can't be assigned to any single item or service sold. Therefore, a *rate* or percentage figure must be established as a guide in establishing a selling price which returns all costs plus a profit.

Suppose, for example, that your own salary and all the other indirect costs of operating your business come to $3,000 a month. Further suppose that the merchandise you sell every month represents a direct cost to you of $7,500 every month. And further, you have decided that you must realize a profit of 10 percent of direct cost on your sales. That means that you must sell that $7,500 worth of merchandise for:

$7,500 (direct cost) + $3,000 (indirect cost)
  + $750 (10% profit on cost) = $11,250
$11,250 − $7,500 = $3,750
$3,750/$7,500 = 0.50 = 50%

That is, you must mark up items 50 percent (one and one-half times your direct cost) to arrive at a selling price. Selling that $3 item at $4.50 will bring back your costs plus a profit, if you continue to sell $7,500 worth (at your cost) of merchandise every month.

Your accountant will calculate your overhead *rate* (we already know that the overhead *dollars* equals $3,000 every month) as:

$3,000/$7,500 = 0.40 = 40%

Of course, he won't do so on a monthly basis, but on an annual basis, because your sales figures will probably fluctuate from month to month, and you would never be able to keep up with recalculating all your costs every month and changing your prices to reflect these.

To put this still another way: It *costs* you 40 cents to sell $1 worth of merchandise. Therefore, you must add that 40 cents to each dollar of what you paid for that merchandise, simply to recover your costs *before profit*.

Now of course you are not free to simply charge whatever you feel like charging, if you want to stay in business. You must be competitive with whatever the market is for what you are selling. If you allow your overhead rate to get out of control and to rise to unreasonable heights, or if you try to get an exorbitant profit, you won't be able to compete successfully. Overhead must therefore be controlled.

Because indirect costs, whether they are all overhead or are subdivided (as they often are), are a rate or percentage of your sales volume, a larger sales volume should mean a reduced overhead *rate*. This can be a decisive factor, as you will see.

Here are some of the typical items of expense which are usually part of your overhead or other indirect costs:

Basic building or facility costs (rent, heat, light, and so on)
Telephones
Advertising and sales

Salaries of non-production people, such as receptionists, clerks, accountants, sales people, drivers, personnel people, officers, and so on
Insurance
Delivery vehicles
Sales commissions
Licenses
Legal fees
Taxes
Fringe benefits (vacations, holidays, sick leave, group insurance)
Expense accounts
Repairs
Depreciation (buildings, equipment, furniture, fixtures)
Interest (on business indebtedness)

On your accountant's ledgers, these various kinds of indirect costs are kept in different accounts or schedules, and even these are broken down further. For more general purposes, all of these may be considered to be overhead costs, and in many cases, all of these will make up what accountants may refer to as the "overhead pool." However, in bidding to the U.S. government, it is wise to separate these costs into overhead and "G&A," which stands for general and administrative costs. Companies which do not do business with the government often do not have such a category, but those who do government contracting usually find it necessary to have a "G&A pool." Here's why.

Many contracting officials, particularly in the Department of Defense, but not necessarily confined to DOD, will not allow certain types of indirect costs to be reimbursed by the government as overhead. They claim, for example, that marketing and sales costs are not properly overhead items, and should not be charged to the government. They admit, however, that these are legitimate costs of doing business, and the contractor is entitled to recover these costs somehow. For that reason, some years ago, the concept of G&A was born, and contracting officials see no problem with paying sales/marketing, officers' salaries, and other related indirect costs, as long as they are listed as G&A, rather than overhead. Actually, this works out to the contractor's advantage, as you will see later in this chapter when we review the cost forms.

Indirect costs are therefore broken into the two broad classes: overhead and G&A. However, some contractors prefer to segregate those overhead costs which are incurred in giving employees paid time-off (vacations and holidays) and other benefits (group insurance, bonuses, and so on). They break indirect costs into overhead, G&A, and fringe benefits.

Direct Costs and Different Types of Direct Costs

We've mentioned only one example of a direct cost: the purchase price of an item which is to be resold. For a merchant, someone who buys at wholesale prices and resells at retail or dealer prices, this is usually the main item of direct cost. But other businesses incur other types of direct costs.

Businesses are often referred to as being either capital intensive or labor intensive. A capital-intensive business is one which requires that a relatively large amount of capital be tied up in inventory, equipment, or both. Ordinarily, capital-intensive businesses use relatively little labor. Labor-intensive businesses, on the other hand, usually have relatively little capital tied up in merchandise or equipment, but depend primarily on what labor produces, and must be able to meet payrolls.

In labor-intensive business, the principal cost is labor, *direct* labor. It is this direct labor that the business sells at a profit to customers. If we substitute one hour of direct labor which costs the employer $3 for that $3 item we used as an example earlier, and we have the same indirect costs, we must resell that one hour of $3 labor at $4.50 to recover all our costs and realize a profit.

The labor-hour is a commodity, just as a physical product is, and the same considerations apply: The business must get back the direct costs of the labor, plus the indirect costs, plus a profit. And, as in the case of the $3 product, the indirect costs are a rate applied to the direct labor. If we have a 40 percent overhead rate, our total cost for that one hour of direct labor at $3 per hour is:

$$\$3 + (\$3 \times 0.40) = \$3 + \$1.20 = \$4.20$$

When we add our 30¢ profit, the selling price is $4.50.

When we prepare a cost analysis for a government contract bid, that is exactly how we must explain our price to the government.

Ordinarily, we have both direct and indirect labor in custom work. If the government has hired us for field engineering a computer, the field engineer assigned to the work and actually doing the work is direct labor. His time is being applied directly to the job, and it is his time specifically for which the government is paying. But the clerk who makes up the bill for that labor and the person who answers the telephones and receives visitors in the lobby is indirect labor. The government is not buying what they do, nor is it possible for us to identify how much time each spends supporting the field engineer (if, in fact, it were desirable to do so). Therefore, they are *indirect* labor, labor which costs us money and must be recovered, but is recovered by making their cost part of our overhead rate.

There are, usually, other direct costs. These are costs which are directly chargeable to the contract and can be clearly identified as costs which would not otherwise be incurred. For example, if we pay the field engineer's travel expenses to the field site, that is another *direct cost.* If he must use a pay telephone or calls the office collect in connection with what he is doing, that is another direct cost. If the project includes a written report, and that report must be duplicated, we can charge the duplicating cost to the job as another direct cost. Any other costs which can be specifically assigned to that job and would not have otherwise been incurred are "other direct costs," and should be recorded and entered on the books as such.

However—and note this carefully—overhead is that percentage of direct-labor dollars, excluding other direct costs and G&A, which we must charge to recover all our costs. That is, the overhead rate is applied to *direct labor only,* and not to other direct costs.

We break down costs, then, into these broad categories, which we must report to the contracting official in making our cost estimates:

Direct labor
Other direct costs
Overhead (to include indirect labor)
G&A

To these we add our fee or profit.

Variations

The above is the general case. But like most things, it has exceptions. For one thing, an organization may report more than one overhead! Here is how that may happen.

Service organizations, which have labor-intensive characteristics, of course, usually run relatively small overhead rates, from a low of 35–40 percent to a high of 100–150 percent. Capital-intensive operations, especially those engaged in heavy manufacturing, usually run much higher overhead rates—400 percent is not uncommon.

The reason for this is (1) the great expense each year of depreciating the equipment which represents the capital, and (2) the great difficulty in identifying direct costs.

Many businesses are both labor-intensive and capital-intensive. Take, for example, a firm developing a new aircraft for the air force.

The early months of engineering design, drafting, testing, and otherwise preparing a set of drawings are labor-intensive operations. The later stages of actually building the prototype unit in the company's shops are capital-intensive operations. Therefore, the engineering department and the manufacturing division are each likely to have its own overhead structures. In submitting its bid, the company must separate the two types of work from each other, and compute the costs for each in the same set of cost estimates.

In still another case, a multi-divisional company may divide a large project among several divisions, and each division may have its own overhead base. Again, the cost estimates will have to report these various overheads.

The government recognizes all these situations and provides cost forms for bidders to accommodate each one. The form used by the Department of Defense is DD 633, and most other agencies use a modification of this, Form 60 (see Figure 10). (And there is still another, Form 59, used occasionally.) All use the same general approach, however:

1. Direct material (parts, subcontracts, and so on)
2. Material overhead (if any)
3. Direct labor (by category)
4. Labor overhead (rate and extension in dollars)
5. Special testing
6. Special equipment
7. Travel
8. Consultants
9. Other direct costs
10. Total direct cost and overhead
11. G&A (rate and extension in dollars)
12. Royalties
13. Total cost
14. Fee or profit (dollars)
15. Total price to customer

This explains why the G&A works to the contractor's advantage. It's applied, as a rate, to just about everything but royalties: purchased parts and subcontracts, direct and indirect labor, other overhead costs, and other direct costs.

"Below the Line" Costs

On some contracts, the government will stipulate that certain items are to be billed to the government at their actual cost to the contractor—that is, without profit. This is often referred to as putting the items "below the line," meaning below the lines on which overhead and fees or profits are calculated. However, this "contractor's cost" is the actual purchase cost plus G&A.

The rationale is, apparently, that the contractor has not stocked the item, has not had money tied up in inventory on the shelf, but has ordered it for immediate use on a contract, and is therefore not entitled to a profit. However, the contractor does incur bookkeeping and administrative costs, and those should be recovered through G&A charges. Ordinarily, when purchased items are to be below the line, they are incidental to the main work of the contract.

The standard cost forms do not make provision for such items specifically, but are readily adaptable to the need by simply listing the items in the appropriate places but not including them in the calculations for overhead and fees.

What the government expects in cost proposals

The "line" referred to in the expression "below the line" is not the same line referred to in "the bottom line." The bottom line shows the cost to the customer, and that line should reflect *all* costs, of whatever kind, plus profit. In short, what difference does it make what we call a cost—direct, indirect, overhead, G&A, other direct, and so on—as long as the bottom line isn't affected?

It makes no difference to the customer in ordinary commerce, because you don't provide a customer with a breakdown of your costs. He is interested in the bottom line only.

Not so the government contracting official. He is very much interested in what your costs are, how they're generated, and how they're distributed (except in those cases where he requires that you supply a selling price only). In a few minutes, you'll begin to see why he is concerned.

For example, let's hypothesize a $500,000 cost-reimbursement contract, for which you estimate the following costs:

Direct labor	$200,000
Overhead	180,000 (90%)
G&A	80,000
Profit	40,000
Total	$500,000

(Text continues p. 118)

Figure 10. Form 60.

CONTRACT PRICING PROPOSAL
(RESEARCH AND DEVELOPMENT)

Office of Management and Budget
Approval No. 29–RO184

This form is for use when *(i)* submission of cost or pricing data (see FPR 1–3.807–3) is required and *(ii)* substitution for the Optional Form 59 is authorized by the contracting officer.

PAGE NO.	NO. OF PAGES

NAME OF OFFEROR

SUPPLIES AND/OR SERVICES TO BE FURNISHED

HOME OFFICE ADDRESS

DIVISION(S) AND LOCATION(S) WHERE WORK IS TO BE PERFORMED

TOTAL AMOUNT OF PROPOSAL
$

GOV'T SOLICITATION NO.

DETAIL DESCRIPTION OF COST ELEMENTS

	EST COST ($)	TOTAL EST COST[1]	REFER-ENCE[2]
1. DIRECT MATERIAL *(Itemize on Exhibit A)*			
a. PURCHASED PARTS			
b. SUBCONTRACTED ITEMS			
c. OTHER—(1) RAW MATERIAL			
(2) YOUR STANDARD COMMERCIAL ITEMS			
(3) INTERDIVISIONAL TRANSFERS *(At other than cost)*			
TOTAL DIRECT MATERIAL			

	ESTIMATED HOURS	RATE/ HOUR	EST COST ($)	
2. MATERIAL OVERHEAD[3] *(Rate ___%×$ ___ base=)*				
3. DIRECT LABOR *(Specify)*				
TOTAL DIRECT LABOR				

	O.H. RATE	X BASE =	EST COST ($)
4. LABOR OVERHEAD (Specify Department or Cost Center)			
TOTAL LABOR OVERHEAD			

		EST COST ($)
5. SPECIAL TESTING (Including field work at Government installations)		
TOTAL SPECIAL TESTING		
6. SPECIAL EQUIPMENT (If direct charge) (Itemize on Exhibit A)		

		EST COST ($)
7. TRAVEL (If direct charge) (Give details on attached Schedule)		
a. TRANSPORTATION		
b. PER DIEM OR SUBSISTENCE		
TOTAL TRAVEL		

		EST COST ($)
8. CONSULTANTS (Identify—purpose—rate)		
TOTAL CONSULTANTS		
9. OTHER DIRECT COSTS (Itemize on Exhibit A)		
TOTAL DIRECT COST AND OVERHEAD		
10.		
11. GENERAL AND ADMINISTRATIVE EXPENSE (Rate ___ % of cost element Nos. ___)		
12. ROYALTIES		
13. TOTAL ESTIMATED COST		
14. FEE OR PROFIT		
15. TOTAL ESTIMATED COST AND FEE OR PROFIT		

OPTIONAL FORM 60
October 1971
General Services Administration
FPR 1-16.806
5060-101

Figure 10. *(continued)*

This proposal is submitted for use in connection with and in response to *(Describe RFP, etc.)*

and reflects our best estimates as of this date, in accordance with the Instructions to Offerors and the Footnotes which follow.

TYPED NAME AND TITLE	SIGNATURE	
NAME OF FIRM		DATE OF SUBMISSION

EXHIBIT A—SUPPORTING SCHEDULE *(Specify. If more space is needed, use reverse)*

COST EL NO.	ITEM DESCRIPTION *(See footnote 5)*	EST COST *($)*

I. HAS ANY EXECUTIVE AGENCY OF THE UNITED STATES GOVERNMENT PERFORMED ANY REVIEW OF YOUR ACCOUNTS OR RECORDS IN CONNECTION WITH ANY OTHER GOVERNMENT PRIME CONTRACT OR SUBCONTRACT WITHIN THE PAST TWELVE MONTHS?

☐ YES ☐ NO *(If yes, identify below.)*

NAME AND ADDRESS OF REVIEWING OFFICE AND INDIVIDUAL

II. WILL YOU REQUIRE THE USE OF ANY GOVERNMENT PROPERTY IN THE PERFORMANCE OF THIS PROPOSED CONTRACT?

☐ YES ☐ NO *(If yes, identify on reverse or separate page)*

III. DO YOU REQUIRE GOVERNMENT CONTRACT FINANCING TO PERFORM THIS PROPOSED CONTRACT?

☐ YES ☐ NO *(If yes, identify.):* ☐ ADVANCE PAYMENTS ☐ PROGRESS PAYMENTS OR ☐ GUARANTEED LOANS

IV. DO YOU NOW HOLD ANY CONTRACT *(Or, do you have any independently financed (IR&D) projects)* FOR THE SAME OR SIMILAR WORK CALLED FOR BY THIS PROPOSED CONTRACT?

☐ YES ☐ NO *(If yes, identify.):*

V. DOES THIS COST SUMMARY CONFORM WITH THE COST PRINCIPLES SET FORTH IN AGENCY REGULATIONS?

☐ YES ☐ NO *(If no, explain on reverse or separate page)*

See Reverse for Instructions and Footnotes

OPTIONAL FORM 60 (10-71)

2

The bottom line is $500,000, of course. But let's take a closer look at overhead. A breakdown reveals that overhead includes rent, heat, light, and other facility costs; telephone, receptionists, clerical, typing, and duplicating; and insurance, taxes, paid time-off, group insurance, and travel.

Note that the overhead is 90 percent of direct labor, a relatively high rate for a service business. Note, too, that there is no entry for "other direct costs." All costs are either direct labor or indirect costs.

This means that typing, travel, long-distance calls, and duplicating done under this contract will be charged off to the general overhead. This is a great convenience because the staff does not have to keep track of all those kinds of expenses incurred under this contract. But it also means that the overhead rate is pushed up. Let's suppose that the overhead figure includes $30,000 worth of such support work which can be traced directly to the requirements of this contract, and hence can be charged to this contract as "other direct costs." What would then happen to the figures?

Direct labor	$210,000
Overhead	150,000 (71%)
Other direct costs	20,000
G&A	80,000
Profit	40,000
Total	$500,000

Note now that the bottom line has not changed, as a result of charging typing and other support labor to *direct labor,* and other such costs to *other direct costs.* But something has changed: the overhead. It has been reduced from 90 percent to 71 percent. What difference does that make? A lot.

Taking the easier way out and charging all support work to the general overhead has not *one,* nor even *two,* but *three* undesirable results:

1. It puts "spike values" in your overhead—expenses which are not usually there, but are caused by the needs of this single contract. It is therefore a *distortion* of your normal overhead, which should be kept as constant as possible, as *predictable* as possible, if you are to be able to prepare cost estimates with any degree of reliability.
2. By raising your "historical overhead," you place yourself at a disadvantage for other bids. Perhaps your overhead will settle back to 71 percent after this contract is over, but what overhead figure will you use in the

meanwhile? You've lost some of your competitive edge—19 percent of it, to be exact.

3. You may have an unhappy contracting officer. Contracting officers do not like to see high overhead figures, and the next paragraph will explain why.

If a contracting officer were to scan the two sets of figures just discussed he would see the government getting less for its $500,000 in the first case (at 90 percent overhead) than in the second case (at 71 percent overhead). In the first case $500,000 is buying only $200,000 worth of direct labor, which is the main objective of the contract. In the second case, for the same $500,000 on the bottom line, the government is getting $210,000 worth of labor applied to its needs, plus $20,000 in other direct costs.

The official sees the overhead as the cost of buying the direct labor and/or other direct costs, which is something like seeing interest as the cost of using money. To the government, overhead is not productive cost and doesn't contribute directly to achieving the goal for which the contract was written. (In fact, overhead is often referred to as the "burden" or "burden rate"!)

Overhead, to most contracting officers, is a measure of your *efficiency* as an organization. The lower your overhead, the more efficient you appear to be. And the more efficient you probably are, if your overhead is controlled carefully. Careful control of your overhead means that *nothing* which can be properly recorded as an "other direct cost" is ever charged to overhead. The benefits of keeping your overhead low are well worth the time and effort to keep track of all costs and charge them off properly. The ideal should be *true* overhead, and true overhead should be only and exclusively those costs which it is impossible or impractical to assign and charge to specific projects.

The government expects a contractor to maintain a reasonably low overhead, and judges a contractor to a large extent by that standard.

Projecting overhead

Overhead is not an absolute constant. Every business has certain fixed expenses (rent, basic telephone service, loan payments, and so on) and certain variable expenses (payroll, light, heat, printing). If you double your sales and activities, but can still conduct all business in your present facility, you incur no increase in rent, and a relatively small increase in telephone, power, and certain other variable expenses. That is, some indirect costs, such as taxes and fringe benefits, will increase in direct proportion to increases in the payroll, but others will not. You probably will not need to expand your accounting department because you have increased sales and payroll, for example.

For this reason, while overhead *dollars* will increase with expansion, the overhead *rate* ought to go down as you spread overhead dollars over a larger labor base or sales base. Since you cannot tell with any great certainty exactly what your overhead rate is at any given moment, the usual practice is to use either your *historical* rate (the rate reported by your accountants when they completed your most recent year's books) or a *provisional* rate.

A provisional overhead rate is a projected rate, an estimated one, and it is a fairly common practice to use a provisional rate for large contracts, particularly contracts which will be subject to audit. (Most contracts of over $100,000 are subject to audit; that does not necessarily mean that they *will* be audited.) The usual requirement to do this is to include such schedules of expense pools as to support the projected rate; that is, show how the rate is arrived at.

If the contract is a large one, and especially if it is a cost-reimbursement contract, using a provisional rate means that the books will probably be audited, at the end of the year, to verify the rate. Adjustments are then made, with the contractor receiving extra money from the government if the rate was higher than that projected, or refunding money to the government if the actual rate was lower than what the government was charged.

There are, of course, limits placed on provisional rates. You might project an overhead rate of 60 percent, perhaps, with a ceiling of 70 percent. If, upon audit, your actual overhead rate for the year was 67 percent, you will be entitled to bill the government for the extra 7 percent you have not been charging. But if your actual rate is higher than the ceiling, say, 72 percent, you will be able to bill only up to the ceiling.

Using a provisional rate offers you certain competitive advantages if you are bidding for a contract whose size will make a fairly large increase in your total year's sales or labor base. Here's why. Let's suppose that you have been doing $1 million a year, with a labor base of $600,000, an overhead of $330,000, and a profit of $70,000 (neglecting G&A, for simplicity). Your historical overhead rate is

$$\frac{330,000}{600,000} = 0.55 = 55\%$$

Your profit is

$$\frac{70,000}{600,000 + 330,000} = 0.0752 = 7.5\%$$

Let's consider a large, new contract, *to be added to* that base, in which you calculate about $300,000 worth of direct labor. Your existing labor base is $600,000. With $300,000 added, you will have a labor base of $900,000. If we cost-estimate the new job at the existing rates:

Direct labor	$300,000
Overhead @ 55%	165,000
Profit @ 7.5%	34,875
Total	499,875

This set of figures assumes that 55 percent is the correct overhead rate. But it neglects the effects of increasing the labor base by one and one-half times, from $600,000 to $900,000. That increase is bound to have a substantial effect on the overhead rate. In fact, it should drive the overhead rate down to at least 45 percent. Your accountants will have to do the calculations, but let's assume, to illustrate the point, that your projected overhead rate, with that new business in the house, does go down to 45 percent. Let's estimate the job now:

Direct labor	$300,000
Overhead @ 45%	135,000
Profit @ 7.5%	32,625
Total	$467,625

This reduces your estimate by $32,250, a substantial reduction which may very well mean the difference between winning the contract and not winning it. And there are no risks involved, if you are confident of keeping that original $600,000 base intact for the term of the new contract, because you have made that lower overhead provisional on winning this new contract. If you don't win it, you have sacrificed nothing. If you do win it, you will be that much more competitive, with 45 percent overhead, for everything else you go after!

Other methods for cutting costs

Costs are always a consideration. Anything you can do to reduce your costs cannot but help increase your chances for winning. One way of reducing costs is this: Don't reinvent the wheel.

It is truly surprising how often a contractor will develop things in-house which he could have bought more cheaply off the shelf—or even have gotten for nothing! Here are a few examples to illustrate this:

Writing a large bid proposal for a Job Corps center (which turned out to be worth some $25 million of business) called for a great deal of work, including planning six complete vocational training programs and an academic curriculum. The work resulted in a three-volume, 1,000-page proposal, which astonished the customer, who firmly believed that we had spent at least $50,000 (in 1964!). In fact, we had spent about $12,000. Here's how:

1. To develop the six vocational programs, which had to be detailed down to a description of and objectives for each hour of instruction, we sent out to the nearest public library and gathered up armfuls of how-to books on the trades we were interested in. We sorted through them and selected one for each of the vocations of interest. An individual was then assigned to draw up a detailed outline of each book, which was then broken down by a training specialist into one-hour increments, and objectives written for all increments. Voila! With relatively little effort, we had designed six vocational training courses.

2. To identify training resources for each, we bought a government publication for $3, which listed 6,000 training films and slide/tape programs. We selected the appropriate ones and listed these as training resources. We did the same with publishers' catalogs to identify texts of interest.

3. We also bought a number of military training manuals for related trades and used them as sources of information and illustrations.

4. When this was all assembled, we wrote the text passages to describe how these programs would be taught and administered, while our psychology department designed the "group life plan," and a former school teacher wrote up an academic course in the "three R's."

This was a great deal of work, but it would have been almost impossible for an organization of our size had we attempted to design everything from scratch. The result was a program far more impressive than anything we could have developed any other way.

In another case, we were to prepare a training program in automation machine technology. This required a great many drawings and illustrations of all kinds, including photos of many types of automatic machines and systems. We drew up a form letter requesting copies of texts, manuals, specifications, photos, and/or drawings, and asked for permission to use them in a training program to be used by government agencies. We promised to give credit lines which would identify the machines and manufacturers and acknowledge their help.

Within less than two weeks, a previously unused desk was piled high with materials we had gotten from some 100 manufacturers, all eager to see their products listed and shown in the program!

I had a requirement to prepare an audiovisual program on the history and culture of the American Indian. The Government Printing Office has an abundance of materials on the subject, but GPO publications have become quite expensive, and I needed a great many resource books and drawings. I therefore called on the Bureau of Indian Affairs with my problem. They were delighted to help. They gave me, without charge, dozens of excellent books, pamphlets, posters, charts, and the like, in addition to lending me an entire library of slides!

In a $78,000 bid for a training program for the Job Corps, we had estimated our art requirement at $8,000. The customer wanted our program, but objected to our price. To reduce it, we again utilized GPO publications, all of which are in the public domain (anyone is free to use the materials). We found almost all the illustrations we needed, in easily reproducible line drawings. Our final art cost: $2,000.

There are innumerable such resources available. Virtually everything published by the Government Printing Office, for example, has been printed at the request of some federal agency, which always takes a large quantity for its own use, and often makes these available without charge to anyone interested! Nothing is free from the GPO today, but what you need may be free from the originating agency.

The National Archives is part of the General Services Administration. An enormous store of information is contained there, including many rare photos. Copies of photos and other materials are available at low cost from the National Archives (the photos can be ordered as slides, also, at low cost).

NASA Headquarters showered me with virtual armloads of beautiful, multi-colored photos of the space program. I could have bought these at the GPO bookstore, of course, but NASA made no charge for them.

As a result of my activities in writing training programs such as these and in producing newsletters, my name has found its way onto many government mailing lists, and hardly a day passes that I do not receive press releases, government newsletters, government monthly magazines, reports, manuals, and many other useful items. Anyone can get on these lists, usually by addressing the Public Information Office which every agency maintains.

The General Accounting Office issues a great many reports throughout the year, some of them "letter reports," some of them thick, bound reports. They issue a monthly guide to reports currently available. It is not difficult to get a single copy of any report free of charge.

Some of this information and material is directly useful in performing under a contract, as explained, but much of it is also invaluable in writing proposals! Anyone bidding seriously to government agencies is well-advised to begin a library of such resource materials. Such a library not only results in far better proposals than can be written from scratch, but greatly reduces research time—and therefore the cost of proposal writing.

Make or Buy?

In business and industry generally, "make or buy" decisions must be made regularly. No one makes everything—even the giant automobile manufacturers buy wheels, carburetors, and many other components of their cars. The dictum "Don't reinvent the wheel" is analogous to that: It's the government contractor's make-or-buy decision. It comes down, in the end, to a matter of cost. But often a buying decision carries within it the seeds of costs never anticipated. Here's an example:

In one company where I had the distinction of being the editorial director, we were spending a fair amount of money every year for printing. The president of the company became aware of this, as he pored over the balance sheets and P&L statements, and came to me with a bright idea: "Why don't we buy a small printing press? A salesman came in the other day and offered me a factory-reconditioned one for only $800."

I tried to explain tactfully that the $800 would only make us "pregnant." We would have to have an operator, a plate-maker, and some sort of binding equipment, at the least. Soon we would wish that we had a cutter (paper guillotine), a camera, an automatic stitcher, and a few other things. Even then, we would have to send much of our work out because we wouldn't be equipped for all kinds of printing. What would we do with our press operator when we didn't have printing for him to do? Where would we house all this?

Sad to report, my arguments were overruled, and Mr. President succumbed to the salesman's pitch and spent the $800. Only a few months later, he sold the machine for as much as he could get, which was considerably less than $800.

In costing your bid, plan to use suppliers for anything which is not properly *part of your business*. Get the best prices you can, and have your bidders supply *written* quotations, guaranteed for a suitable period of time.

Who creates the costs?

In many companies, particularly the larger organizations, engineers, psychologists, and other technical/professional specialists write technical proposals and proclaim complete ignorance of and no responsibility for costs. They never get any closer to the accounting function than to question a payroll deduction on their checks, nor are they interested in the mysterious world of costs.

After all the specialists have designed the proposed program and written the technical proposal, the job of costing the project falls to the accountants in these companies. Those hapless individuals spend many weary hours with the technical specialists assigning dollar values to their specifications. Typically, the boss sees the final proposal and hits the ceiling when his eyes fall on the bottom line; his mouth drops open in disbelieving shock. Then follow frantic efforts and gallons of midnight oil to chip away at an obviously overpriced project.

The technical specialists shrug. Costs are not their problem. The accountants shrug. They can only cost out what they've been given.

The *mechanics* of costing are the accountants' domain and responsibility. But costs are the creation of the designers—the proposal writers. Only their own ingenuity can cut the costs and give the organization a competitive advantage over less-shrewd competitors.

Let's illustrate this, to show clearly how much impact on the bottom line different approaches to a project can have. Let us take a rather simple project of writing a training manual. Here's a first analysis of what is going to be needed:

- Development of a "book plan," to be reviewed by the customer and approved. Will include complete outline of content, format, list of illustrations.
- Development of complete draft, to be reviewed by customer, returned with comments. 20 copies of draft required.
- Revision, per customer comments. Resubmit to customer for final review, final comments, and approval to complete. 20 copies required for review.
- Set type, ink illustrations, size final art, print 200 copies, deliver.

There are several ways to approach this job. Obviously, the main work will be done in-house, by your own expert staff. But suppose you do not have an artist on staff or an existing in-house typesetting capability. You can rent a typesetting machine for about $150, and a good typist can learn to operate it. Or you can use outside services from subcontractors or vendors. Which is the best way to go? See Table 1 to compare the breakdown of costs.

Table 1(a). Cost of project using in-house staff only.

Direct Labor	
Planning and writing	$15,000
Typing and proofing	3,000
Staff artist	2,500
Typesetting	1,000
Total direct labor	$21,500
Indirect Costs	
Overhead @ 60%	12,900
Printing 200 copies	1,100
Subtotal	35,500
G&A @ 7%	2,485
Subtotal	37,985
Fee @ 10%	3,799
Total price	$41,784

Table 1(b). Cost of project using both in-house staff and subcontracted services.

Direct Labor	
Planning and writing	$15,000
Typing and proofing	3,000
Total direct labor	18,000
Indirect Costs	
Overhead at 60%	10,800
Illustrating, sub-contracted	3,000
Typesetting, sub-contracted	1,200
Printing 200 copies	1,100
Subtotal	34,100
G&A @ 7%	2,387
Subtotal	36,487
Fee @ 10%	3,649
Total price	$40,136

The difference between the two bottom lines is $1,648, a considerable sum. The saving is effected despite paying an outside contractor a bit more than we would have to pay a staff person, because we are *saving overhead:* We don't have to provide the contractor with fringe benefits, a place to work, a telephone, or a desk, or pay taxes, and so on. We have also reduced the risks. Suppose our staff artist is unable to complete the work within $2,500 worth of time?

A dollar added to direct labor costs affects the bottom line this way:

Direct labor	$1.00
Overhead	.60
G&A	.11
Profit	.17
Total	$1.88

Conversely, every dollar which can be cut in direct labor saves $1.88 on the bottom line! Even exchanging a dollar in direct labor for a dollar's worth of outside services or products eliminates that 60¢ in overhead.

Proposal writers should always be aware of every dollar of cost they are creating, and what they are cutting on the bottom line by every economy they can effect in their planning and designing.

Once, in my lofty position as editorial director, I found myself plagued with an enormous oversupply of "light editing." My editors were never finished tinkering with the camera-ready copy. Each time the copy they had corrected was returned to them for review and approval of corrections, they found more corrections to make, and provoked still another cycle of changes.

One Friday afternoon I assembled a half-dozen of these extremely conscientious people in my office, and seated them before my desk, on which I had piled that week's collection of corrections, a rather large pile of "repro masters."

"I have here before me," I announced dramatically, indicating the stack of paper, "the third cycle of changes to the masters for the _____ program. I have spent most of the afternoon going through them. They average about six changes per sheet, and there are over 600 sheets. Most of the changes are to punctuation; a few are minor changes in grammatical construction. I've consulted with the manager of our typing pool on what it costs to make these changes. It works out to about 50¢ per change, or about $3 per page. A small amount of money. Until we multiply it by the number of pages. Altogether, it will cost us more than $2,000 to make these changes."

I paused for dramatic effect, as six pairs of eyes widened apprehensively—perhaps in shock.

"Tell me," I then went on, "do you believe that you have worked $2,000 worth of improvement in this program? Would you pay $2,000 more for this program as a result of these changes?"

I never had to say another word about excessive cycles of editing and changes to anyone on that staff. Proposal writers, like editors, must be made to understand the cost of the work they do.

Collecting your money from the U.S. government

There's a myth that the U.S. government takes forever to pay its bills. The myth arises from the fact that it's true—in a few cases. In general, however, the government pays more promptly than do many commercial accounts. Being a giant bureaucracy, the government reacts the way all bureaucracies react. When a small, administrative problem arises, lower-level people do . . . nothing. They simply wait for someone else to do it. Here is how the system is supposed to work.

You submit your bill to the contracting office (contracts specify how and to whom the invoice is to be submitted), citing the contract number, and so on. The contracting office sends it on to receiving or the government's project manager to approve (certify that the goods were delivered or services performed and all is satisfactory). The contracting office, having already checked the contract, and past payments, if any, to verify the correctness of the bill, approves the bill and puts it on a schedule for payment by the Treasury Department disbursing office. The bill is then paid, usually, within less than a week. Bills should be paid 20 to 30 days after submittal (some government offices manage to do it in 15 days), especially if you have a 20-day prompt-payment discount. (All contracting officers are under standing orders to take advantage of all discounts.)

Delays are almost always due to either someone's lethargy (your bill is lying on a desk) or carelessness (someone has mislaid your invoice). Here is what you can and should do about delays in payment:

1. Submit your invoice in at least *two* copies. Otherwise, the agency must duplicate, another delay. It doesn't hurt to submit in triplicate; some agencies need three copies.
2. Wait not more than 30 days (but more than 21) unless the agency has advised you otherwise. There are some specific cases in which the normal payment cycle is six weeks, for example. Then assume that something has gone wrong, as it almost certainly has, and take action.
3. Start telephoning and find out exactly where your invoice is (at what stage in the process) and what you can do to move it along. Don't let people simply promise to "get back to you," unless they can deliver on that promise within a reasonable length of time. Frequently, that's a stalling tactic. Don't settle for anything less than finding out exactly what the holdup is—why it has occurred.

These measures are usually sufficient to get you paid within days. If they do not do the trick, go *up* in the hierarchy, to the Chief of the Contracts Division, for example, or even to the agency head if necessary.

NOTE: It is a good idea, when doing business with an agency you have not done business with before, to find out in advance exactly how their system works. (There are specific differences among the various agencies.) This helps you to troubleshoot if someone slips up later. However, in many cases, you can *walk* your invoice through the first couple of steps, and thereby avoid the most frequent hazard of misplaced paperwork or simple lethargy. For example, sometimes you can *start* with the government's project manager and have him or her approve your invoice, then hand-carry the approved invoice to the contracts office, thereby completing the first two steps immediately and avoiding the cause of the most common slip-ups.

7

The proposal game

Nothing happens until somebody sells something

What is a proposal?

While waiting my turn as a guest lecturer at a seminar one day, I heard several other speakers explain to an audience of proposal novitiates that a proposal is a "contractual document." I listened with growing impatience and some sense of outrage, because these speakers were supposedly all proposal experts, and the trusting neophytes listening to them were drinking in every word.

Those speakers were referring to a proposal as a contractual document in order to caution proposal writers that they would be held to what they promised in their proposals. To the extent that the contract will incorporate the proposal, the characterization is true. That is, the government has bought what the proposal offers, and the contract seals the bargain.

However, that characterization is misleading. Strictly speaking, the proposal *will become* a contractual document—if the customer "buys" it. Until then, it is *not* a contractual document; it is a proposal. To put this another way, it is something the writer *hopes* will become a contractual document. Every word in the proposal should be carefully calculated to maximize the probability that the customer will accept it and it will become a contractual document.

Until such time as the customer accepts and a contract is executed, the proposal is *an offer* to do something for a stipulated price. The proposal is a sales presentation, for only as a sales presentation does a proposal make any sense. If it is not an effective sales presentation, you need never have any fears about it becoming a contractual document!

When are proposals required?

There are many reasons for requesting potential contractors to submit proposals rather than sealed bids.

1. The work or product required is to be to custom specifications, and the customer wants to evaluate the qualifications of the various aspirants for the contract.
2. The customer wants the freedom to make a choice on qualitative grounds, rather than be compelled to accept the lowest bid.
3. The customer is not absolutely certain of what the problem or need is and is seeking the contractor with the greatest ability to identify it.
4. The customer is not up to date on the relevant technologies and therefore is not absolutely certain of what the possible solutions are. That customer is seeking "state of the art" solutions—those that are possible *today*, but might not have been possible yesterday.
5. The customer needs a problem identified and/or solved, which calls for skills not available to him except by contract with private industry.
6. The customer needs more hands and feet; he simply does not have the in-house staff to get the work done.
7. The customer needs a person with some special qualifications that no one on staff has.
8. The customer needs a facility or resource (such as a laboratory) not available except via contracted services.
9. The customer needs a new product or piece of equipment developed (an R&D job).
10. The customer needs an outside study done to validate a program or funding he or she has requested.
11. The work can be done cheaper by a contractor than it could be done by federal employees.

There are many reasons for needing more hands and feet for a program. The program (and the need) may be a temporary one, making it impractical to hire more federal employees. Or it may be politically impossible to hire more employees because of "freezes" on federal hiring, which are not rare (they occur at least once during virtually every new administration).

A great deal of controversy exists over whether a project can be handled more efficiently (that is, at lower cost) by contract than by federal employees. The federal employee unions always insist that the work is carried out at lower costs by federal employees, but they are hardly impartial observers. Opponents of using federal employees for all programs point out that few privately employed people get the fringe benefits of federal employees and enjoy as little pressure to get work done.

The Office of Management and Budget has taken a hand in this and issued OMB Circular A-76, which establishes policy and guidelines for judging whether to contract-out or have a job done in-house. The chief bone of contention has been the allegedly low value assigned to federal retirement benefits. OMB has fixed their value, for the time being at least, at 20.4 percent of salary.

Under the terms of the circular, a project is to be done by whichever appears to be lower in cost. If an existing program can be cost-reduced by 10 percent or more, it is to be contracted-out if it is being done in-house; or, it must be done in-house if it is currently being done under contract. Some $10 billion of work being done in-house is to be scrutinized, as well as about $30 billion currently done under contract. (The remaining contract work is not in dispute, at present.)

Here are some typical procurements, which reflect the kinds of needs and problems contract work is intended to solve:

• Many federal computer systems are operated by contract personnel under "facility management" contracts. Contract personnel, in these cases usually working on government premises, operate the computers, write programs for them, and otherwise perform all the services associated with running computer systems.

• Contract personnel are used often for engineering tasks of many kinds, for test and maintenance work, for writing, and for a variety of other technical/professional skills. In some cases, the experience of the organization and its ability to design and manage programs is the chief consideration, although the evaluators are always interested in the individual qualifications of the staff proposed. But in many other cases, the chief organizational credential desired is evidence that the organization can supply qualified personnel and manage them, under technical direction of the customer's project manager. (To a large degree, the contractor's project manager is a conduit for instructions from the government's project manager, who, by law, cannot give orders directly to the contractor's personnel.)

• Ordinarily, "personal services contracts" are strictly verboten. These are contracts in which a contractor (or the contractor's employees) are personally directed by a civil service employee or which state as a requirement that the services of some specifically named individual are required. There are exceptions, however, especially to the second case. In one instance, NASA wanted a book written on celestial mechanics, a specialty in the field of physics dealing with astronomy, the motion of heavenly bodies, and navigation in space. The world's leading authority on the subject was a Japanese physicist who was rather elderly and whose number of remaining years was a matter of conjecture. He was therefore bound under a personal services contract to write the definitive work which, probably, no one else in the world could have done nearly as well. At the same time, a contract was let for an American scientist who could edit the physicist's manuscript competently. The latter, however, was not a personal services contract.

• When the military services want to take advantage of new technology to design a faster airplane or a more accurate radar, they issue invitations to submit proposals, with the intention of evaluating basic design concepts offered by the proposers, as well as their general credentials. In many cases, where the effort calls for design, R&D, or problem-solving in general—no matter what the end-product is to be—it is the proposer's approach or initial concept which is most critical in the contest. Ordinarily, the chief bidders for such contracts are all experienced firms, with good track records. All are quite competent, technically, but one will put forth a concept or design approach which captures the customer's attention.

There are many cases where the customer could, logically, use an IFB, calling for sealed bids, to get acceptable bids. But, as discussed in Chapter 5, this creates the possible problem of being forced to accept as a contractor someone whose qualifications are doubtful. Theoretically, the customer may disqualify a bidder as not showing the necessary technical competence, but in practice it will fall on the government to prove the bidder's lack of technical competence, and that can and usually does prove to be nearly impossible. Hence the resort to an RFP when such eventualities are feared.

There is still another situation which appears to call for an IFB, but which often is handled by soliciting proposals and engaging in negotiated procurement: When the customer expects few bids, perhaps only one, but wants the opportunity to negotiate a price, something that cannot be done with sealed bids. This situation often comes about simply because the item is so painstakingly detailed in its specifications that there are few suppliers who can "meet the spec." In such a case, the supplier usually has a realistic appraisal of the competition and the asking price may be a high one. Hence the need for negotiation.

Sole-source procurements

As our technology advances, we see more and more sole-source procurement taking place. Sole-source procurement, sometimes referred to as selected-source procurement, is buying by negotiated procurement methods from a single, selected source, without inviting bids or proposals from others. The procurement regulations provide for such exceptions to the general rule of competitive procurement, and there are several possible circumstances in which such bypassing of the normal competitive bidding is justified.

- A single firm may be peculiarly qualified by virtue of having done some predecessor work, which results in its being the only firm that can handle the new requirement efficiently. Any other firm would have to learn a great deal to qualify equally well, which would elevate the costs substantially.
- The sole-source procurement may be justified because the selected contractor has some proprietary knowledge, equipment, or patents which represent the only practicable approach to the program.
- The new contract may be an extension of or modification to an existing contract.
- Or, the sole-source procedure may be based on an unsolicited proposal.

Unsolicited Proposals

Unsolicited proposals are somewhat controversial. In theory, an unsolicited proposal is one offered by an individual or organization at his, her, or its own initiative, often based on proprietary ideas; that is, ideas and concepts developed by the proposer at the proposer's expense. An unsolicited proposal results in a non-competitive award, if it is accepted. The government does not have the right to make the proposer's idea known to others and to solicit proposals from others. The government either accepts the proposal, with or without negotiation, or rejects it.

Many contracting officials are suspicious of any proposal purporting to be unsolicited. They suspect that a government executive may have used the unsolicited proposal provision as a convenient means to circumvent the normal procedures, which represent a great deal of work and time. A statement of work must be written, solicitation packages must be sent out, with time allowed for recipients to prepare proposals, proposals must be evaluated, and negotiations conducted. This normally requires six months or more before a project can actually get under way. But an unsolicited proposal avoids the writing of work statements and evaluation of proposals. So there is always the possibility that a government executive has actually suggested to a contractor that he offer an unsolicited proposal to do something the government executive wants done!

Therefore, many contracting officials examine all proposals purporting to be unsolicited with a close and piercing scrutiny, and demand extensive evidence that the proposal is a truly unsolicited one, prepared entirely at the initiative of the proposer and not prompted by the government.

In 1977, following a study of five government agencies, the General Accounting Office reported that most federal agencies appeared to be abusing the provisions for non-competitive procurements. This does not appear, however, to have reduced their incidence a bit.

"September Buys"

One of the causes for at least some of the non-competitive procurement lies with the U.S. Congress. Unfortunately, despite the fact that the government's fiscal year has been changed so it now ends on September 30 instead of on June 30, Congress still rarely completes all its funding authorizations by the end of the fiscal year. In fact, in many cases, funding is not completed until after the end of the calendar year.

That places the various agencies in the position of not knowing how much money they will have to carry out their programs until well into the new fiscal year. As a result, they have considerably less than 12 months to plan and implement their various projects, since all funds must be spent before the end of the fiscal year.

That requires a bit of explanation, too. For one thing, when Congress finally completes the funding allotments for a given agency, the funds allocated to the agency are "authorized." Except for those few cases of "full funding" (programs which have been funded for their anticipated lifetimes, rather than year by year, as most programs are funded) the funds are to be used during the fiscal year, and may not be carried over into the next fiscal year. Any funds remaining beyond September 30 must be returned to the Treasury.

This, however, does not mean that the funds must be literally "spent" (disbursed). It means that the funds must be "obligated."

Obligated funds may be disbursed or spent after the end of the fiscal year. Authorized funds are funds the agency has available to spend. Obligated funds are funds allocated specifically, for example, by contract, to a given program or cost center. That is, if a new contract for $500,000 is signed on September 30, the $500,000 is obligated and does not have to go back to the Treasury.

Given the constraint of completing all contracting and other program implementation for the entire year in the span of perhaps six months, agencies tend to be under pressure to spend money, especially when the current fiscal year begins to dwindle and approach an end. Having money left over is considered to be a cardinal sin in government circles. Even the White House gets upset at spending shortfalls and tries frantically to reduce them, as the fiscal year approaches its end. Add to this the usually lengthy periods necessary for formal competitive contracting, and many government executives feel bound to seek shortcuts which will enable them to spend their allocations before September 30. Those frantic, last-minute buying efforts are sometimes referred to as "September buys," and in many cases they are the principal reason that officials resort to non-competitive avenues of procurement.

Multiple awards

At the opposite end of the spectrum from sole-source awards are multiple awards. These are contract requirements in which a number of awards will be made; that is, this is the exception to the only-one-winner-in-the-contest rule. Situations do arise, from time to time, in which the government believes that several contracts are merited, for whatever reason, and this is usually made known to the proposers.

A good example of this was the initiation of the Job Corps, some 15 years ago. There were to be seven Urban Job Corps Centers, plus a then-unspecified number of Rural Job Corps Centers. However, the Centers were not awarded in seven separate proposal contests, but proposals were accepted for Center operation, and the Office of Economic Opportunity selected seven contractors, one by one, assigning each of them one of the Centers.

In the case of the NASA Headquarters contract for publications support services, for example, it was the practice to award four contracts. The chief rationale for this was, apparently, that many of the requirements were sudden and on a short fuse (they required a rapid response). Having four contractors available lessened the possibility that the task would not get done on time, because each contractor had the privilege of passing up a task if he felt that he could not meet the schedule requirement, and the government could then call the next contractor on the list and offer that contractor the task. For contracts of that type, requiring sudden, quick-reaction services, it is not unusual to award several contracts.

There are other situations in which multiple awards are considered desirable. One of them is where the products or services are used by many federal agencies throughout the country, and the agencies require a local or nearby source of supply. In such cases, there may be many contractors on a "schedule," with copies of the schedule distributed to the various agencies, with instructions for ordering from their nearest supplier.

Formal versus informal proposals

Most RFPs call for formal proposals, and they usually specify what information must be supplied in the proposal. A case in which the proposal may be informal is usually identified as a "letter proposal." A letter proposal is essentially that: a letter in which the writer makes his offer, supplying only a cursory proposal. This is most often the case with small purchases. Here is a typical situation which results in a letter proposal:

Several years ago, I called on OSHA, spending several hours meeting different executives and discussing their possible needs. I finally met a gentleman who had a problem which was a suitable target for the services I offered. As we discussed his problem, I suggested remedies I could supply. Finally, he became seriously interested and invited me to submit a letter proposal.

A few days later, I submitted a two-page letter, in which I reviewed his problem briefly, described the services I would provide and the result I promised, and quoted a price for my services. My description of the problem and services to be provided became the statement of work, which he transcribed to a government purchase order and awarded to me as a contract.

In most cases, however, a full-blown, formal proposal is required, and this may be of almost any size, from 25 to 50 pages for a small job, to many hundreds—even thousands—of pages for a major award.

The essential nature of the proposal

At the beginning of this chapter, we posed the question, "What is a proposal?" The answer supplied was "an offer—a sales presentation." What remains to be explained and defined is, "What is a sales presentation?" To answer that effectively, we must look at salesmanship, its basic nature and principles. For the basic nature of a proposal, a *successful* proposal, that is, is salesmanship.

Look around, and you'll find more examples of bad salesmanship than of good salesmanship. Far too many writers of what is supposed to be sales copy write testimonials to themselves, rather than sales copy. The single most common error is that they do not give the customer *a reason to buy* what they offer.

Volkswagen commercials of a few years ago were a good example of clever, entertaining advertising which didn't sell anything. Likewise, one series of Alka-Seltzer commercials constituted great "advertising art" which succeeded in winning everything but sales.

It isn't cleverness with phrases or even with illustrations that sells. The cleverness that sells is *empathy*—understanding the prospect's viewpoint and catering to the prospect's desires. Consider beer commercials on TV: Do they try to sell beer? Certainly not. They promise good times at the beach or at the local tavern. Dishwasher detergent is sold by promising bright, sparkling dishes that win admiration from friends and family—they sell the admiration, not the detergent.

But what has all this to do with proposals offered to the U.S. government? Just this: The U.S. government is *people.* They are no more objective than are other people, and although they buy with the government's money, rather than their own, they are influenced by many personal considerations. After all, their own careers are involved!

Advertising men and sales experts will tell you that there are four elements in the process:

A: GET ATTENTION
I: AROUSE INTEREST
D: GENERATE DESIRE (to buy)
A: ASK FOR ACTION (close)

Of course, with our predilection for acronyms in today's society, they preach the dandy little acronym which has the same name as the opera: AIDA. In their anxiety to be clever, they overlooked a few things, and became a bit cryptic. However, we can use their acronym as a point of departure to explain why the proposal is not entirely dissimilar from any other sales presentation or advertising campaign (which operate on the same principles of salesmanship). There is one major difference, however, which we should note immediately.

"Asking for action," or closing, means asking for the order, and is often considered the most critical part of selling and the most common failure of inexperienced (and even experienced) salespeople. In proposing to government agencies, we don't have to "ask for action." The government intends to buy, and doesn't have to be persuaded to order, but rather to select you as the proposer from *whom* to order. That brings our acronym, for proposals, down to AID.

However, the government already has a desire to buy. That's why the RFP was issued. The question is only which offer (proposal) to accept. So we might modify that "generate desire to buy" to "generate desire to buy *our* offer."

The key question, then, for each element—A, I, and D—is *how? How* shall we get attention (and why?), *how* shall we arouse interest, *how* shall we generate desire to buy from us? It's the "how," as well as the "what," which is the art of effective proposal writing, and the subject of the rest of this chapter.

The elements of the successful proposal

The element left out of selling, in that dandy little AIDA acronym, and which is most essential in selling anything, is *credibility.* The most modest claims will not sell if they are not credible, believable by the prospect, and the most outrageous claims will sell if they *are* credible. The mistake so many writers make is to fail to furnish evidence of truth, to make the claims believable.

Many sales presentations are good up to the point of credibility. They get attention, they offer benefits (reasons to buy), they are easy to understand—and then they fall on their faces because they fail to *convince.* They fail to compel belief that they will deliver, as promised.

In TV commercials, actors posing as druggists or laboratory scientists are often used to generate that believability through the "white coat" approach, if the product lends itself to the use of such authority figures. Candidate Dwight Eisenhower was a shoo-in for the presidency, although he had few qualifications for the job, because he was believable, an authority figure, a father image.

The chief problem is that so many writers mistakenly believe that *claims* are *evidence.* Typically, such a writer will say some such thing as, "J. Black and Company is the largest tool manufacturer in our industry," which is obviously a claim, the writer's *opinion*. The adjective, "largest," is the giveaway. Lay off the adjectives and adverbs, and stick to the nouns and verbs. As Walter Brennan used to say in one of his TV characterizations, "No brag; just fact."

Let's take that claim of being largest. Suppose we said it this way: "J. Black and Company employs 7,000 employees in 43 plants throughout the United States." That's *evidence*. No claims; just reporting the facts.

Getting attention has a certain importance, as you shall see shortly. But a successful sales argument has just two objectives:

1. To explain, clearly and unmistakably, what will result (benefits to the buyer) from buying what you offer (the reason for buying).
2. To prove your case. To present the evidence that will enable the prospect to believe that you can and will deliver exactly those promised results.

It may take hundreds of pages to do this, and it does take a great deal of explanation to demonstrate the many subordinate elements in achieving the two objectives just stated. But except for a few techniques for getting the customer's attention—you can't get your message home if the person is not paying attention—every word and illustration in a proposal is aimed at one or both of these objectives: Give the customer the reasons for buying and the reasons for believing. Anything which does not contribute to this is superfluous, a distraction which can do no good and may do harm.

The following points should be covered in a good proposal. See if you can relate these to the two objectives just stated:

- A general introduction, briefly stating who the proposer is, why that person is interested in bidding for the contract, and the general qualifications, to be expanded on later.
- A general statement or review of the requirement that demonstrates an understanding of it.
- A somewhat lengthy and in-depth discussion, exploring various considerations in satisfying the requirement (analysis), that logically arrives at a specific plan that will satisfy the requirement.
- A specific plan for implementing the approach arrived at, which is, in fact, the proposal (*this* is what becomes the contractual document).
- Qualifications (resumes) of the proposed staff.
- Qualifications (experience and resources) of the proposing organization.

Note the logical flow of this presentation: We are the such-and-such company, with x number of years in the business of satisfying just such needs as you describe. *We see your need as being thus and so.* There are several ways in which this need can be addressed, but each alternative method has its pros and cons. (Discussions of methods, analysis of each.) *Therefore, we believe the approach described to be the best method, offering the fewest problems and the greatest probabilities for complete and unqualified success. Here is exactly how we propose to proceed.* (Detailed plans.) *We have an excellent staff of well-qualified people, whom we propose for key roles in the project.* (Resumes.) *We have ample experience and resources, to demonstrate both our capability and track record of success.* (Experience and qualifications of organization.)

This takes the reader of your proposal through the entire analytical process by which you have arrived at the plan you present. This is a necessity because it must never be assumed that the customer recognizes the merits of your approach and your plan. He may or may not be an expert; that is, he may be equally, more, or less knowledgeable than you are in the field of interest. Therefore, he must be made to *understand* all the elements: the benefits, the methodology, the rationale for the methodology, the rationale for choosing the approach you recommend over other approaches which might have been offered (*and may be offered by competitors*). This is to say that you may have to *educate* your reader in order to sell him, just as general advertising often includes educational material to educate the consumer on the pros and cons of electric refrigerators, automobiles, and cough syrup. It's part of the credibility ammunition.

The common mistakes of proposals

A typical solicitation for proposals may bring in 5, 10, 20, or even over 100 proposals to be read and evaluated. But the number of proposals submitted does not reveal the true competition. In all cases, a percentage of the proposals submitted are rejected on first reading, sometimes before being read all the way through. The percentage rejected can vary widely. One government contracting official reveals that in some proposal competitions, as many as *9 out of 10* proposals submitted are rejected summarily. It is safe to say that an average rejection rate is at least 33.33 percent. Fully one-third of the proposals submitted in a typical competition are considered to be not worth the time to read them!

The swift death knell of these is justified by the simple characterization of the proposals as being non-responsive. That phrase can cover many faults, but the most common one is that the writers of the proposals appear not to have read the RFP with any great care. Evaluators of proposals have been heard to mumble to themselves, "They just don't seem to understand the problem."

This is often reflected in listed evaluation criteria, where points are awarded for "understanding of the requirement." The customer is sending a message, loud and clear, which says, "Don't start writing your proposal until you have studied the requirement and understand exactly what we seek."

There are many ways in which a proposal can be non-responsive to an RFP. One is, of course, by simply failing to reflect an understanding of the requirement; that is, by offering something other than what the RFP has called for—perhaps by offering a solution to which there is no problem!

There are organizations which have developed their pet solutions, perhaps a proprietary package or process, and who insist on reading into each RFP a need for their own, pet solution. In writing their proposals, they will consciously or unconsciously insist on distorting the customer's description of the need to make it fit their solution.

There is also the problem that many organizations, lacking enough work or trying desperately to break into new fields without adequate preparation, will simply play roulette. They'll bid for work they really know nothing about, hoping to be struck by the lightning of a contract award.

This situation is readily apparent at openings of sealed bids for specialized work. In a typical situation of this type, the U.S. Forest Service had solicited bids for the preparation of a small programmed-instruction course in office procedures. A proper price range for the job, the prevailing "market" for such work at that time, would have been approximately $8,000–$10,000. The bids read aloud at the opening ranged as high as $80,000! The $80,000 bidder obviously was completely unfamiliar with the work or had not read the RFP.

In all fairness, however, a typical RFP and work statement does offer many opportunities to be non-responsive. Some statements of work include lengthy lists of specifications, and failure to respond to even one of these may be construed as non-responsiveness, if the customer chooses to so construe the failure.

An RFP usually sets out certain qualifications and conditions required, to warn off unqualified bidders so that they do not waste their time and money preparing proposals for work they cannot qualify for. In that list of qualifications, there may easily be a few which do not match the characteristics of an otherwise well-qualified proposer. To simply ignore these is to risk being non-responsive, whereas in many cases the proposer can persuade the customer that he is well-qualified and should be considered, despite failure to match the customer's ideas exactly. Being non-responsive does not mean failing to match every particular set forth, but can mean failure to acknowledge and respond to every point on which information or opinion is solicited by the RFP.

Such failure can apply to *any* element of the proposal—understanding of the requirement, staff resumes, company qualifications, delivery dates, management provisions, physical facilities, and so on.

Cosmetics versus Content

Some organizations have the notion that the cosmetic niceties of proposals, the type, paper, and bindings, are highly important because they focus attention on those aspects rather than on content. There is no doubt that a proposal is enhanced by a good physical appearance. However, no amount of cosmetic surgery or makeup can compensate for weaknesses in content. Proposals which have been carried to the extremes of elaborate typesetting and expensive bindings are rejected as swiftly as are the most simply typed and stapled proposals, if their content does not merit further consideration. In fact, most RFPs include a statement emphasizing that elaborate printing and binding is neither desired nor appreciated, and may be construed as evidence that the proposer is lacking in suitable cost-consciousness!

This is not to say that a proposal may not be typeset, printed, and bound suitably. It should be made as attractive as possible without going to extremes. But it should never be made attractive at the expense of content. Many proposals that are typed neatly, duplicated on an office copier, and stapled in the upper left-hand corner have won out over competing proposals printed and bound in heavy covers. Content is always more important than packaging.

The Attempted Snow Job

One scathing comment often made by evaluators as they read pompous, overblown phrases is, "Madison Avenue!" The effort to overpower readers by obscure phraseology, by purported scholarliness, by buzz words, by extravagant and unsupported claims, and by other such devices simply does not work. One manager in the Department of Labor reports that he is amused by such tactics—but he swiftly goes on to read other proposals, often without even finishing the one which has amused him so mightily. At the same time, he says that he is adversely impressed, "turned off," he says, by careless use of language. He believes that spelling errors, poor grammar, and other such weaknesses are most "unprofessional," and that anyone who is that unprofessional when preparing and submitting a proposal is likely to be equally unprofessional in carrying out a program! Further, this manager told me that he has often canceled a procurement entirely because he did not believe that *any* of the proposals submitted merited award.

The Rambling Wreck

A great many proposals simply ramble, without apparent plan or direction. An individual seems to have sat down and begun to write, putting words on paper as thoughts presented themselves, with little plan and no concrete objectives in mind. The proposal drifts with the currents, expanding into great detail when the author happens across a topic of especial interest and in which he feels knowledgeable, scampering quickly across the shoals of little-known subjects, and arriving wherever it finally arrives because the current has taken it there.

At least, that's the impression one gets from reading some of these. This may come about because the RFP and statement of work (SOW) are not particularly well organized. Often they are not, because the writer of the SOW is not a disciplined writer. The proposal writer (or writers; the word "writer" is used here to include both the singular and the plural) has perhaps attempted to write a proposal in sequence and synchronism with the SOW. Doing that is usually a mistake. Few SOWs are that well organized. Many ramble badly, offering items of information and instruction completely out of any logical sequence, and are often highly redundant. The fact that the person responsible for the SOW (who is likely to be an evaluator of your proposal) is not a good writer does not necessarily mean he can't judge the quality of somone else's writing.

However, there is one major reason for bad writing and bad organization in proposals, and it is this: Most proposals are written by individuals who are not professional or experienced writers, and they attempt to write well in their first draft! The have not learned that hardly anyone can compose a good first draft or even organize the information well in the first draft. It is quite apparent to even the untrained eye that a large proportion of the proposals received in government offices are first-draft proposals which should never have been seen by other eyes than those of the organization's writers and editors.

The phases of proposal development

The actual act of writing the proposal is the final stage in proposal development. Other phases should have preceded it:

1. Bid/no-bid analysis and decision.
2. Requirement analysis.
3. Identification of the critical factor(s).
4. Formulation of the approach and technical/program/pricing strategies.
5. Formulation of the capture strategy.
6. Establishing the theme.
7. Planning and outlining.
8. Design and presentation strategy.
9. Writing.

The quality of the proposal and its chances for success will depend even more heavily on these early phases than on writing skills, important though those are. Each of these is a subject in itself and will be examined individually, although we have touched on some of them already.

Bid/No-Bid Analysis and Decision

Obviously, proposal development begins with a decision to make the bid, to write the proposal, and this is itself an analytical and decision-making process. However, the information gathered during this analysis is—should be—a first input to the proposal-development process itself.

Many factors must be considered when deciding whether to bid or submit a "no bid" to the customer. Some of these are "constants"; they result from fixed policies or conditions; others are variable, according to the circumstances of the moment: An RFP which your organization might have wished to respond to in January may not be attractive in August, as you will soon see when you review the factors to be considered in arriving at a bid/no-bid decision. Here are the types of questions to which you must seek answers in reviewing the RFP:

1. Exactly what is it that the contractor is to do or supply? Is it in our normal field of operation, or would we have to gear up especially for this contract? Is it some field we are eager to enter?
2. What are our strengths for this contract? Our weaknesses? Can we overcome our weaknesses? Will our strengths be adequate to carry the day? In short, how credible can we be?
3. What other bid opportunities do we have, at the moment? Are bid opportunities plentiful or scarce? What is our backlog? How badly do we

need additional contracts right now? How attractive is this contract, compared with others we might pursue? What do our chances for this one appear to be, compared with others we can go after?
4. What or who is the competition? How strong are they? How do we compare with them? Do we have any natural advantages? Specific disadvantages?
5. What staff do we have available to write the proposal? How big an effort will it be? What is it likely to cost us in dollars? Is diversion of staff needed elsewhere?
6. What is (are) the most compelling reason(s) for bidding this? Potential profit? Follow-on contracts? Breaking into new fields? What are reasons for not bidding it?

The answers to many of these spawn secondary sets of questions. If, for example, you decide that you lack many of the strengths you need for this proposal, yet you'd like to pursue this contract for one reason or another, you may wish to consider bidding with another firm—co-bidding, that is. Frequently, that can win a contract otherwise probably unattainable. Here's an excellent example of that.

Approximately 10 years ago, when NASA had issued an RFP for management and operation of its Scientific and Technical Information Facility in College Park, Maryland, there was a persistent rumor that the customer was unhappy with its incumbent contractor, and would welcome a new one. The contract ordinarily comes up every three years for renewal, at which time proposals are accepted from all bidders. It's a large facility, which then employed approximately 360 people and was worth approximately $5.5 million per year in billings. The contractor installs his employees and manager on the government's own site in College Park, and operates a large complex of computers and printing equipment, turning out a variety of technical documents.

One of the contenders was a relatively new firm, Informatics, an aggressive marketer. At the time, Informatics was simply not large enough, nor did it have all the qualifications needed to be completely credible for the contract. However, Informatics "teamed" with another firm, Computing and Software, which also was not a large corporation, but had a good track record with NASA as a supplier of computer programming specialists and manager of on-site computer operations. Together, they formed a third entity, in partnership, Technical Information Systems Company or TISCO, as it soon became known. That alliance won the contract, and is still operating the facility today.

It is extremely unlikely that either firm could have won the contract by itself. But together, they showed enough strength to satisfy NASA, and they have obviously done a satisfactory job for these past 10 or more years. Better half a loaf. . . .

Teaming with another firm (co-bidding) is obviously one way to overcome a weakness. Another way is to recruit additional staff, whose resumes may be used. These may be individuals to be hired or consultants to be retained for the contract in the event of award. Still another way may be to devise a technical plan or approach which is somewhat different from that suggested by the RFP, but still a legitimate approach and one that you believe you can "sell" to the customer. Here is an example of how that may sometimes be done:

The Post Office Department (before it became the U.S. Postal Service) issued an RFP calling for a basic ordering agreement for computer programming services. The requirement was for a contractor who had on staff and available for assignments on short notice a wide variety of computer specialists with a wide variety of skills. The statement of work listed specialists rated on an ascending scale from the most junior programmer to systems design specialists, with experience in many types of machines, and with knowledge of a wide variety of computer languages. Taken at face value, the RFP required the contractor to be able to produce, on short notice, any combination of skill level, machine familiarity, and computer-language knowledge. The permutations of these several parameters are, of course, a staggeringly great number.

The successful bidder had relatively few computer programmers on staff. However, he had an exceptionally well-developed recruiting capability, because that was one of his chief services: supplying specialists, under contract, for long or short periods of time. He therefore turned his weakness into a strength by taking the calculated risk of modifying the requirement somewhat, in this manner:

He stated to the customer that the *real* requirement was not to have this stupendous mix of specialists on staff (and that it was most unlikely that *anyone* did), but, rather, to be able to *produce* any specialists required whenever a request was made. He went on to explain his company's great strengths in doing just that, citing case after case of having done it in the past. He won the contract without difficulty.

It is frequently of critical importance to *interpret* or *translate* the requirement, as stated by the customer, into another set of terms. Obviously, you should interpret it so as to support your own approach and proposed program.

However—please note this—it is also important to interpret the customer's stated requirement *for your own benefit.* The case just cited is a good example of the customer misstating his own need. Of course it was not required that the contractor actually be the permanent employer of all the specialists called for, but only be able to *supply* those specialists, when needed; the customer readily agreed with the proposer's interpretation. This is a rather common condition: The customer does not always explain the need clearly enough, and frequently it is essential that the proposer spend a good bit of effort studying that requirement closely and reaching a better interpretation or definition of the need.

There are times when bid opportunities are plentiful—three to six months before the end of the government's fiscal year. Most contractors, at times like these, have far more bid sets on their desks than they can possibly respond to. Therefore, they must classify the bid sets in terms of desirability and possibilities of winning, in an effort to select those best worth their time and effort. However, the contractor who has not been very successful during the "proposal season" may have a slender backlog, and therefore will bid for jobs ordinarily spurned.

In any case, the next phase begins when and if a decision is made to bid, of course. And that should begin where the bid/no-bid decision-analysis process began: With a hard look at the requirement and what it means. Even though some study of that was made in the bid/no-bid analysis, additional effort to refine the interpretation further is almost always a good investment.

Requirement Analysis

The discipline known as "value engineering" or "value analysis" is excellent preparation for RFP requirements analysis, for the major objective and address of VE (value engineering) is the study of *function,* especially the *main* function or *basic* function, as value engineers prefer to describe it. In the case of the Post Office Department contract described a few paragraphs ago, a value engineer would have automatically said, "The basic function is to provide computer specialists, so it can't really matter whether they come from the contractor's own staff or from other sources, as long as they are provided." The value engineer has been trained to regard an item (which may be a physical object, system, person, document, or almost anything else) and seek an answer to the question, "What does it do?" (Or, "What is it *supposed* to do?") That's the first step in identifying or defining a basic function, which is the objective of or the reason for the existence of the item (or requirement).

Some time earlier, you learned that the customer has one of several basic conditions or needs which underlie his request for contract help, and that you will be asked, as the contractor, to do one of the following:

Solve a problem.
Provide additional staff to carry out a program.
Provide specialized resources—physical facilities, staff, or know-how—to carry out a program.

As a first step in bid/no-bid analysis, you will have already decided which of these categories the job falls into. Now you want to take a closer look at your earlier judgment. The distinctions are not always as clear-cut as they may appear when stated categorically, as they have been here, and sometimes the customer's statement of work can be misleading. Government people often tend to believe that their requirements are very specialized and have no true counterpart elsewhere in commerce and industry, and they are often right about that. But the uniqueness of their requirement may be due to their own notions of how the job should be done, a misconception of their true problem or need, or a lack of familiarity with how similar problems are handled in the commercial/industrial environment. That is, what is presented as a special or unique problem may be a routine problem, which has a well-known solution. Whether you point this out in your proposal or not is a matter to be settled later, when you consider approaches and strategies; for now you must decide whether such is the case or not. Therefore, you should be analyzing the requirement by another series of questions to which you must seek answers.

• *If stated as a problem to be solved:* Is it truly a *problem* problem, or something occurring commonly and readily solved? Will it be difficult to solve? Is there any doubt about eventual success? Has the customer a true understanding of the problem? Has he really identified the problem or its symptoms? Has he obscured the true problem with a miasma of trivial and extraneous information? Is he gilding the lily—calling it a problem, knowing well that what he requests and needs are really routine services, in an effort to glorify his own project? Or has he some other reason for such obscuration?

• *If the requirement appears to be a need for a set of specialized services and/or skills:* How "special" are they? Will they require staff of rare qualifications? How specialized does the customer appear to think they are? (As distinct from what *you* think?)

• *If the need appears to be simply more hands and feet of one sort or another:* How specialized must the hands and feet be? How well qualified? Will they work as a unit on a single project or be utilized in various ways and locations? Will there be an extensive management requirement?

Once you have satisfied yourself that you have answered these questions satisfactorily, or as far as they can be answered, you are ready to proceed to the next step: identification of critical factors. However, this analysis (analyses) is not totally sequential and discrete. Iteration is often necessary, and as you proceed you may find it necessary to return to an earlier analysis and modify your conclusions drawn there. Therefore, operate on the assumption that every conclusion you draw is a tentative one and is subject to change. You will find that these analyses are all interconnected as one overall analysis. I have separated them here as an illustrative device to help you see some logic and order in the process.

Identification of the Critical Factor(s)

As you begin your search for the critical factor(s), you will begin to grasp the true significance of some of the secondary questions suggested in preceding paragraphs. You will see, also, where this is leading: to the formulation of approaches and strategies. The latter are based on the answers you develop to these questions, and to formulate them without asking and answering these questions is to stab wildly in the dark, hoping to "strike a nerve."

In most cases, there is some overriding consideration in the customer's mind. That consideration may have been clearly stated in the explanatory text, in the explanation of evaluation criteria and their weights, or in both. Or, you may not have been given any idea, overtly, at least, as to what is of uppermost importance to the customer. And frequently there is some factor or set of factors which is critical, upon which success really hinges, sometimes in spite of what the listed evaluation criteria are!

For example, in many cases, the resumes overshadow everything else in importance. Sometimes the resume of the proposed project director is by far the most important of all the resumes. A strong proposed project director may carry the day, even though the other resumes offered are not particularly meritorious, and a weak resume for the proposed project director may scotch the proposal despite strengths everywhere else. The customer feels, with a great deal of justification, that the government is entrusting a great deal of money and a most important program to the contractor's project director and is understandably concerned that the project director be qualified to the nth degree.

There are other things which may concern the customer. He may feel that the project requires an especially strong management plan. Or he may be working on a tight budget and be compelled to accept the best he can get for the price—ergo, price becomes a critical concern. He may want an innovative plan (a state-of-the-art approach), or he may want a conservative approach (the tried-and-true foolproof method). He may want a take-charge kind of contractor, who will require a minimum of attention in running the program, or he may want a contractor who will "touch base" with him almost continuously.

Admittedly, it is not easy to learn all this and usually takes a great deal of detective work. Yet, the clues are there in the RFP/SOW, in most cases, and the alert analyst can ferret them out.

However, they are not always obscure. In many cases, they are so obvious that they are overlooked completely! When Secretary of Defense Robert McNamara wanted an airplane that both the Air Force and the Navy could use, only one of the bidders for the job saw clearly that their proposal must trumpet "commonality" throughout, to let the Secretary know that they understood his objective loud and clear. That bidder won, due in no small measure to that strategy, as well as to a generally sound proposal and capability. Other bidders were more subtle, promising commonality, but never spelling it out distinctly, much less reiterating and reinforcing it frequently.

That critical concern of the customer is the keystone of the entire proposal effort. Understanding what the customer wants and what he says he wants—whether they are the same messages or not—is fundamental to the approach, the strategy, and the theme (which is part of the strategy, of course).

I lost one proposal because I did not understand what the customer really wanted in spite of the fact that the contracting officer had taken me aside and urged me to give him a crackerjack proposal because he wanted me to have the contract. (So much for "fixes" when you don't also write the winning proposal!) It happened this way:

There were some unclear points in the statement of work and I felt we had to ask the customer some questions. Since we did know the officials well, and they were highly receptive to our having the contract—if we gave them a good enough proposal—I sent an assistant over to make inquiries about those points which appeared unclear to us.

It happened that he talked to the man who would manage the contract for the customer. What we did not know was that the individual sharply disagreed with his superior about the conduct of the project, and had written the work statement in his own manner, evidently being deliberately obscure about a few things he wanted to do differently than his superior did. Therefore, he explained *his* intent to my assistant, and we wrote the proposal accordingly. But his superior rejected our proposal because it didn't agree with *his* idea of what was needed to do the job the way *he* wanted it done. (We did, however, win the next two contracts for the same work, once we understood the situation.)

Formulation of Approach and Strategies

There are several types of strategy you will use. There is the technical or program strategy—how you propose to design and carry out the project, how you will manage it, and so on. There are pricing strategies, some of which were discussed in Chapters 5 and 6. And there are presentation strategies, which we will discuss presently. Any one or combination of these may represent your "capture strategy"—the main strategy, which you anticipate will sway the customer in your favor for the contract.

Your proposed approach is the key to the technical/program/ pricing strategy. That is why all are considered here, in a single discussion. You may devise an approach to suit your strategy or vice versa, but you cannot really consider one seriously without the other.

If, for example, you have judged price to be the critical factor, being a low bidder is your capture strategy, but you must devise an approach and technical/program strategy which permits you to be a low bidder without appearing to sacrifice quality or compromise the prospects for a successful project. Logically, you would begin by considering the various possible approaches, selecting the one which appears to suit your purpose best, and designing a program to match the approach. In practice, you may be so familiar with the work that you grasp almost instantly all the possible alternatives and can go almost directly into program design. However, for the sake of logical progression, let's assume that you must ponder this matter at length.

Suppose that at first glance, the project appears to require the full-time services of six highly qualified specialists, who alone would cost the customer on the order of $200,000–$240,000 per year, with overhead and support services. There are several possible approaches to reduce this cost:

1. Use of a lesser number of specialists, supported by junior staff who will be closely supervised so that the end-result will be as though six specialists were used.
2. As in (1) above, but using up to six specialists for part of their time, rather than all of it.
3. Use of consultants, who will cost less because of reduced overhead on consultants.

The criteria for selecting which of the above to use would include (a) total cost savings which could be realized, (b) relative risks to project success which each alternative entails, and (c) affect on customer's judgment of your plan and its suitability.

In any case, no matter which alternative you finally select as the one to be proposed, you will have to *sell* your approach to the customer. You will have to make him agree that your approach and plan are practicable, do not in any way compromise prospects for a successful project or the quality of the service or products of the project, and are more economical to carry out.

To do this, you will have to make a careful analysis and gather up an amount of evidence to prove your point. It is not sufficient to simply assure your customer that you have studied the matter and reached the conclusion that these cost savings can be effected without risk to quality or success; you must prove that by providing enough evidence to convince your customer of that truth.

Any time you promise a markedly better cost saving, an innovation of some sort, or a startlingly greater guarantee of results than your competitors can offer, you automatically strain the customer's credulity, and you must take suitable action to establish the credibility of your proposal. The more you offer or promise, the more evidence you must produce to overcome the instantaneous skepticism.

For example, you may discover an inherent paradox in the RFP, for such paradoxes do occur. One of the many RFPs issued by the Job Corps in its earlier days called for the development of an instructor-based course in electrical appliance repair. The statement of work explained that the target population was "functionally illiterate," a phrase commonly used to describe Job Corpsmen, almost all of whom were school dropouts (some of them never reached even high school before dropping out). Ergo, it was an article of faith in dealing with Job Corps generally that most read at fifth-grade level, at best, and were almost entirely deficient in arithmetic and other academic basics.

To give anyone even a minimally acceptable skill in electrical appliance repair, the student should certainly be able to work from the maintenance instructions published by the manufacturers, and be able to read simple electrical circuit diagrams. The repairman also should be able to order parts and should understand the workings of the equipment at least well enough to substitute equivalent parts when original replacements are not available, as is often the case. This, in turn, means understanding a few basic electrical laws, such as Ohm's Law and, probably, Kirchhoff's Laws (not necessarily in the formal sense of being able to quote and interpret them in language, but to grasp their application to simple electrical equipment, at the least). And this, in turn, calls for a grasp of simple algebra. Whether or not the repairman ever does actual calculations to calculate replacement values for circuit components, he must at least understand the calculations to learn the Laws and their significance.

So, in analysis, we come upon a paradox: How can students who can't read acceptably well, much less perform algebraic manipulations, be taught electrical appliance repair?

It was exactly this paradox which formed the basis for the approach and strategy of the successful proposal. Having reasoned out these problems, which seemed to indicate that the program should not be undertaken at all, the successful proposer proceeded on the assumption that a method must be found to make the project work despite the problem. The approach proposed was to develop a maximum of nonverbal teaching methods, plus several proposed shortcuts which would minimize the need for algebraic manipulations and calculations, plus a great deal of hands-on, work experience—almost an OJT (on-the-job training) environment in the classroom-workshop.

The strategy was to dramatize the problem, which was the paradox of the entire procurement, and to then offer an innovative solution, with the goal of persuading the customer that any other approach proposed was doomed to failure from the beginning. (One way to handle competition!) The strategy worked well, for the proposal was priced "out of sight," but it was so enticing that the customer offered to negotiate, and settled for a highly satisfactory price, which was still considerably higher than that of competing proposals.

As we proceed to other aspects of proposal development, we'll return to this outstanding example and discuss the evidence offered to support the dramatically different proposal.

Formulation of the Capture Strategy

The capture strategy—that aspect of your entire proposal which you are depending on to bring home the bacon—is rarely a single entity, although it may be, in a few cases. Usually, it is the sum of several strategies and techniques. In the case cited above, the main strategy was to be different from all other proposals by drawing attention to the paradox, and utilizing it. The proposal went about it somewhat along the following lines:

1. First, after introducing the proposer and establishing his general qualifications as a bidder for the project, the proposal summarized the stated requirement, and then launched into a brief rationale which pointed out that the skills to be taught entailed certain academic education and ability lacking in the target population, and so on. That section ended with a promise to present sound and reliable methods for coping successfully with this problem.

2. The proposal then went into a lengthier discussion, driving home the arguments summarized in the introductory paragraphs, to prove beyond doubt that conventional teaching approaches could not be expected to work in this situation, and that the project must be undertaken on a completely different basis if it was to have any chance of succeeding at all. It went on to discuss the specific areas of training required, the normal problems of teaching those, the special problems the Job Corpsmen could be expected to have, and the nonverbal methods and learning aids available, or which the proposer could devise, such as Ohm's Law calculators, nomograms, simplified diagrams, picture diagrams, and other devices.

3. The specific plan to develop these things and produce the entire training package was then offered in detail, with many sample materials, such as an Ohm's Law paper slide rule and simplified, multi-color picture charts.

This reflects a number of strategies, although all are part of the capture strategy. Here they are, as they were intended to operate and as they apparently did operate successfully:

First note paragraph (1), which discusses the introductory portion of the proposal. It indicated the inherent problem and probably alarmed the customer thoroughly about the basic soundness of the entire plan. (In so doing, it automatically alerted him to things he should be watchful for in competing proposals: Had the other proposers spotted the problem? If so, were they honest enough to point it out and clever enough to provide a solution?) But after alarming the customer, the proposal went on to assure him that relief was coming, if he would only read on!

If there were lingering doubts as to the proposal's initial claims and allegations, the next section, discussed in paragraph (2), presented much more evidence that the proposer's analysis was sound and dependable, and that failure to see this and provide against it was predictive of failure. (Here the proposer is telling the customer what to look for in competing proposals and how to spot their weaknesses, but in a thoroughly objective tone!) That second section went on to prove that the proposer was capable of developing and delivering the kind of program he advocated, by offering details of the kinds of special learning aids and *job performance aids* which would be provided. (Even the student who never succeeded in learning the basic electrical laws would not be stranded, since he could use the job performance aids, instead of doing the simple calculations!)

Proof was offered, finally, in providing actual samples of some of the devices and aids promised, in the section describing the specific program and project proposed.

So supporting strategies included indirect blows at competing offers, dramatic presentations, and solid evidence of actual "for instances."

A capture strategy, however, should not be a helter-skelter assortment of everything and anything which you think may help. It should be a carefully designed and constructed chain, with a clearly defined main strategy (the main reason the customer should buy *your* proposal) and subordinate strategies which support, reinforce, and strengthen your main strategy. Capture strategy is, then, *all* the strategies you have conceived, but organized to make the net effect greater than the simple sum of the parts.

Therefore, once you have identified the critical factor(s) and have devised your main strategy and approach, you must develop and design those other, subordinate strategies which will reinforce your main strategy and maximize the probability of it being decisive in the competition. The points to consider are these:

What does the customer appear to be most concerned about?
What is most likely to be decisive in the evaluation and in the customer's mind? What is his *real* need?
How does the RFP lend itself to the purpose? What inherent problems are there in what the customer wants to do?
What special *advantages* can your capability and ideas offer the customer?
How can you *dramatize* your presentation?
How can you be *different, yet credible?*

From these and similar questions you can construct a capture strategy.

Analytical Methodology

Small proposals are usually written by a single person; large proposals almost always require several people. But even the small proposal often requires discussion and analysis by a group of people before writing begins. Each proposal is an individual, custom effort, usually for a custom job or product. Each therefore requires an individual analysis and study: creative effort.

Brainstorming is a method often used successfully to synthesize the ideas of several people, invented by Alex Osborne, a New York advertising executive. A group of people gather in a room, address a clearly defined question or problem, and give free flow to their ideas. The basic rules for brainstorming are these:

1. There is a leader who manages and controls the process. He postulates the question or problem to be addressed, keeps the people from wandering off the subject, and enforces the rules.
2. No judgments are to be made. No one is to cheer, jeer, or otherwise react subjectively to an idea put forth. (This is to avoid discouraging anyone from articulating ideas for fear of ridicule.)
3. All ideas are recorded by someone present to do just that.
4. Anyone may "piggyback" his idea on another thrown out, or project an idea provoked by another one.
5. The session continues until the people have exhausted their ideas on the subject.
6. *Now* the ideas may be judged. Ideas may be discarded, studied more closely, modified, combined with other ideas, and so on.
7. Final choices are made from the ideas found acceptable.

The advertising industry has used this method for developing advertising approaches, slogans, and copy. But the basic idea has been adapted for other purposes. It has become a standard method for value engineering, for instance. Value engineering is usually conducted by a team, and value engineering is primarily one of analysis, first, followed by synthesis. Proposal writing also follows that pattern. First there is the analysis of the requirement and the many factors to be considered in developing the proposal, then the syntheses of the approach, strategies, and actual proposal. Brainstorming has therefore proved itself most useful in proposal development, and is usually a far more efficient method for the overall process than are the alternatives available.

A method which is often used when a group of technical/professional specialists are working together on a proposal is to have a general meeting, in which the RFP is discussed and the major requirements identified. Each individual then goes off to his own office to work on some assigned portion or element of the proposal, usually with little instruction or control. The results are often disastrous. This uncoordinated effort yields an assortment of write-ups from various team members which rarely match each other in style, content, level of detail, or any other characteristic, and are hardly suitable even as the roughest of drafts. It's an eminently unsatisfactory technique.

The time frame for most proposals is usually on the order of three to six weeks, and is rarely much longer than that. Time is simply too short for wasted motion. Although it was noted here earlier that few writers, even the professionals, write good first drafts, there is not enough time to do extensive rewriting. In almost all cases, the bulk of the proposal must be "rewritten" through heavy editing, with only partial actual rewrites, if the proposal is to meet the submittal deadline. To achieve this and still have a reasonably well-written and well-thought-out proposal, a great deal of control over the process is needed. It simply cannot be allowed to happen, but must be made to happen.

Adaptation of the brainstorming technique offers a large part of such control, as well as several other benefits. It is an excellent way of analyzing the RFP/SOW and sorting out the definition of the requirement and the critical factors, and it also combines several minds in devising approaches and strategies. In addition, instead of having the discrepancies in ideas surface in written drafts two or three weeks into the actual proposal writing, they can be identified during the brainstorming session and resolved there.

If two minds are better than one, how much better several trained minds must be! In a brainstorming session a synergism usually emerges, and the group often comes up with far better results than even the most gifted individual would have been able to achieve alone.

Even an individual writing a proposal alone can benefit from the method by discussing the requirement with one or more other people at an early stage. In fact, I've used his method quite often in writing my solo proposals, and it works quite well. At the very least, it gives me a Devil's advocate point of view against which to test my ideas. The other party usually makes more substantial contributions than that, and helps greatly in devising strategies, directly or indirectly.

Graphic Aids to Analysis

Most requirements involve a great many steps, although the work itself may not be especially complex. In nearly all cases, it is difficult to explain any but the most simple concepts in words alone. For example, try to describe a piece of furniture in your home in such detail that the reader can get an accurate picture in mind. We use photographs, drawings, charts, diagrams, and anything else to help convey an understanding and complete a description.

If diagrams help one understand what a text says, perhaps they can help us understand and *analyze* an RFP/SOW. However, only rarely has the writer of a work statement included diagrams to aid us in following his words and their meaning. We can, however, "fix" that. We can develop our own diagram, as we study the SOW, translating the words into the functions, actions, and relationships which can only be shown effectively in a diagram.

Consider the proposal-development process I have described (*prescribed*) so far. Does it begin to confuse you? Would it be clearer if you had it in front of you in an overall diagram? Let's try sketching out the words we have used in a graphic presentation, starting with the stages of proposal development. A simple set of blocks would look something like Figure 11(a). The text explains that the steps shown are not necessarily discrete and in sequence, but may be iterative; in fact, they usually are. That can be shown graphically too, as in Figure 11(b). The feedback lines show that the process is iterative: the output of any box may be fed back to modify, refine, and improve earlier decisions. This defines, far better than the text can, that all this analysis is really a single, continuous process, rather than a series of isolated steps.

This is known as a flowchart because it illustrates the logical flow of events, actions, decisions, and other functions. (Sometimes it is referred to as a functional flowchart.) All functions should be defined, identified, and shown in their logical *relationships* to each other—sequential, parallel, and so on.

Translating an RFP into such a chart compels identifying the various functions and phases of the project, the general flow of events leading to the required end-result, and the various interrelationships among the functions and events. It therefore pins down and highlights any anomalies or gaps in the RFP and facilitates, also, identification of problems which may be anticipated. Charting the project as described in the RFP is an excellent aid to analysis. Modifying and refining the

Figure 11. The stages of proposal development.

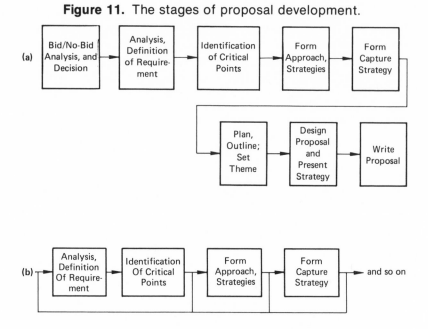

chart to reflect a proposed plan of action is a shortcut to *synthesis* (design) of the proposed program. And it is the process of converting the *de*scriptive flowchart (the one describing the project as stated in the RFP) to the *pre*scriptive flowchart (the one presenting the proposed program) which enables the formulation of effective approaches and strategies, often based on critical points unearthed during the analysis.

Flowcharting can facilitate intelligence-gathering. Many RFPs and their work statements are not nearly as clear as their writers intended, and can confuse prospective proposal writers. Flowcharting the program points up all anomalies, redundancies, and gaps, and this itself often answers questions raised by the RFP.

Large and complex projects may require several flowcharts, one for each major phase or portion of a program, or flowcharts at several "levels" of detail. For example, we might begin to develop a more detailed flowchart than the original one in Figure 11. The box in 11(a) labeled "bid/no-bid analysis, decision" can be expanded, as shown in Figure 12.

Of course, if we expand the entire flowchart in this detail, the result

Figure 12. Portion of a detailed flowchart.

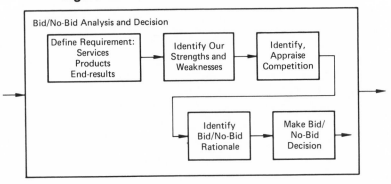

is a rather long chart. Many proposals are, in fact, submitted with charts running to six or more feet in length! However, the proposal team must judge each case on its own merits, to decide whether such detailed charts serve any good purpose. Usually, for any large or complex program, it is advisable to have one overall flowchart, at a relatively "high level," revealing the major steps, phases, and/or functions. The proposer must then decide whether additional, detailed flowcharts are needed to explain, define, or "sell" the program in its various aspects. In general, however, a routine function or step which involves nothing especially different or important needs no detailing. On the other hand, anything in your program which is innovative, especially striking, or one of the keys to success should be detailed.

The clue to this is really the amount of detailing and study you have put into the function in your planning. If you have found it necessary to draw up detailed flowcharts for your own analysis and planning of some step or function, the chances are that the customer should be similarly shown what you have planned and why you planned it that way. To do this effectively, it is usually necessary to provide all the details to the customer, to educate him in your thinking. At this point, we're talking about the flowchart as an analytical tool, but the chart(s) will also be useful selling tools.

Establishing the Theme

One of the great weaknesses of many proposals is that they have no theme. It is futile to attempt to impose one artificially on a "rambling wreck" of a proposal.

"Theme" is what a proposal is all about. It's a unifying concept, closely related to the overall approach and strategy of the proposal. It's a selling message which should be pressed home to the reader as often and as forcefully as possible, to remind him of what he is being asked to buy and why he should buy it. Therefore, in a proposal, the theme should be a sales message.

In the case of the contract for a common Navy—Air Force plane, the theme of the winning proposal was commonality. The customer was constantly reminded that commonality was what was asked for and commonality was what was being offered. Rivals stressed technical/engineering facets of their proposals, which were far more subtle, and far less effective, themes.

In the case of the Job Corps competition for an appliance-repair training course, the successful proposal had "nonverbal learning methods" as its theme, which was the basis for all the strategies and approaches.

The theme might stress low cost, innovative methods, outstanding management, unusual experience, or any of dozens of possible ideas. But it must tie in directly with the main strategy and approach, and it must be a unifying factor which characterizes and distinguishes the proposal. That is the reason for deciding on a theme now, in the planning stage.

A theme should be expressed through some sort of slogan or brief phrase, if possible, and should be strongly woven through the fabric of everything said in the proposal. It is far better to be explicit than to be clever and subtle. The slogan or phrase itself does not have to be chosen or constructed now, in the planning stages; that can come later. But the substance of the theme, its definition, ought to be settled now, if the proposal is to hang together properly and not become one of those rambling wrecks.

Theme may also be thought of as something to be proved by the proposal. If your theme is a more efficient way of getting the job done, all the proposal sections should be written to demonstrate the validity of that, to *prove* it. Theme is therefore a guide for the proposal writers, reminding them of where they are "going" in the proposal, what they must demonstrate and prove.

Planning and Outlining

Most RFPs (there are occasional exceptions) provide at least some general information on what is required in your proposal. Some are more detailed than others, and they range from offering little or no clues to what is required to a detailed, mandated format, although this latter is much more the exception than the rule. Obviously, if the customer requires you to organize and present your information in some prescribed format, you must do so. Otherwise, you're on your own.

A general approach to proposal organization and format has been suggested earlier in this chapter. The major elements include an introduction, a précis of the requirement, an extended discussion of the requirement, a specific proposed program, and a presentation of the offeror's qualifications, for a total of four sections (the précis of the requirement is part of the introduction). This works out well for most small- to medium-size proposals, but often has to be expanded for large and complex proposals. This is by no means the only way to organize a proposal, nor even necessarily the best way. However, it is the format I have used for years, and it has worked out well, lending itself to most of the proposals I have written or directed. But here are some of the considerations which may lead you to design your proposal along somewhat different lines:

If an RFP/SOW makes it clear that some single element is far and away more important than anything else, it may be wise to design the proposal so as to stress and focus on that element. For example, suppose the RFP makes it clear that the customer believes management to be the most critical part of the program. It may be that it is better to launch into management needs immediately after introducing yourself, and make that the major section of your proposal. In fact, some proposal writers do this exactly, in all their proposals, on the assumption that management is always important enough a topic to be discussed first.

There may be some particularly difficult specification or technical requirement. For example, a requirement to design an airborne device of some sort may specify some weight or physical-size requirement which is most difficult to meet. Obviously, the customer is going to study your plans to see if they meet the size/weight requirement. In such case, you will probably want to make that discussion the *pièce de résistance* of your proposal.

Still, I have found the standard format I advocate adaptable to almost all situations, in this manner: That section which I regard as the introduction (although not necessarily called that, for reasons to be made clear later) includes only a brief description of who the bidder ("offeror") is and why he is responding to the RFP, and then goes swiftly to the requirement itself, with a (relatively) brief interpretation or view of it. Here, in this introductory interpretation of the customer's requirement, you may highlight, stress, and focus on just about *any-thing you want to.*

An extended discussion follows that, in a second section or chapter, and here again, you may concentrate on whatever you deem most important.

The third section is your proposal per se, and again you may use this section and its presentation to stress whatever you believe is most gainfully stressed.

And, finally, the fourth section presents your credentials as an organization, and you can (and should) shape that presentation to support those most-critical aspects of the requirement.

Using this standardized approach for most of your proposals makes outlining and planning the actual writing effort relatively simple. A detailed outline appears at the end of this chapter under the heading "Proposal Guide." This is, however, a model, and the model must be adapted to each individual case.

Design and Presentation Strategy

On at least one occasion of which I know specifically, my proposal never had a chance for serious consideration because it was buried under an avalanche of competing proposals and was hardly noticed. Later, a follow-up with the evaluator caused him to re-read the proposal, and he confessed that it was at least as good as the one he accepted and awarded the contract to. But he had read so many proposals every day, to the point of exhaustion, that many had hardly registered, especially those he read late in the day and toward the end of the whole stack of proposals. Mine, unfortunately, was among the forgotten.

How many other times this may have been the case I shall never know, of course, but it's a safe assumption that it happened on other occasions.

There is a way to combat this and get special attention. In fact, there are several ways to almost ensure that your proposal will be noticed. In many cases a good proposal won't have a chance if it doesn't get noticed, especially if you are not a well-known organization whose very name commands attention.

How to make your proposal distinctive in some way is a proper subject for study during the design phase. Don't be misled by this. Presentation pyrotechnics will not win the contract nor even enhance your proposal content, and it certainly will not substitute for good content, but it will help ensure that your proposal is not overlooked.

Let's return to that proposal to develop an appliance-repair training program for the Job Corps. You may recall that we offered the customer samples of the learning aids we promised to develop. One of these was to be a large number of oversize multi-color charts. We did, as we promised, develop about a half-dozen of these for the proposal. And they were done oversize, as most illustrators prefer to do them, because it is much easier to work on a large-scale drawing than on a small-scale one, and because small imperfections tend to disappear when the large drawing is reduced photographically for printing on an 8½ × 11 inch page. Therefore, the original drawings were on large art boards, about 3 × 5 feet each.

Having had the printer reduce these for printing a standard-size proposal, we were through with the posters, and I returned them to our art department, where we had had them made. Our art director asked me what I wanted done with them. I shrugged and told him, "I'm through with them. I have no more need for them."

"It's a shame to throw them out," Frank said. "They're really pretty good."

Then an idea struck me. I took the posters back from him, and made them "exhibits" to our proposal. I packaged them all together, wrapped them in brown paper, and presented a "proposal" which was about 3 × 5 feet. I delivered the package several days before the official opening date, so that the unusual proposal could stand in a corner of the procurement office arousing curiosity and comment for several days!

Perhaps we didn't need this extra touch to what was already an excellent proposal, and perhaps the customer would have congratulated us on an "outstanding" proposal in any event. But it didn't hurt, certainly, to have become the talk of the agency with that submittal. There was no possibility that we (our proposal) would be overlooked.

Having thus almost accidentally stumbled over an attention-getting device which appeared to work, I subsequently used it on many more occasions, even those in which the proposal did not require posters, by creating a few "twists" on the original ones. In one case, we developed a flowchart so constructed as to reflect all the significant milestones by which progress could be measured and noted, with tentative target dates on each, and "overlaid" it with a sheet of clear acetate suitable for making grease-pencil markings which could be easily erased. After photographing and reducing the original for the proposal, we enclosed the large board exhibit when we delivered the package. The gentleman who was to manage the project for the government was delighted to pin that chart on his wall and use it to help manage the program he contracted out to us!

For another customer, who was in the habit of requiring a pre-award presentation for every contract, we saved the original charts (copies were in the proposal, of course) for the presentation. We used the large originals at the presentation to illustrate our review of the project, as we proposed to handle it.

For an exceptionally complex logistics program, we developed a chart which ran to about 7 feet, and then combined it with two other charts of parallel activities by running three parallel "tracks" on the chart. Of itself, the chart was an attention-getter because the technique was unusual (as far as I know, it's never been used before or since) and also because it was rather long, although 7 feet is no world record; I've seen charts much longer. However, after incorporating the chart in the proposal, folded down to 8½ × 11 inches, of course, we mounted the original on art board and hinged it so that it would fold down to a convenient size, yet be amenable to being mounted on a wall to serve as the centerpiece for presentation and discussion.

In still another case, the statement of work was incredibly difficult to translate. The project, overall, was to provide on-site computer services and related functions to EPA for its pesticide-registration program, which was already far behind schedule and under heavy fire from Congress and other critics. (Moreover, most of what had been done previously was defective and was to be scrapped and done over!) The lengthy statement of work described many tasks and functions, none of them presented very clearly. We had a strong suspicion that the customer did not really understand his own needs very clearly, and had simply assembled words from a number of staff people, all of whom were struggling to "get their acts together."

After hours of studying the text, we could discern no unifying force or theme in the RFP; as far as we could determine, at that point, it appeared to describe a large number of tasks, most of which showed little or no apparent relationship to each other. That's not a unique situation. Many support contracts call for a contractor to provide general support, as the need appears. Yet, we somehow suspected that this was not the case here and that there had to be some central relationship among all these tasks and functions called for.

A brainstorming session with the technical experts on the subject, during which we sketched the major tasks and functions out graphically, finally exposed the logical chain of events, and enabled us to put every described task into its proper "pigeonhole" in the flowchart. The proposal we developed from that was probably the best definition of the entire program produced to date by anyone. Certainly, the customer could not deny that our organization had demonstrated an understanding of the requirement, and ours was possibly the *only* organization that truly did. It also turned out that it was impossible to reduce that chart to page size; the smallest we could make it without losing legibility was the size of two pages. We wanted to use it on the cover, as an attention-getter. (We felt that we were entitled to crow a bit, after the effort required to develop *that* chart.) We solved the problem by "inventing" the fold-out proposal cover!

A job requiring warehousing and access to dockside-loading was a case in which the physical facilities of the bidder were of especial importance. We used photographs of the facilities, with "callouts" identifying each requisite element (in aerial views), and sent the original overall photo along mounted on art board.

Bidders have sometimes sent along audiotapes, slides, and other presentation devices with their proposal to draw attention and create a greater impact than an unadorned proposal does. All of these are dramatic devices which do help the proposal get special attention. But there are some other approaches, resulting from the content and from the style or techniques used in the writing, that should also be considered.

Proposal Writing

Although the attention-getting devices and the graphics are important, the quality of the writing is a critical factor, and its importance is not to be minimized. Given the impact of a powerful strategy, a persuasive theme, dramatic presentation techniques, and an effective general format, a large burden still falls on the writing itself—the style, the technique, the effectiveness of words. Even with the help of graphics, the words must bear the principal burden for accomplishing several things:

1. They must *communicate*. A fine plan is for naught if the reader does not understand it.
2. They must *sell*. Other proposals present what appear to be fine plans too. Yours must be sold: the reader must be persuaded to believe.
3. They must *educate*. The reader must be educated sufficiently to follow your arguments, so that he may understand why your plan is superior.
4. They must arouse and sustain interest. If the reader has many other proposals to read and has lost interest in yours, he will skim over it or even lay it aside and go on to the next one.

5. Words should also be used to get attention, to make the reader sit up in his seat, widen his eyes, and turn pages rapidly to find out what is coming next.

To some extent, making the reader eager to see what's on the next page *is* the art of writing. Writing that is not read is like a symphony played by a machine on a desert island with no human in earshot. A philosophical argument can be mounted on whether there is even a sound, if no human ear is present to hear it.

Fiction writers use "narrative hooks" to get the reader's attention at the outset. The heroine wears a bikini in February on a city street; a man strolls through the jungle at noon in white tie and tails; a gorilla is seated behind the wheel of a Rolls Royce tooling along a boulevard; and so on. The intent is the same in each case: to arouse the reader's interest, even if by describing a bizarre situation. But, having gotten the reader's attention, the writer must *keep* the reader interested.

Obviously, we cannot use such a device as this. And yet, we can *adapt* the idea to proposal writing. That is, we can and should open the proposal with the most intriguing or startling idea we have to offer. Such an item of information may not be an attention-getter for the layman, but may well be for the technical/professional specialist who is reading the proposal. For example, if I offer a radar design which will accomplish 300 360-degree horizon searches a minute, while retaining the capacity to guide 60 missiles and track 40 hostiles, that might be of no consequence to the layman. But if the customer is seeking an improved radar capability and I open my proposal by telling him that I am about to reveal my design for accomplishing the feat just described, there is little doubt that he will begin turning pages with some eagerness, if only to determine whether I know what I am talking about or am a complete lunatic!

It need not necessarily be that startling. Perhaps I can offer the services of one of the most prestigious specialists in psychological testing to a customer who is seeking a firm to develop a battery of industrial personnel tests. Or I may have some rare laboratory facility which is highly relevant to the requirement. Or I may be able to promise that I am going to reveal a revolutionary new way to reduce tooling costs. Whatever it is, I would like it to meet as many of the following criteria as possible (and it *must* meet some of them):

- It should be startling enough or interesting enough to command some immediate attention.
- It should promise desirable end-results (benefits) to the customer.

- I must be able to *prove* its validity.
- It should, preferably, be a unique claim, one my competitors can't match.
- It should be something important—a trivial fact might command attention and even arouse interest, but I need something *important*.

But suppose you have no special abilities, no special staff people, no special facilities, no startling ideas. What then? Here is where the art of writing, using skill and imagination, can come galloping to the rescue. The presentation itself, although it may have nothing really new, different, or startling to offer, can be made interesting through the skillful and imaginative use of language.

For example, in the training business, especially following the mid-1960s, anyone who proposed developing a training program of any sort without a "task analysis" risked being branded a charlatan, a fool, or, at best, an amateur. Task analysis was definitely *de rigueur* for serious educational technologists and behavioral scientists. Ergo, every proposal for training proposed task analysis. Ultimately, through its overuse and abuse, task analysis came to be almost meaningless. It was originally applied to the study of a given task or skill to observe and record the specific *behaviors* required to perform the task, and to then translate these into *behavioral objectives,* another absolute must for serious training developers. But as the methodology began to grow up a bit, it became clear that the analysis had to extend to frontiers well beyond those of task analysis, to include such things as the environment, the prior knowledge of the trainee, and other factors.

Thereupon, one gentleman renamed what he did, calling it "front-end analysis," and achieved some local fame and recognition for his "invention." And the term front-end analysis was itself an attention-getter in a proposal. It was something new and demanded attention! (I switched to "needs analysis," which soon came into vogue also.)

With time, our "new" terms and our inside jargon or technical idiom become somewhat shopworn and lose their original impact. Moreover, in many cases, the original phrases were not very descriptive or definitive to begin with, and the term would benefit greatly from a fresh *nom de guerre,* which will attract a bit of attention as well.

In one proposal which succeeded in winning a tidy sum of money, the customer wanted to develop a number of educational materials. His RFP made it clear that he wanted some new and fresh ideas, although the end-products he suggested in the RFP were pretty shopworn. We were brainstorming for some fresh ideas to offer the customer in our proposal, when the thought came to me that perhaps the customer would be pleased to join in the brainstorming session and be an active participant in generating new ideas. We therefore worked the idea into our proposal, suggesting that the customer sit down with us in an initial session immediately after contract award and brainstorm with us for new ideas.

But as we were doing the final writing, it struck me that brainstorming was kind of an obscure name and had been around long enough to become a bit ragged at the edges. We changed it to "ideastorming," which we thought more descriptive.

The invention of new techniques to solve old problems can be most intriguing to the customer. One of the troubles in training development which crops up constantly is overtraining, teaching trainees things they do not need to know to do the job. Traditional task analysis, which helps screen out unnecessary training, is somewhat less than perfect in identifying all the training needs. On two occasions we developed new ideas to cope with the problem and won both contracts.

In one case, the need was to develop on-the-job training for technicians responsible for maintaining the complex of equipment to be used in the new bulk-mail centers. Quickly reviewing this problem in our proposal, I drew attention to our plan by stating that I would solve this problem by "asking the equipment" what it needed in the way of maintenance, and confine the technicians' training to only that which the equipment "asked for." To make good on this startling promise, I invented a new method for front-end analysis or needs analysis, which I called "failure-probability analysis." I described a complete scheme for analyzing each piece of equipment, according to well-established knowledge and statistical methods, so as to be able to predict incidence and frequency of failures with great accuracy.

This was less radical an idea than it may seem. Had it been too radical, it would never have flown. There is a well-established and accepted discipline called reliability analysis, which I used as a reference to demonstrate that failure-probability analysis was respectable too. (It was indeed an entirely legitimate idea.)

In another case, I borrowed the PERT or CPM (Critical Path Method) scheme, used widely in the construction business to plan and program construction operations, and adapted it to needs analysis, through a method I won't go into here, to present another perfectly practical idea.

The point is that an imaginative writer or designer can take many worn, old ideas and create fresh, new ones from them; sometimes fresh, new names, sometimes fresh, new methods.

To keep your reader turning pages, keep making promises. That is, keep dropping broad clues as to evidence and information yet to come. Keep the reader's appetite whetted for more. For example, in the second section, you will discuss the need and the possible approaches. You will reason logically to the selected approach. You will promise to reveal the specific methods you propose to use in implementing that approach. *But you don't reveal those specific methods until you get into the next section.* Don't give all the goodies away too soon, or you'll have nothing left for an encore.

You're still selling

Somewhere, several thousand words ago, you read the comment that every word in a proposal should contribute to *selling.* Let's expand that a bit: *Everything* in a proposal including illustrations, for example, should contribute to selling. It almost makes me want to cry when I see the missed opportunities for selling in most proposals. Let's take a look at how most proposal writers title their illustrations, for a sad example:

Illustration: A flowchart of the project overall.
Title: Flowchart of the XYZ Project.
  What that title should have said:
The most efficient flow for maximum results in the XYZ Project.
  Or:
Zambesi Corporations's plan for most efficient XYZ-Project completion.

A chart showing your new concept for solving an old problem might merit a title such as: "A Revolutionary Method for Reducing Loss." Or, preferably, it could be even more specific. The method I referred to earlier, shown conceptually in a chart, might be titled: "Failure-Probability Analysis: A new, scientific method for precision training design."

Don't strive for short, snappy titles, if you have to do so at the expense of communicating or selling. It's far better to have a long title that *says* something, that *sells.* Keep reinforcing your main messages, your theme, your strategy. Keep reminding your reader (read "customer") of the benefits he's to get from your plans and your unsurpassed capability.

If there is anything that marks professional bureaucrats, as a class (although there are some individual exceptions), it's insecurity. Government executives on the rise are about as secure as are most Hollywood luminaries. They need constant reassurance that your plan is going to work brilliantly, and their program will be a complete success with your support. But bear this insecurity in mind in the amount of innovation you propose, too. Be careful that none of your plans are so different as to seem radical, "harebrained," or "wild" to the customer. He'll want to feel that he can defend his decision to award you the contract, and he will look to your proposal to furnish the ammunition for that defense, should defense become necessary. Anything innovative must therefore be carefully justified and made as "respectable" as possible.

Some More Common Mistakes in Proposal Writing

Here are two of the most common and most deadly mistakes many proposal writers make. In a sense, it's really one mistake, practiced in two areas of the proposal, however. The mistake is this: Use of "boiler-plate" or standard resumes and company-qualifications materials. Having made all the effort to devise a good plan of action, and having gone to all the expense and trouble of developing a powerful proposal, many companies then go into their files and exhume—that's the right word, in this case—a collection of tired and out-of-date resumes and write-ups of the company's past projects, and plug these, unchanged, into the proposal. Rarely do these boiler-plate write-ups and resumes fit well. A proposal is a custom job of writing that offers to do a custom job of something or other, for a customer who may be a new customer, to you.

Rewrite the resumes so that they *fit* the proposal and *sell* the individual in the project position for which he is proposed. And ditto for those little blurbs which describe the company's past projects, the physical facilities, the many resources, and the reporting order.

It's worth the trouble.

Proposal guide

A basic outline which serves well for most proposals has the four basic sections discussed earlier in this chapter: introduction, discussion, proposed program, and proposer's qualifications. There are, however, numerous other elements necessary to reinforce and strengthen the basic presentation. The following list/outline describes or identifies all the elements which should be in most proposals, and a brief discussion or explanation of each such element follows. The titles used for the sections and subsections are not necessarily those you will use, but are selected here purely for descriptive purposes. The elements are presented in the order in which they would normally occur in a proposal, with brief comments.

Element	Remarks
Cover	Should strive to be attention-getting, should identify the RFP, the agency, the proposer, and the fact that it is a proposal (technical, management, or cost).
Letter of Transmittal	Original goes to contracting officer, but common practice is to bind a copy inside the cover of the proposal.
Title Page	Purely conventional. Repeats cover, plus date of submittal, plus proprietary notice, if any.
Executive Summary	Intended (nominally) for top-level people who won't read entire proposal, but want the "meat" of it. However, the summary will probably be read by everyone concerned; hence, it is important to get as much "up front" as possible. Use your best points and most persuasive arguments. Some RFPs require an Abstract, which might take its place; however, I recommend that the executive summary be used here in all cases.
Table of Contents	List all elements, starting with the executive summary, including all major headings. Be sure to provide ready reference to key elements, such as resumes.
Response Matrix	Not always used, but most helpful to both government officials and the proposer. See discussion which follows.
Introduction	Contains two subdivisions: (1) a brief introduction to proposer, with précis of qualifications and summary of chief benefit(s) offered, and (2) a discussion demonstrating an understanding of the requirement. This should be in your own words; do not parrot the RFP. Keep it brief.
Discussion	This is possibly the most important section, certainly one which calls for the greatest writing skills. Expand demonstration of understanding of the requirement into a full exploration and analysis; look at all alternatives and consider pros and cons of each; lead logically to your climax, which is the approach chosen, and give all the reasons for selecting that one.
Proposed Program	Detailed presentation of everything offered and proposed: *specifics* of project organization, management structure and plans, procedures, staffing, tasks and subtasks, manloading, descriptions of deliverables, schedules, resumes. As specific—*quantified*—as possible. This is section which will become part of contract, if successful.
Qualifications	"Resume" of your organization. Include past projects, facilities, resources, management and functional structures, key officials, corporate backup of project, backup resumes of others who can be made available as necessary, and references, especially other government agencies, with specific names, addresses, telephone numbers.

Explanations and Brief Discussions

   Cover. Many companies use a standard proposal cover, which they have had printed. This is not absolutely necessary, but should your company choose to do so, opt for a bright cover stock which will stand out, such as yellow, red, or gold. A bit of artwork on the cover also helps make it an attention-getter. Some of the ideas used in the past have included copying the customer's logo on the cover; printing a screened-back functional chart of the job, with the other material sur- printed (printed over the chart); using two colors; and so on. Don't go to extremes, however, as that may create an unfavorable impression about your cost-consciousness.

   Letter of Transmittal. The original of this goes to the contracting of- ficer, in a separate envelope. This is the only page (other than the cost breakdowns) that you may be *sure* he will read. Some people use the letter of transmittal in a purely mechanical way. However, it is an ideal place to present those arguments which are most appealing to the con- tracting officer: price and dependability. A good letter of transmittal presents a main argument and helps the contracting officer to gain at least a general understanding of the proposed project.

   Executive Summary. Many people consider this the most important element. Its purpose is ostensibly to summarize the proposal, but it is good marketing to use this to summarize *reasons for accepting your proposal.* Bring out all your heavy guns, the best arguments for your proposal, and stress all the benefits to customer, with brief and per- suasive rationale. Use graphic techniques such as changes in type- faces, capital letters, boldface, italics, and so on to *dramatize* and get attention.

   Table of Contents. If you have chosen your titles and headings carefully, the table of contents will present the reader a more detailed version of the executive summary. Use selling headlines, and your table of contents will be a sales presentation. But be sure to structure it so that readers can find what they want with ease.

   Response Matrix. This can be the most important part of your pro- posal for maximizing your technical-point score. It should list *every* itemized requirement or specification in the RFP/SOW, *especially those listed as evaluation criteria,* with (1) a brief statement of your response and (2) page and paragraph numbers in your proposal where readers may find your specific response(s) to each. Doing this ensures that you will not allow anything to slip between the cracks, that the customer will be alerted to your response to each requirement without any confusion, and that the customer will find it *easier to score your proposal,* as a result. Tip: Leave an extra, *blank* column in the matrix for the customer to enter check-marks, notes, and numerical scores for each item listed. That all but guarantees a top technical score.

A typical response matrix format is shown below. Your matrix will vary depending on the size of the project. The key items, however, are those shown here.

Requirement or Specification	RFP Ref	Proposal Response	Notes
Understanding of the problem	p. 7	Sec. I, pp. 3−6	
Innovative approaches	pp. 17−19	Sec. II, pp. 14−33 Sec. III, pp. 6−9	
Weight restriction	p. 3, Attach. I	Sec. II, pp. 3−5; Sec. III, pp. 12−14	

This can be many pages long, depending on how detailed the RFP and requirement are. Some organizations include a column in which they summarize, in a short phrase or two, their response to the specific requirement and then refer the reader to the proposal pages where the detailed information is presented.

Introduction. Establish your theme here, along with something to command interest. For example, "Black and White Consultants, Inc., is pleased to be able to offer to the Bureau for Social Rehabilitation the services of the renowned authority, Dr. Wilhelm Maven, as the leader of our innovative approach to the problem presented in RFP No. XXX-345—OZD." (That is, if Dr. Maven *is,* in fact, a well-known authority in the field.) If your firm is not well known or, at least, not known to the customer, describe its qualifications briefly: "B&W Consultants, Inc., has carried out many social research programs for HUD, the Labor Department, and the U.S. Army. Details will be presented later in this proposal." Be brief here, however; this is not the time for credentials. Merely qualify yourself as a proposer to be taken seriously.

The second part of this first section or chapter consists of presenting the customer with a brief recap of the requirement, in your own words. Do not simply restate what the customer has said in his RFP. The purpose here is not merely to prove that you have read the RFP and SOW and understand the customer's words, but to demonstrate that you understand the *problem* or *need,* which is not the same thing at all. For example, if the customer has stated the problem or need in thousands of words, including a great deal of extraneous detail and trivia, your recap should cut through all that and address the core or essence of the need. Or, if the customer has stated symptoms, without describing the problem, point that out. (For example, "The existence of inaccurate computer-generated reports is not necessarily a computer problem but may be the result of the following, or a combination thereof: poorly designed data forms, poor recording practices, faulty programming, malfunctions in the program, or other causes.") Having established that, you have opened the door to the extended discussion to follow, and possibly to your own unique approach. At the least, you have demonstrated that you are expert in your field, that you can think clearly, that you have analyzed the problem, and that you are honest.

Discussion. This is the section where you do the bulk of your selling. Here you must expand your rationale through analysis, offer your approach, and sell your approach. Many people neglect this opportunity and assume that the reader will readily see that the proffered approach is obviously the best. Not so. For one thing, the reader may or may not be as expert as you are in your field. For another, even if the reader is an expert, it is necessary to explain your logic and your reasoning, rather than expecting quantum jumps from your premises to your conclusions.

Proposed Program. The keynote here is this: *Be specific.* This is where the customer will ask the question: "What are you going to do with all my money, if I give it to you?" Obviously, the more money involved, the closer the scrutiny of how you propose to spend it.

The customer may or may not agree with every facet, every particular, every small detail of how you propose to operate the project. If the contracting officer likes your plan generally (and if your price is within an acceptable range or reasonably close to it) you are likely to be called in for negotiations, and may be asked to change anything the customer doesn't agree with. But if you have not been specific, if the customer really has no idea of how you propose to spend the money, it is almost certain your proposal will be passed by. Your proposal must be written so a contracting officer can justify to superiors why *you* were awarded the contract. Even when the customer knows you, likes you, trusts you, and wants you to have the contract, you have to give him the material to justify the award. And that means a highly detailed, specific program.

Quantify. Don't offer "a manual"; propose a manual of some *estimated* number of pages, illustrations, tables, and so on. If you are as qualified as you purport to be, as qualified as you should be to win the contract, you should be able to estimate what you will deliver and when. The customer *expects* that.

This is the best place to present the resumes of the *key* individuals proposed for the project staff. If you want to offer other resumes to document your overall capability, put them in the next section. Don't dilute the impact of this section by incorporating unrelated information. Discuss here only what you specifically propose for the project in question, but put all of it in here.

No one ever lost a contract for providing more information than that required, but many contracts have been lost by not providing enough information.

Manloading is part of the proposed program, and often one of the most important parts. It shows the customer your conception of the various tasks and subtasks, which staff members you will assign these, and how much time you expect each staff member to spend on each task or subtask. The most efficient way to present this is in a chart, somewhat along these lines:

Phase/Task/Subtask	Project Director Hours	Data Manager Hours	Writer Hours
Phase I: Analysis			
1. Survey literature	48	64	
2. Draft field study plan	16	40	40
3. Submit for review and approval			
Phase II: Carry out field study			

In this chart, a slot is established for each key staff member (do not include clerks, typists, and so on) with estimates of hours for each task, as shown. This enables the customer to gauge your grasp of the realities, your understanding of the need, your ability to plan in detail, and serves also as a basis for your cost estimates, presented separately in your cost proposal. For a large project, this chart can run many pages, but is an essential part of quantifying, and a large part of that persuasive detail which makes your plan credible. Too, it is a basis for substantiating your cost estimates and an extremely useful reference during final negotiations. In fact, many RFPs specifically request that you furnish such information.

Qualifications. This is your company "resume." This is where you demonstrate that your organization is well qualified and capable, and that you not only *can* deliver, but *will* deliver. That's not a fine distinction at all: Many companies fail to live up to their capabilities, and it's much easier to prove that you *can* than it is to prove that you *will*.

That latter is best proved by your track-record—the projects you have carried out successfully and on schedule. Describe them in this section, selecting those which most closely resemble the project you're bidding for, not only in the general type of work and overall objective, but also in the nature of the problems and obstacles to overcome. It is very important to demonstrate your success in the past with *approaches resembling the one currently proposed*. Take advantage of the opportunity to brag a bit about the difficult curves thrown at you, and the clever and dedicated ways you handled them to achieve complete and unqualified success.

Back this up with references, letters of commendation from previous customers (if you don't have them, ask for them; they're valuable convincers), names, addresses, and telephone numbers of past customers; draw on both contracting people and program people. Include anything else to bear the evidence out, such as drawings, photos, and so on.

8

Special buying arrangements and opportunities

Everybody keeps his own store

If you sell common commodities . . .

The Federal Supply Service, one of the major divisions within the General Services Administration, operates 20 supply depots and 75 stores in the United States. Those establishments store nearly six million separate items, which the Federal Supply Service stocks to supply the rest of the federal establishment. In addition to stocking and distributing these huge numbers of "common use" items, the Federal Supply Service arranges annual supply contracts for any other products which it does not carry in stock and for services, spending approximately $3 billion a year for this.

Another major division of GSA, the Automated Data and Telecommunications Service (ADTS) "manages" the procurement of many other items, principally those required in connection with computers and telecommunications systems.

In addition, the Veterans Administration also buys centrally for the large number of VA hospitals, and is a major government purchaser of food and hospital supplies.

The Department of Defense must supply and support the various armed forces and their many military bases, and is therefore also a major buyer of foods and many other items, both military and nonmilitary in nature. Department of Defense buying is handled through the

Defense Logistics Agency, which operates six Defense Supply Centers in the United States.

There is also the U.S. Postal Service, which buys centrally for the vast chain of post offices and the huge Postal Service motor vehicle fleet of over 100,000 vehicles (second in size to only that of the U.S. Army). The Postal Service main supply depot is at Topeka, Kansas.

To reduce the duplication of purchasing which resulted inevitably from this multiplicitly of procurement and supply organizations, a National Supply System has been created, on paper, at least. Gradually, agreements are being worked out among the several procurement organizations to assign responsibility for each class of supplies to one or the other. For example, despite the size of the Postal Service motor vehicle fleet and the estimated $25 million annual purchase of spare parts and maintenance supplies, the Postal Service orders its tires through the GSA; nonperishable food items are "managed" by the VA and the DLA (Defense Logistics Agency), the Federal Supply Service having surrendered management of all nonperishable food items to these agencies.

These agencies do not stock all the supplies the U.S. government needs and buys every year, but only common-use items, which are used regularly and predictably, and are usually available commercially. Such items may be bought for stock as the stocks dwindle, by competitive bids, or they may be bought from suppliers with whom contracts for an entire year's supply have been negotiated, usually following normal competitive bids.

But these are not the only buying arrangements. There are several other conditions and situations which must be accommodated. It should be borne in mind that the various purchasing arrangements are not whimsical or arbitrary, but represent an effort to solve the many different kinds of supply problems encountered by the various government establishments.

There are many items which federal agencies are almost sure to buy during the year, yet it is almost impossible to predict which agencies will want them, when they are likely to want them, or in what quantities they will want them. For example, it's likely that there will be some demand for valves of various kinds, but no one can predict what kind, how many, or where they will be needed. For many of these items, individual orders may be rather small; however, the overall total of such orders will be great enough to make buying at retail or using imprest funds (a form of petty cash fund) prohibitively expensive. In addition, the individual orders are often small enough that competitive bidding is impractical; the need is often for quick delivery, so the time necessary for competitive bidding would be unacceptably long. In some instances, the nature of the procurement is such that it is necessary to buy locally: A military base cannot afford to order milk and eggs from a supplier 2,000 miles away, or have laundry and dry cleaning service provided by a distant firm.

These varying needs and conditions can account for the rationale behind the many procurement methods and instruments. They explain, too, why one bid is for a single, one-time order, another is for a year's supply, another is for a multiple of shipments to various points, and so on. And they help to explain why a given agency may choose to order something independently, despite the fact that they could purchase the item through one of the centralized purchasing and supply services.

Figure 13 shows several items from a recent issue of the *Commerce Business Daily* which illustrate some of what has been said. Among these notices, which are typical and may be found almost every day in the CBD, are represented the annual supply contract, the multiple-shipment contract, and the single-shipment contract.

Procurements such as these tend to be formally advertised (sealed bids with public openings) but they may also be negotiated contracts, for any of the reasons explained earlier.

The same considerations apply to services, as the notices in Figure 14 indicate. These, too, tend to be procured via formal advertising, but may appear as negotiated procurements. And, while many of them are for rather standardized services, many others are for novel services, so that success in winning government business may, and often does, depend on the willingness and ability of a bidder to adapt the services to the needs expressed, or to design a set of services to meet the need.

The Federal Supply Schedules

The Federal Supply Service maintains approximately 300 Federal Supply Schedules, plus approximately 200 other annual supply agreements which are similar in nature. (See Appendix 4 for a list of Federal Supply Schedules.) The general purpose of the schedules is to arrange for the various federal agencies to be able to buy from suppliers in any quantity at wholesale prices, and to be able to buy from suppliers who are nearby and/or can fill orders spontaneously and on short notice.

Figure 13. Notices for goods,

---

85 Toiletries.

---

85 - - TOOTHPASTE Definite Quantity—IFB BO/DQ-M-00133, Bid opening: 21 May 79. (107)
GSA, Business Service Center, Rm L-1, J.W. McCormack PO and Courthouse Bldg, Boston MA 02109

---

99 Miscellaneous.

---

99 - - ARKANSAS RIVER WATER, 1400 Acre-Feet for FOB delivery to any one of the following 3 Bureau of Reclamation East Slope, Storage Facilities: 1) Twin Lakes Reservoir, 2) Pueblo Dam, 3) Turquoise Reservoir. RFQ 9-01-73-00570 to be issued about 8 May 79.(109)
Department of the Interior, Bureau of Reclamation, LM Region, Building 20, Denver Federal Center, Denver, CO 80225, ATTN: MS. Meyer (303) 234-3135

---

❶ **99 - - IDENTIFICATION PLANTES**—Fabricated from No. 18 gage aluminum. 1½"x3", letters no less than 3/16" gothic or futura. holes ⅛". IFB DLA002-79-B-0004. Bid opening 18 May 79. See notes 12, 32, 56 and 80. (109)
Defense Industrial Plant Equipement Center, Attn: DIPEC-TC, Memphis, TN 38114

---

99 - - CONDENSER TUBES AND FERRULES Tubes shall be ¾" O.D. x 13'- 2½" long x #18 B.W.G.—IFB DACW66-79-B-0044—Bid opening 3 May 79. (107)
Memphis District, Corps of Engineers, Attn: C. P. Williamson, 668 Clifford Davis Federal Bldg, Memphis TN 38103

---

99 - - ARTS AND CRAFTS MATERIAL, NSC 9999-NONE, IAW description cited in IFB—Quantity and Destns unknown—IFB —Quantity and Destns unknown—IFB DLA400-79-B-2003—Bid opening 18 May 79—For Tech. info. contact Mrs. Sarnecky, 804/275-4473. See notes 72, 73 and 80. (106)
Defense General Supply Center, Richmond, VA 23297, Tel: 804/275-3350

from *Commerce Business Daily.*

---

84 Clothing, Individual Equipment, and Insignia.

84 - - COVERALLS with elastic waistband 6.0 oz. polyester long sleeve, navy blue, one piece—RFQ 17-095-79 Bid opening 3:00 PM—26 Apr 79. (088).

Procurement Officer, Seventeenth Coast Guard District, PO Box 3-5000, Juneau AK 99802.

88 Live Animals.

88 - - SWINE, unbred females. Delivered f.o.b. destination within consignee's premises to Beltsville, Maryland, RFQ 11427 due 6 Apr 79. (082)

U.S. Dept. of Agriculture, SEA/GSB, Rm 318H, Administration Bldg., Agricultural Research Center-West, Beltsville, MD Attn: Dawn Foster 301/344-3360

● **88 - - HORSES, GELDING,** 15 hand high, 3 to 7 years old, broke for riding and packing, Stehekin District, North Cascades National Park Complex. Verbal quotes approximately 16 Apr 79. (088).

National Park Service North Cascades National Park 800 State Street Sedreo Wolley, WA 98284

89 Subsistence.

89 - - POTATO CHIPS AND CORN CHIPS for Naval Air Station Memphis, Millington, TN—Requirements Type Contract for period 1 Oct 79 through 30 Sep 80—Estimated requirements as specified in IFB N00612-79-B-0119—Deliveries required within 7 days after receipt of order—Opening date o/a 18 Jun 79—Mrs. Mary F. Southard, 803-743-4781—Availability of the solicitation is limited and will be furnished on a first received, first served basis.

89 - - BEVERAGE BASE, FRUIT FLAVOR—Requirements Contract—Estimated annual quantities Fruit Punch, 2000 GL, Grape, 1500 GL, Orange 2000 GL, Black Cherry, 1000 GL—Delivery to NAS Memphis, Millington, TN—IFB N00612-79-B-0121—Opens o/a 12 Jun 79—J.J. Bridges—803-743-6483—Availability of the solicitation is limited and will be furnished on a first received, first served basis.

89 - - BEVERAGE BASE—Cola, Lemon-Lime and Root Beer flavors—Indefinite quantities for period 1 Oct 79 through 30 Sep 80—Estimated annual requirements as specified in IFB N00612-79-B-0120—Deliveries within 72 hours after receipt of order—Opening date o/a 11 Jun 79—J. Bridges, 803/743-6483—Availability of the solicitation is limited and will be furnished on a first received, first served basis. (135)

Commanding Officer, Code 200, Naval Supply Center, Charleston, SC 29408

Figure 14. Notices for services,

---

① **Z - - MAINTENANCE PAINTING** Exterior, Bldgs. 102, 103, 409, 416 and 436 at the Air National Guard Base, 8030 Balboa Blvd., Van Nuys CA 91409 (Los Angeles County)—DAHA04-79-B-0031—Bid opens 25 May 79—Magnitude of Proposed construction is between $25,000 and $100,000. (110)
Office of the U.S. Property and Fiscal Officer for California, PO Box G, San Luis Obispo, CA 93406, Attn: Contracting Office, Mrs. Roulis, Tel: 805/544-4900, Ext 214

---

① **Z - - REMOVING OLD AND INSTALLING NEW GUTTERS,** various buildings, VAMC Dublin, Georgia. Project 79-105. Bid opening 30 May 79. Bid material available 1 May 79. Estimateds $25,000 - $40,000.
① **Z - - REPLACING LOUVER DOORS,** VAMC Dublin, Georgia, Proj. 79-112. Bid opening 30 May 79. Bid Material availalbe 1 May 79. Estimated $12,000 - $18,000. (113)
Veterans Administration Medical Center /134, Dublin, GA 31021

---

① **Z - - REPAIR ROOF,** building 94 (R18-78) Naval Air Station, North Island, San Diego, CA. The work includes, but is not limited to, removal of existing gravel surfacing and installation of new roofing and clean gutters and down spouts, complete and ready for use. N62474-78-B-9096—between $100,000 & $500,000—21 May 79. (113)
OICC, Navy Public Works Center, Box 113, Naval Station, San Diego, CA 92136.

---

① **S - - CUSTODIAL SERVICE,** VA Drug Dependence, Clinic, Houston, TX — 1 year(s) - IFB GS-07B 20687, Bid Opening 6-7-79 (134)
GSA Business Service Center, 819 Taylor Street, Fort Worth, TX 76102

---

① **S - - FIRE PREVENTION AND PROTECTION SERVICES** for Castle Dome Heliport, US Army Yuma Proving Ground, AZ—IFB DAAD01-79-B-0049. Estimated opening date 8 Jun 79—See note 18. (134)
Procurement Directorate, US Army Yuma Proving Ground, AZ 85364.

---

① **S - - GARBAGE, TRASH AND REFUSE COLLECTION &DISPOSAL** at Marine Corps Air Station, Laurel Bay, Station Housing and Naval Hospital, Beaufort, S.C. Job IFB 06-79-42442. Bid opening 12 June 79.
Officer in Charge of Construction, MCAS, Beaufort, S.C. P.O. Drawer Y, Burton, SC 29902

from *Commerce Business Daily.*

S Housekeeping Services.

---

❶ **S - - NIGHT DESK CLERK SERVICES**—The Contractor will disburse additional linens, receive and issue dormitory keys, control and issue dormitory recreational equipment, assist in the even to fdormitory disturbance, and monitor the National Mine Health and Safety Academy s cardkey control system. Performance shall be during night and weekend periods. IFB S2701005. Estimated bid opening July 6, 1979. See Note 12.

S - - GARBAGE AND TRASH REMOVAL at the National Mine Health and Safety Academy, Beckley, West Virginia. The Contractor will furnish all necessary labor and materials to render complete trash, edible and non-edible garbage removal daily except Sunday. Dumpster type containers are required. Containers shall have a minimum of 16 cubic yards. IFB S2701004. Estimated Bid Opening 2 Jul 79.

S - - LINEN AND LAUNDRY SERVICES at the National Mine Health and Safety Academy, Beckley, West Virginia. Pickup, delivery and professional laundering of aprons, wash cloths, bathtowels, sheets, pillowcases, tablecloths and similar items. IFB S2701002. Estimated bid opening 3 Jul 79. (130)

U.S. Department of Labor, Mine Safety and Health Administration, Branch of Management Operations, PO Box 25367, Denver Federal Center, Denver, CO 80225.

X - - ASA SOFTBALL OFFICIALS for 400 Intramural games and 86 playoff games, 16 May 79 - 11 Aug 79, Fort Richardson, Alaska. RFP DAKF70-79-R-0062. Negotiations will be conducted with Polar Bear Sports Officials Association, Fort Richardson, Alaska. (110)

Department of the Army, Procurement Division, P.O. Box 5-525, Fort Richardson, AK 99505, Attn: Mrs. Lyon 907/863-8283

---

❶ **J - - PREVENTATIVE MAINTENANCE ON ELECTRICAL EQUIPMENT** at Federal Center, 74 N. Washington Avenue, Batttle Creek, MI Solicitation No. 5PF7B-79-0041. Offers Due by 21 May 79. Willnot exceed $10,000.00. Contract period 1 Jun 79 through 31 Aug. 79 (113)

General Services Administration, PBS, Federal Center, 74 N. Washington Avenue, Battle Creek, MI 49017

J - - MAINTAIN INTRABASE RADIO SYSTEM at Altus, AFB, Oklahoma—IFB F34612-79-B0016—O/A 26 Jun 79—1 Oct 79 through 30 Sep 80—See Note 56. (131)

Base Contracting Div., Altus Air Force Base, OK 73521 ATTN: Dorotha Lovett 405/481-7321

A supply schedule is therefore a basic ordering agreement with each supplier, under which the supplier agrees to fill orders at some stipulated discount from his normal list prices for some term, usually one year. The discounts may be on a sliding scale, depending on quantities ordered.

There are three general types of Federal Supply Schedules:

> *Multiple-Award Schedules,* which cover ordering agreements entered into with a number of contractors for the same types of supplies and/or services.
>
> *Single-Award Schedules,* which cover ordering agreements entered into with a single supplier for the class of goods or services listed in the schedule.
>
> *New-Item Introductory Schedules,* which enable contractors to introduce new/or improved items to the supply system.

Under these schedules, contractors may enter even unique or proprietary items into the system. For example, many publishers of books, manuals, and newsletters may enter their publications in the 76 group of schedules (see Appendix 4, listings 76 I through 76 III B).

Generally speaking, the multiple-award schedules afford the agencies an opportunity to select from among a large number of suppliers so they can take advantage of the largest discounts or the most convenient delivery, or otherwise accommodate the service to their needs. Contractors listed in multiple-award schedules are usually required to supply catalog sheets to the agencies describing their listed products and providing ordering information.

In most cases, the single-award schedules are for items covered by federal specifications, although in some cases the contractors are required to furnish descriptive literature and ordering information to those agencies listed as the relevant "buying activities."

The Federal Supply Service reviews applications for entering items on the new-item introductory schedule and decides whether an item merits inclusion there. Ultimately, if the item generates sufficient demand among the buying activities, it may be transferred to a regular supply schedule or there may be a new supply schedule established to cover it.

A typical multiple-award schedule is reproduced in Appendix 4. That one is for publications of several kinds, as listed on the cover page. A copy of the schedule is supplied to each of approximately 2,500 federal buying activities that are usual buyers of the products listed, for example, schools, libraries, military installations, laboratories, and so on. The contractor is furnished a list of the buying activities, on labels, and is required to send each a catalog or price list which includes ordering information and discounts, and a form listing the contract number and other specifics of the contract terms.

Getting on the Schedule

Getting on the schedule means bidding for and being issued a contract or ordering agreement. No money is committed in this agreement. When a buying activity wishes to order, the buying activity issues a government purchase order, citing the contract as authority.

Note that in the schedule shown in Appendix 4 both publishers and their dealers are listed, but the schedule does not indicate what publications are offered by each nor the prices asked. That's why contractors must mail a catalog or price list to the many buying activities. In practice, many of the buying activities, having received their copies of the schedule, will write to each contractor listed and request copies of their catalogs.

Figure 15 is an example of the information which the contractor must send along with the catalog sheets. The government does not have an official price-list form, but GSA furnishes a sample for the contractor to follow. Note the sliding discount scale, according to the size of individual orders. Note, too, that the minimum order-size is set (the contractor has a range he may select from to stipulate his minimum order) and so is the maximum order-size. That points up another feature of the supply schedules: Ordinarily, under the Small Purchases Act, a federal agency is limited to $10,000 maximum per purchase order. However, when an agency issues purchase orders under an existing ordering agreement, the limit is set by the ordering agreement, rather than by statute, and can go quite high; even $50,000 purchase orders are not unusual, in these circumstances.

Being listed on a schedule and getting such a contract is actually not at all difficult. In fact, it's virtually routine, as long as all procedures are followed and some discount is offered. However, there are no guarantees that orders will be issued; it's up to the contractor to go out and do some selling, to pursue the business. (For that reason, some contractors call the Federal Supply Schedule a hunting license.) There are no limits placed on the total amount of business you can do under these schedules, and they can be a valuable source of business and an entree to federal procurement offices which might otherwise be all but closed to you.

One difficulty with these schedules is that there is really no central

Figure 15. Contractor's price-list form.

```
                     GENERAL SERVICES ADMINISTRATION
                        FEDERAL SUPPLY SERVICE

AUTHORIZED FEDERAL SUPPLY SCHEDULE CATALOG AND/OR PRICE LIST

SCHEDULE TITLE:  FSC Group 76, Part I, Publications

GSA MAILING CODE:                      CONTRACT NO: GS-01S-06899
CONTRCATOR:  Government Marketing News, Inc.
             P.O.Box 6067                PERIOD:  February 9, 1979 through
             Wheaton, MD 20906                    January 30, 1980

CONTACT:  Ms. Sherrie Holtz     TELEPHONE:  301-460-1506

MANUFACTURER'S CODE:            BUSINESS SIZE:  Small

AWARDED SPECIAL ITEMS:  426-3, 4


GEOGRAPHIC COVERAGE:  The 50 States, Washington, DC, and Puerto Rico

MINIMUM ORDER:  $10

TIME OF DELIVERY:  45 days

PROMPT PAYMENT TERMS:  1% 10 days, ½% 20 days

PRICES:  Prices as approved on original offer dated 11/10/78 and letter of 12/14/78


FOB POINT:  Destination

QUANTITY DISCOUNTS:  1-50 copies, 10% discount
                     51-99 copies, 20% discount
                     100 or more copies, 30% discount


FOREIGN ITEMS:  None

POINTS OF PRODUCTION:  Washington, DC

ORDERING ADDRESS:  3110 Whispering Pines
                   P.O. Box 6067
                   Wheaton, MD 20906

PAYMENT ADDRESS:  Same as above

WARRANTY PROVISIONS:  Replacement of copies received in damaged condition.
```

coordination. Different schedules are issued by different GSA regional offices (and there are 10 of those) at different times of the year. Moreover, you can apply for some schedules at any time of the year, whereas others are "open" for new contractors only once a year. The Federal Supply Service does not maintain a list of where schedules are issued and when they are open for applications. The list shown in Appendix 4 is handled in Boston, at the Region I GSA office, and is for the period February 1 to January 31 of the following year. That means that bids are accepted late in the year, and must be in the hands of the contracting officer well before the end of the calendar year to qualify. Note on that schedule that although the contract is to run—nominally—from February 1, 1979 to January 31, 1980, the schedule was not issued until March 9, and the contract was mailed from the Region I GSA office on February 9, 1979.

To run down a particular schedule, under present conditions, it is necessary to call or write the Federal Supply Service Information Center in Crystal City, Arlington, VA. Their mailing address and telephone number are

General Services Administration
Schedule Information Center (FPS)
Washington, D.C. 20406
(703) 557-8177

The Information Center is actually located in Room 726, Crystal Mall Building No. 4, Arlington, VA. In this room are stored copies of every Federal Supply Schedule, and the people who work there can check the cover page of any schedule which interests you and advise you as to which regional office of GSA handles it and what the issue date is. Other than this, it is a laborious task, involving many letters and/or telephone calls to track down the schedule so that you can determine where to apply for inclusion!

Once you do ascertain that, the matter becomes somewhat simpler. You simply write the appropriate GSA Contracting Officer, request a solicitation package, and submit your bid, as you would any other. If it is a multiple-award schedule, you are likely to receive a telephone call from the contracting officer some weeks later to pursue a telephone negotiation, in which the official strives to get from you the best discounts you are willing to offer. Once that is settled, it is only a matter of time until you receive your contract and are finally listed on the schedule. Ultimately, you will also receive the mailing list, although that will probably come from the Denver GSA Office, regardless of where the schedule is managed.

The majority of the schedules are for supplies of various kinds. There are, however, a few schedules for services. One of the more popular of these is Schedule 733 III, for providing graphic arts services of various kinds. These are necessarily on a local basis because they are for small orders. The Washington-area schedule for these services, for example, is issued to contractors who maintain offices within a 50-mile radius of the GSA Region III office, which is in Washington. Other regions operate their own local 733 III Schedules, but all are issued from the Region III GSA office, for some reason. This was changed only a few years ago. At the same time the Region III GSA office was required to take over all 733 III Schedules, it became available for new contractors only once a year, whereas it was once open the entire year for additional contractors.

The procedure you must follow, then, is to check the listing of Federal Supply Schedules (see Appendix 4 for current listing), reach the Information Center by letter or telephone, and check (1) whether the schedule is still operative (they do change), (2) which GSA regional office manages it, and (3) what the dates of the term are. Then you apply to the GSA office concerned and get on the bidders list.

The Defense Logistics Agency

The Defense Logistics Agency (DLA), referred to in many older government publications as the Defense Supply Agency (DSA), is the major buyer and supplier of common-use items for the various military arms. DLA operates six Defense Supply Centers, administers the Federal Supply Catalog, and manages the Defense Contract Administration Service, among other things. In addition to the six Defense Supply Centers, DLA operates six Defense Service Centers and four Defense Depots.

Like GSA, DLA buys both centrally and locally, and both by one-time procurements and by annual ordering agreements. However, DLA does not do all the buying for the military departments, just as GSA does not do all the buying for the civilian departments. Each department has its own centralized procurement and supply organizations, and each separate establishment does at least some buying of its own. (See Appendix 2 for listings.)

DCAS small business specialists

One of the several functions of the Defense Contract Administration Service (DCAS) is to aid small business in winning a share of government contracts and subcontracts. Each of 21 DCAS offices has at least one small business representative, to whom you may apply for counseling and other assistance in pursuing Defense Department business. (See Appendix 2 for listings.)

Doing business with the military

Many firms do business with the military agencies entirely. The range of military needs is such that although many of their needs are unique (for supplies and services that only a military organization would have use for), they also buy almost everything else that any other agency might need.

The Department of Defense and the military departments that make up DOD have always depended on commerce and industry for their supplies and equipment and were, until recent times, at least, always the largest market in the government. It is therefore not illogical that the Defense Department and the various military organizations have the most highly organized procurement systems. (Most other federal procurement is patterned after military procurement regulations, forms, and procedures.)

When you request a Form 129 (application for bidders list) from the military, you are usually given, in addition, a form which lists a great many items of supplies and services, and you are asked to check off those which interest you. This information is then supplied to a computer and stored, so that the agency may ask the computer to select a candidate list of potential bidders for any given procurement. (Similar systems are used by NASA and other agencies which do a great deal of procurement and/or buy a great variety of goods and services.)

The military agencies also have a great many more specifications than do most civilian agencies (although some civilian agencies invoke many of the military specifications for their procurements). In most cases, the specifications invoked are available for inspection or may be ordered from the Navy Publications Forms Center, 5801 Tabor Road, Philadelphia, PA 19120.

To assist small businesses and implement the socioeconomic requirements of federal procurement generally, DOD places certain requirements on its major prime contractors. For example, any prime contract of $500,000 or more carries with it a requirement that the contractor maintain a Defense Small Business, Minority Business Subcontracting, and Labor Surplus Area Program, and that he designate within his organization a Small Business–Minority Business Liaison Officer to administer (implement) the program. Recent regulations require that bidders for larger contracts actually furnish specific subcontracting plans before awards are made.

There are, however, many opportunities for sales within the military establishments:

Direct sales, on a local basis, to the military bases.
Both central and local sales to military exchanges.
Central and local sales to military commissaries.
Local sales to military R&D centers.

Department of the Army

The major organizations within the Army, as far as procurement is concerned, are the following:

U.S. Army Corps of Engineers
U.S. Army Medical Department
U.S. Army Forces Command
U.S. Army Training and Doctrine Command
U.S. Army Ballistic Missile Defense Advanced Technology Center
U.S. Army Communications Command
U.S. Army Materiel Development and Readiness Command (DARCOM)

Specific installations and procurement offices of the Army are listed in Appendix 2.

Department of the Navy

The major portion of procurement in the Navy is the responsibility of the Chief of Naval Material, who heads the Naval Material Command. Within that command are five major subdivisions:

Naval Air Systems Command
Naval Electronic Systems Command
Naval Facilities Engineering Command
Naval Sea Systems Command
Naval Supply Systems Command

The Chief of Naval Material also is responsible for some of the procurement for the U.S. Marine Corps, which is part of the Navy.

A separate Navy organization which does some buying is the Military Sealift Command, and some buying, especially of R&D services, is done under the command of the Office of Naval Research. Buying offices and commands of the Navy are listed in Appendix 2.

Department of the Air Force

Major Air Force organizations which do most of the buying for various Air Force needs include the following:

Air Force Logistics Command
Air Force Systems Command
Military Airlift Command
Air Training Command
Air Force Communications Service
Aerospace Defense Command

Buying offices and organizations of the Air Force are listed in Appendix 2.

Research and Development

Research and development (R&D) is carried out by many government agencies, with the bulk of the work done under contract with private industry. The military agencies provide by far the greatest opportunity for such contracts, but other technological agencies also offer some contracting possibilities in R&D. The largest of these are NASA (National Aeronautics and Space Administration) and DOE (Department of Energy). However, some R&D is also carried out by the Department of Transportation, which includes the Coast Guard and the Federal Aviation Administration among its divisions.

All three military services (Army, Navy, and Air Force) maintain a number of R&D facilities, which conduct both basic and applied research in many areas, including communications, weapons, medicine, human behavior, electronics, and data processing, among other things. Some of the projects are funded by grants, rather than contracts, although grants are almost always awarded to nonprofit organizations, such as universities. (There are occasional exceptions, and grants can go to for-profit organizations.)

A listing of federal R&D facilities is included in Appendix 2.

Unsolicited Proposals

An unsolicited proposal is one offered voluntarily by an individual or organization, and is more commonly found in R&D areas than in most others, because it is almost inherently an offer to do something innovative, based on a proprietary idea, product, or capability. Because it is unsolicited, it has no competition; if the customer likes it, negotiations follow.

There is no prescribed format for an unsolicited proposal, but the Department of Defense suggests that two copies of an unsolicited proposal should be submitted, and that the proposal should contain at least the following information and elements:

1. A cover sheet
2. An abstract
3. A narrative
4. A cost proposal (separate)

It is recommended that the cover sheet include the following information:

Name of agency to which offered
Name of proposer
Address of proposer
Title of proposer
Proposed project manager or principal investigator, with telephone number
Address of project manager, if different from above
Individual to contact for discussion, negotiations, and so on
Address of above
Date of submittal

The abstract, which should be part of the "front matter" (that is, appear before page 1 of the proposal proper), should state the basic purpose of the proposed effort, give a brief summary of the work to be done, and describe the expected end-result and end-product of the proposed work. DOD suggests that the abstract be approximately 200 to 300 words long, but obviously that will vary, depending on the size of the proposal being abstracted.

The narrative should make clear how the proposed work relates to the mission of the agency to which it is submitted, the problems it will solve, and whatever other justification the proposer believes appropriate. The proposer's qualifications should be presented also, of course. The objectives of the proposed contract should be made clear and should be detailed as clearly as possible. Obviously, the customer is not likely to fund a fishing expedition. It is necessary to present a convincing case for the proposed contract, and present good evidence that the proposed work will contribute substantially to the mission of the agency and have a good prospect for success in achieving the stated objectives.

Any preliminary or preparatory work out of which the proposal grew should be mentioned, as it will contribute to the probability that the proposal will be accepted by the customer.

In general, what has been said about competitive proposals applies for the most part to unsolicited proposals as well—perhaps even more so, since the customer has not felt the need for such work prior to submittal of the unsolicited proposal, and must be convinced that the work and result will be a worthwhile and justified contribution.

In presenting the offerer's qualifications, the suggestions made earlier in connection with proposing competitively should be followed, but the information submitted should also include the following:

___(name of proposer)___ is a ___(type of organization)___, organized under the laws of the state of _____, having its principal office and doing business in the city of _____.

If the firm is incorporated, furnish names of chief officers; if it's a partnership or sole proprietorship, furnish names of principals. Indicate the number of employees, state whether yours is a small business, a minority enterprise, or a woman-owned business, and whether it is in a labor-surplus area (as defined by Department of Labor in quarterly designations of labor-surplus areas). State where the proposed work will be performed, whether you are currently doing related work or whether related work has been done in past, and your other general qualifications.

State whether subcontracts are contemplated. If they are, state what will be subcontracted and to whom, if known.

State whether you have or have not retained a company or person to secure the proposed contract, and express willingness to furnish information to the contracting officer regarding this.

State whether working capital is available or, if not, where you intend to turn for working capital.

Describe where the work is to be done, describe the facilities and resources to be used, and mention any other pertinent details.

In practice, it is unwise to ever offer an unsolicited proposal with no advance discussion, since it is most unlikely that the customer will buy an unsolicited proposal which comes in cold and completely unexpected. However, many unsolicited proposals are funded every year, and are a major source of income to many firms.

One word of caution: Many, if not most, contracting officers are automatically skeptical about proposals purporting to be unsolicited, since many government people "arrange" to have favored suppliers submit "unsolicited" proposals which have actually originated in the government executive's mind. It is highly advisable to take all possible steps to document the unsolicited proposal as truly unsolicited.

Military Exchange Services

Military exchanges buy merchandise for resale such as foods and other consumer goods. Officially, Army and Air Force exchanges buy everything offered in the various exchanges through one or more of five regional exchange offices. In practice, some goods may be sold to individual exchanges, particularly if the item is suitable for local sale only. For example, the cost of some local products would be excessively high if they were shipped elsewhere, and custom orders are taken for some items, such as custom-stenciled T-shirts. Most purchases, however, are via regional offices.

For overseas exchanges, all buying is done via the Army and Air Force Exchange Service Headquarters at Dallas, TX 75222. Any information on Army and Air Force exchange procurement may be addressed to the Command and Public Relations Division there. (The telephone number is (214)330-2763.)

The Navy invites suppliers to sell Navy exchanges through the Navy Resale System Office (NRSO) at Brooklyn, NY, or the NRSO Branch Office at Oakland, CA, or by sale directly to the individual exchanges.

To sell to Marine Corps exchanges, contact the Marine Corps Exchange Service.

Specific name and address listings for the various exchange offices are included in Appendix 2.

Military Commissary Stores

Most commissary resale items are purchased by brand-name contracts issued by Headquarters, Defense Personnel Support Center, Defense Supply Agency, 2800 South 20th Street, Philadelphia, PA 19101. However, each commissary store may also make direct purchases of resale goods and services, within prescribed dollar limits. Navy commissary stores do most of their purchasing through the Navy Resale System Office, the same organization which buys for Navy exchanges.

The U.S. Postal Service

The U.S. Postal Service is a government corporation today, rather than a Department, as it once was. However, it is still an official agency within the U.S. government and subject to the same statutory control in its purchasing as are other agencies. But its needs are somewhat different from other civilian agencies, and the Postal Service has long had its own centralized purchasing and supply system, with its main warehouses and depot at Topeka, Kansas.

The Postal Service orders some of its supplies from GSA and the Federal Supply Service, and at one time used a great deal of military surplus, especially motor vehicles. However, it requires many specialized supplies and types of equipment, such as sorting machines, cancellers, carts, computers, scales, vending equipment, and other devices to support its automation efforts. Much of that equipment is custom designed under contract, some developed at the Postal Service R&D laboratory in Rockville, Maryland. However, aside from extensive purchases of capital equipment, the Postal Service buys a great deal of transportation services to move the mail from city to city and a great deal of service and supplies to maintain its huge fleet of motor vehicles.

Motor vehicle maintenance is carried out by some 300 Vehicle Maintenance Facilities (VMFs) which are part of the Postal Service, and many VMFs are supported by "satellite" VMFs. The Baltimore VMF, for example, maintains a satellite VMF in Annapolis, to avoid the long tow of a disabled Postal Service vehicle from Annapolis to Baltimore. However, many localities have no VMF within reasonable range, and in such cases the Postal Service relies on local commercial facilities (service stations and garages) to service its vehicles.

Each VMF has its own parts room and parts clerk, and attempts to stock those parts considered necessary to keep vehicles in good operating condition and minimize "down time." However, inevitably many occasions arise when the needed part is not in stock. In such cases, the VMF buys the part locally from nearby dealers. (Since most Postal Service vehicles are standard commercial models, this is entirely feasible.)

One major need of the Postal Service is for construction services. As suburban communities continue to grow, new post offices must be built. Hardly a day passes that the Postal Service cannot offer opportunities to bid for new construction and/or renovation and repairs to existing buildings.

When it was reorganized as a government corporation, the Postal Service employed approximately 670,000 workers, with an annual budget of approximately $10 billion. The budget has grown as a result of both inflation and increased load (about 92 billion pieces of mail per year, currently), although the workforce has grown more slowly, since U.S.P.S. has invested heavily in automation so as to become slightly less labor intensive. However, there are some 30,000 post offices, plus a number of other buildings in the Postal Service System, making it a major market for many services and supplies. Buying is done through both the Procurement and Supply Office at Postal Service Headquarters in Washington, D.C. and through its many offices. A list of major offices is located in Appendix 2.

The Government Printing Office

The U.S. Government Printing Office (GPO) is one of the old-time agencies of the government, dating back to June 23, 1860. Unlike most of the other agencies, GPO is not part of the Executive Branch, and therefore does not report to the President, but is part of the Legislative Branch and reports to Congress, which has a Joint Committee on Printing that acts as the Board of Directors for the GPO.

Virtually all printing done for the government must be done either through GPO or by other means authorized by GPO. Agencies that want to have a private contractor do printing for them must persuade the GPO to authorize it through a waiver. There are, however, a number of agencies operating their own small printing plants, presumably with GPO blessing.

GPO is presently handling approximately $500 million worth of printing for the various agencies every year. However, GPO contracts out about 70 percent of this work to commercial printers through its own headquarters establishment in Washington, D.C., and its 13 Regional Printing Procurement Offices in Atlanta, Boston, Chicago, Columbus, Dallas, Denver, Hampton (VA), Los Angeles, New York, Philadelphia, St. Louis, San Francisco, and Seattle. And, of course, GPO also buys paper, ink, and other supplies, as well as equipment of various kinds.

In addition to printing, GPO contracts out typesetting and some special services, such as maintaining subscription lists for periodicals, soliciting subscriptions, and so on.

Many small print shops do GPO work exclusively or as a large portion of their total volume. Satisfactory contractors to GPO can expect continuous invitations to bid. To apply for inclusion on GPO's many bidders lists, the bidder must first ask for GPO's standard package of materials, which includes forms on which the bidder will list and describe the facility and equipment. This enables GPO to determine what kinds of jobs the bidder can handle and therefore which bid sets that company should receive. The large number of bids every day would make it too time consuming and difficult to require sealed bids and hold public openings, but the bids are normally let on the basis of low bid. The bidder receives a *detailed* estimating form on which to calculate prices—even to the extreme of pricing the staples used in binding, for example. However, GPO usually gives a generous amount of time to complete a job.

GPO has many different types of printing requirements, from newsletters to slick magazines; from simple, side-stitched manuals to casebound books; from letterheads to snap-out forms and other specialties. Many are simple, one-time requirements, while others are annual "programs," which furnish continuing work for an entire year, just as many other agencies do.

Locations of key offices of the GPO are listed in Appendix 1.

Opportunities for individuals

There are many self-employed individuals who find frequent employment on small government jobs, usually arranged by informal purchase order, sometimes by a simple letter contract. Individuals are frequently retained to lecture, write, consult, and handle other small assignments which are usually performed more efficiently by an individual than by an organization.

In some cases, an individual is retained to do a study or write a book for an agency because he or she is peculiarly qualified, perhaps uniquely qualified. In others, it is simply because the individual has taken the trouble to track the need down and sell the job. For such small tasks, simply "making the calls" is appropriate and adequate for the need. And the individual can develop a "following" of satisfied customers who will call the individual back again and again. Or such jobs can lead to long-term assignments.

There are, for example, some consultants who furnish two or three days a week to an agency for many months, on a semi-permanent basis. At OSHA (Occupational Safety and Health Administration, Labor Department), a fairly large staff of "consultants," all contracted for individually, handle the public information, write press releases, publish a monthly magazine, and perform a variety of such chores.

Many of those who lecture in government classrooms are outside "consultants," hired because of special competence in some subject and an acceptable "platform" presence.

Only about $10 billion worth of government services are considered to be necessarily done by federal employees because of the nature of the duties. All the rest, probably in excess of $100 billion (no one, in or out of the government, knows exactly how much), is done by outside contractors. Work is done by federal employees in-house only if and when it is deemed to be less costly to do it that way. The federal employee gets 20.4 percent of his or her base salary in retirement benefits, plus up to 10 weeks paid time off from work, plus almost-guaranteed annual increases and promotions, so it is increasingly difficult for agencies to demonstrate that they can do the job less expensively than an outside contractor can do it. Therefore, the opportunities for government contracts have been growing steadily, rather than declining. Paradoxical as it may seem, presidential moves toward austerity and economy invariably lead to additional contracting opportunities. "Economizing" almost always means reducing the federal payroll—without reducing the work federal agencies are required to do. They must still carry out the same programs. Frequently, the requirement for a consultant is precipitated by and directly due to the fact that the agency has had a freeze put on hiring, and therefore uses money available for contracting to get the job done.

9

Government freebies
you can use

The large print giveth and the small print taketh away

Some of the best things in life are still free

The IRS taketh, as most of us know, but most of the rest of the U.S. government giveth, freely. They giveth welfare, grants, specially created jobs, and many other things, some of which are useful to the business seeking to sell to the government agencies. One major item is information, primarily in the form of publications of many sorts.

The Government Printing Office is the publisher, at this time, of about 25,000 publications, ranging from slender brochures and leaflets to case-bound books, full-color magazines, and many other items. Only a few years ago, many of GPO's smaller publications were offered to the public free of charge, while many others were at such low prices that they were obviously subsidized. That is no longer true. Except for a small catalog or two used as "advertising" for GPO publications, GPO now gives absolutely nothing away. Everything has a price, and the prices are not below cost; in fact, they're not even competitive with those of private industry. It is obvious that the Government Printing Office is what some contracting officers would refer to as a high-cost producer.

For example, take the annual *Statistical Abstract of the United States,* a much-prized publication. The GPO offers it to the public at $10 a copy. A commercial publisher, Prentice-Hall, reprints the volume and sells it at $8 a copy! That's legal because almost everything the GPO publishes is "in the public domain," unprotected by copyright, and is legally the property of the public. That's as it should be, for public money (taxes) have paid for developing and publishing the book.

However, you can get those expensive GPO publications free of charge, as well as many other GPO publications which are never offered to the public for sale. Here, in general, is how the system works:

An agency submits an order to GPO to have something typeset, printed, and bound for use and/or distribution by the agency. The agency is billed for the work by GPO, of course, based on the quantity ordered for agency use, and they must take some quantity for their own use. GPO decides whether the general public would be interested in the publication; if so, they run a quantity for offering to the public, setting a price on it, and list it in their price lists. And, while it is still a new publication, they will usually display it in the GPO bookstores, of which there are 25 throughout the United States. (A list of these appears in Appendix 1.)

In the meanwhile, the agency is busy giving the publication away! In fact, there is little else they can do, since there is no provision for most agencies to accept money for the U.S. government. Payment would be an embarrassment for them. For example, every agency which does a sizable amount of contracting has a brochure or manual of its own on how to do business with its various divisions, and in some cases there are several manuals. Many of these are offered for sale by the GPO, despite the fact that the agencies have ordered them to give away to anyone who inquires about business opportunities with the government.

The National Archives and Records Service, which is a division of the General Services Administration, is a favorite research library for writers and scholars. In its stacks are voluminous records, photos, and other documents, available for examination and copying. For example, the Archives contain many photos, some of them rather rare. For a small sum, anyone can get copies of the photos or even slide versions of the photos. (We used this service to gather slides for a training program on American Indians.) National Archives branches are listed in Appendix 1. NASA Headquarters has given away thousands of copies of original color photos of its programs, including many moon-landing shots.

The GPO is also the largest subscription service in the United States, publishing over 400 government periodicals. Many of these are available only by paid subscription, but there are others which are free to anyone who asks.

Another source for information is the General Accounting Office, which publishes reports on a regular basis. Most of these are offered for sale, but single copies of letter-reports are free, as are some of the larger reports.

One major government resource which is available and is vastly underutilized by the public is the library system. Almost all agencies have their own in-house libraries, some of them quite large and extensive, and for the most part they are readily accessible by the general public. The Library of Congress, however, is probably the granddaddy of all libraries. It was established on April 24, 1800 with an initial appropriation of $5,000, for the use of Congress, and it has been growing ever since. The public may use most of its vast research facilities free of charge, although certain collections have carefully controlled use.

Reference specialists in the Science and Technology Division will answer brief inquiries concerning bibliographic entries, without charge, and the Library also provides a free referral service to those wishing to engage the services of professional researchers.

On request, almost every agency will send you a bundle of literature about how to do business with them. In some agencies, this is handled by the contracting or procurement division, while in others it is the function of the office of public affairs. However, if you happen to address the wrong office, your request will ultimately be routed to the correct office. The list of free publications included in this chapter is far from complete. In fact, if it were possible to assemble an absolutely complete list, it would be impractical to include it all here. It could easily occupy a large volume of its own. However, a great many representative publications are listed here. When requesting any of these, be sure to ask the agency for any other information available on the subject; new publications are generated constantly. Here, then is a partial list:

Publication(s)	*From whom to request*
Guidelines for Preparation of Unsolicited Proposals	National Science Foundation, Washington, D.C. 20550
Selling to the United States Air Force	Office of A.F. Small Business Advisor, HQ USAF/LGPF, Washington, D.C. 20330
Monthly List of GAO Reports	General Accounting Office, 441 G Street, NW Washington, D.C. 20548

Publication(s)	*From whom to request*
Selected U.S. Government Publications *Government Periodicals and Subscription Services, Price List 36*	Monthly listing from GPO of new GPO publications. Request from Superintendent of Documents, GPO, Washington, D.C. 20402
How to Do Business with the Government Printing Office, A Guide for Contractors	Any GPO Procurement Office (see Appendix 1 or Printing Procurement Department, GPO, Washington, D.C. 20402
Library of Congress Publications in Print *Calendar of Events* (monthly listing of Library of Congress programs and exhibits)	Central Services Division, Library of Congress, Washington, D.C. 20540
OMBE Access (monthly magazine) *OMBE Funded Organizations* *Franchise Opportunity Handbook* *Report of the Task Force on Education and Training for Minority Business Enterprise* *Federal Procurement and Contracting Training Manual for Minority Enterprises*	OMBE, Information Center, Department of Commerce, Washington, D.C. 20230
General Information Concerning Patents *General Information Trademarks*	Patent and Trademark Office, Department of Commerce, Washington, D.C. 20031
How to Do Business with the Defense Logistics Agency *An Identification of Commodities Purchased by the Defense Logistics Agency*	DLA Small Business Advisor (DLA-PS), Room 4B110, Cameron Station, Alexandria, VA 22314
HEW—People Serving People, A Common Thread of Service	Information Center, HEW, Humphrey Bldg., 200 Independence Avenue, SW, Washington, D.C. 20201
Publications of the U.S. Department of Labor	Information Office, Department of Labor, 200 Constitution Avenue, NW, Washington, D.C. 20210
How to Do Business with DHEW *NIH Guide for Grants and Contracts*	Director of Business Affairs, DHEW, Washington, D.C. 20201 Grants and Contract Guide Distribution Center, Division of Research Grants, NIH, R-219, Westwood Bldg., Bethesda, MD 20014
Contracting with the United States Department of Transportation	Department of Transportation, Office of Procurement, Washington, D.C. 20591

In addition to these few listed here, all agencies have many small brochures and leaflets describing their many programs. The Department of Commerce, for example, has leaflets covering the activities of the Economic Development Administration and its several programs to assist American business in winning sales overseas; OSHA has many leaflets and small brochures describing their training programs, and the various occupational hazards and health hazards; and so on.

Most agencies also have press officers, and issue press releases regularly or intermittently. Many of these releases are, in actuality, lengthy treatments of subjects, with charts and full presentations. The Department of Energy publishes what really amounts to a weekly newsletter, as a press release, listing many kinds of events and activities in the energy field. The Office of Management and Budget releases information every week about its activities, including the full text of its many presentations to congressional committees.

Press releases from the Economic Development Administration of the Commerce Department are particularly valuable as sales leads, because they announce grants and loans every week, identifying the community or firm receiving such aid, and to what use the money will be put. A typical month's collection of these releases will represent $30 to $50 million in funds for construction, economic stimulation, and related purposes.

Agencies that have substantial grant money available, such as the National Science Foundation and the Foundation for the Arts, publish rather elaborate manuals on their grant programs, some of them detailing the preferred methods for seeking grants successfully and writing grant proposals. These publications are available free, on request.

Many agencies have movies which can be borrowed, on request, free of charge. And many also have speaker's bureaus, supplying speakers without charge.

The largest bonanza of free and low-cost publications of interest to small business is that of the Small Business Administration. Every SBA office, and there are approximately 90 throughout the United States, has a number of small brochures and leaflets, but a larger library of free and low-cost SBA publications is available to the public. At any SBA office (see listing of offices in Appendix 1) you can get a complete list of these, with instructions for ordering them.

The SBA also offers a great many other free services to assist small business generally and minority-owned and woman-owned businesses especially. Some of them are general counseling and guidance services; others are specific consulting services in prescribed areas, and still others are training programs.

SBA will also aid small businesses seeking government contracts in at least three ways:

1. The general programs of information, training, and counseling.
2. The Certificate of Competency process. Under this program, should a small business be denied a contract award on the basis that the agency alleges the firm lacks the proper technical capability for the work, SBA can delay contract award until it investigates the bidder's capability. Should SBA judge that the bidder is capable of handling the contract, SBA may issue a Certificate of Competency to the firm, which invalidates the contracting officer's objection.
3. Financial assistance. Should a bidder be denied an award on the basis that it lacks the financial resources to handle the contract, SBA may delay the award until it attempts to aid the firm in finding money (either by guaranteed loan or direct loan) so that the firm will qualify as financially responsible.

A visit to the GSA Business Service Center will also be rewarding in the information offered. Each GSA Regional Office has a Business Service Center, staffed by specialists who can answer your questions about doing business with GSA. You will also gather up an armload of publications and forms to get on bidders lists.

There are a number of publications for which you will probably have to pay, but they are worth the investment. Those are listed in Appendix 5. However, it may be advisable to hold off ordering these until you see how many will be offered you without charge. A great many of the books in my own library carry substantial GPO price tags, but were given to me free at various agencies. In some cases, priced government publications are laid out in public racks in agency offices, with an invitation to help yourself to any which interest you.

Freedom of information

Many people approach government offices with hesitancy, as though they feared they were intruding on some individual's or organization's privacy. And on occasion, a government employee may behave as though he or she thinks that such is the case. The Freedom of Information Act and the Government in the Sunshine Act make it abundantly clear that you and I have the *right* to visit these offices and to get any information that is not classified and/or does not invade any individual's privacy. We ask, courteously, but we can *demand,* if necessary.

This happened on a fairly recent occasion, when I called the contracting office of an agency to inquire into what was currently being paid to a contractor for certain services. The gentleman at the other end of the line told me that he had no intention of giving out that information. I responded that I had a right to ask and get the information, and that I was now invoking that right, under the Freedom of Information Act, and that I would press the matter with higher authorities should that be necessary. At that, the other man became a bit uneasy and asked me to wait a moment. (He obviously wanted to confer with his superior.) In literally a minute or two he returned to the telephone and released the information I had requested.

Federal Information Centers

The General Services Administration has established a national network of Federal Information Centers, which citizens may write to, telephone, or visit for information. These offices are supposed to assist you in getting any information they cannot provide spontaneously. These centers, some of which have toll-free tie-lines, are listed in Appendix 3.

The PASS program

All federal agencies operate under the legal requirement and presidential directives to support socioeconomic programs by singling out appropriate procurements for small business, minority enterprises, woman-owned enterprises, and enterprises which provide (or would provide) jobs in "labor surplus" areas. In many cases, when an agency wishes to do so, they have the problem of finding suitable firms to issue bid invitations to, and they often turn to the SBA for help. But until now, the SBA did not have a central source of information.

The SBA is now operating the PASS (Procurement Automated Source System) program by registering firms qualifying under these various descriptions, and making the computerized directory available to other agencies.

One thing which may help is to get into the system. You need only write or call your nearest SBA office and request the registration form for PASS.

Appendixes

The best is yet to come

Appendix 1

Agencies and offices of special interest to business people

The United States is divided into 10 federal regions, and most government agencies maintain an office in each region. However, several of the agencies are designed to help business in various ways, through their programs, and these usually maintain a large number of district or field offices, in addition to their regional offices, so that everyone may have ready access to the services.

Those which are of special interest to business people seeking information and aid in selling to the U.S. government or getting the aid offered in federal programs are listed in this appendix.

The Small Business Administration and the Department of Commerce both maintain an unusually large number of field offices because both are concerned almost entirely with supporting American businesses. However, the General Services Administration and the Government Printing Office also maintain many offices for the convenience of the public, and all are listed here for the convenience of the reader in finding those closest to his or her own establishment.

(Note that these are offices and agencies offering information and help to those seeking government business, whereas in Appendix 2 are listed many government procurement offices—those which do the actual buying.)

SMALL BUSINESS ADMINISTRATION REGIONAL AND DISTRICT OFFICES

Headquarters office:
1441 L Street, NW, Washington, DC 20416

Region I
60 Batterymarch, Boston, MA 02110
150 Causeway St., Boston, MA 02203
302 High St., Holyoke, MA 01040
40 Western Ave., Augusta, ME 04430
55 Pleasant St., Concord, NH 03301
1 Financial Plaza, Hartford, CT 06103
87 State St., Montpelier, VT 05602
57 Eddy St., Providence, RI 02903

* Both Regional and District Offices

Region II
26 Federal Plaza, New York, NY 10007 *
111 W. Huron St., Buffalo, NY 14202
Carlos Chardon Ave., Hato Rey, PR 00918
970 Broad St., Newark, NJ 07102
100 S. Clinton St., Syracuse, NY 13202
180 State St., Elmira, NY 14904
99 Washington Ave., Albany, NY 12207
100 State St., Rochester, NY 14604
1800 E. Davis St., Camden, NJ 08104
Franklin Bldg., St. Thomas, VI

Region III
1 Bala Cynwyd Plaza, Bala Cynwyd, PA 19004 *
Charleston National Plaza, Charleston, WV 25301
109 N. 3rd St., Clarksburg, WV 26301
1500 N. 2nd St., Harrisburg, PA 17108
1000 Liberty Ave., Pittsburgh, PA 15222
400 N. 8th St., Richmond, VA 23240
7800 York Rd., Towson, MD 21204
1030 15th St., NW, Washington, DC 20417
20 N. Pennsylvania Ave., Wilkes-Barre, PA 18701
844 King St., Wilmington, DE 19801

Region IV
1375 Peachtree St., NE, Atlanta, GA 30309
1720 Peachtree Rd., NW, Atlanta, GA 30309
111 Fred Haise Blvd., Biloxi, MS 39530
908 S. 20th St., Birmingham, AL 36205
230 S. Tryon St., Charlotte, NC 28202
1801 Assembly St., Columbia, SC 29201
2222 Ponce de Leon Blvd., Coral Gables, FL 33134
1802 N. Trask St., Tampa, FL 33607
215 S. Evans St., Greenville, NC 27834
200 E. Pascagoula, Jackson, MS 39205
400 W. Bay St., Jacksonville, FL 32202
502 S. Gay St., Knoxville, TN 37902
600 Federal Pl., Louisville, KY 40202
404 James Robertson Pkwy., Nashville, TN 37219
211 Federal Office Building, Memphis, TN 38103
701 Clematis St., W. Palm Beach, FL 33402

Region V
219 S. Dearborn St., Chicago, IL 60604 *
550 Main St., Cincinnati, OH 45202
1240 E. 9th St., Cleveland, OH 44199
34 N. High St., Columbus, OH 43215
477 Michigan Ave., Detroit, MI 48226
575 N. Pennsylvania St., Indianapolis, IN 46204
122 W. Washington Ave., Madison, WI 53703
500 S. Barstow St., Eau Claire, WI 54701
540 W. Kaye Ave., Marquette, MI 49855
517 E. Wisconsin Ave., Milwaukee, WI 53202
12 S. 6th St., Minneapolis, MN 55402
1 N. Old State Capitol Plaza, Springfield, IL 62701

Region VI
1720 Regal Row, Dallas, TX 75202
1100 Commerce St., Dallas, TX 75202
5000 Marble Ave., NE, Albuquerque, NM 87110
4100 Rio Bravo St., El Paso, TX 79901
500 Dallas St., Houston, TX 77002
611 Gaines St., Little Rock, AR 72201
222 E. Van Buren, Lower Rio Grande Valley, Harlingen, TX 78550
3105 Leopard St., Corpus Christi, TX 78408
1205 Texas Ave., Lubbock, TX 79408
1001 Howard Ave., New Orleans, LA 70113
50 Penn Place, Oklahoma City, OK 73118
727 E. Durango, San Antonio, TX 78205
500 Fannin St., Shreveport, LA 71163

Region VII
911 Walnut St., Kansas City, MO 64106
1150 Grand Ave., Kansas City, MO 64106
210 Walnut St., Des Moines, IA 50309
19th & Farnam Sts., Omaha, NE 68102
1 Mercantile Tower, St. Louis, MO 63101
110 E. Waterman St., Wichita, KS 67202

Region VIII
1405 Curtis St., Denver, CO 80202
721 19th St., Denver, CO 80202
100 E. B St., Casper, WY 82601
653 2nd Ave. N., Fargo, ND 58102
618 Helena Ave., Helena, MT 59601
125 S. State St., Salt Lake City, UT 84111
8th & Maine Aves., Sioux Falls, SD 57102
515 9th St., Rapid City, SD 57701

Region IX
450 Golden Gate Ave., San Francisco, CA 94102
211 Main St., San Francisco, CA 94105
1130 O St., Fresno, CA 93721
Ada Plaza Center Building, Agana, Guam 96910
1149 Bethel St., Honolulu, HI 96813
301 E. Stewart St., Las Vegas, NV 89101
350 S. Figueroa St., Los Angeles, CA 90014
112 N. Central Ave., Phoenix, AZ 85004
880 Front St., San Diego, CA 92101
2800 Cottage Way, Sacramento, CA 95825
300 Booth St., Reno, NV 89101

Region X
710 2nd Ave., Seattle, WA 98104
915 2nd Ave., Seattle, WA 98104
1016 W. 6th Ave., Anchorage, AK 99501
216 N. 8th St., Boise, ID 83701
501½ 2nd Ave., Fairbanks, AK 99701
1220 SW 3rd Ave., Portland, OR 97204
651 U.S. Courthouse, Spokane, WA 99210

GENERAL SERVICES ADMINISTRATION

Headquarters office:
18th and F Sts., NW, Washington, DC 20405

Headquarters, Federal Supply Service
1941 Jefferson Davis Highway
Arlington, VA 22202

Mailing Address
Washington, DC 20406

National Archives and Record Service
8th Street and Pennsylvania Ave., NW
Washington, DC 20408

Regional Offices and Business Service Centers

Region I	John W. McCormack Federal Building, Boston, MA 02109
Region II	26 Federal Plaza, New York, NY 10007
Region III	7th & D Sts., SW, Washington, D.C. 20407
	600 Arch St., Philadelphia, PA 19106
Region IV	1776 Peachtree St., NW, Atlanta, GA 30309
Region V	230 S. Dearborn St., Chicago, IL 60604
Region VI	1500 E. Bannister Rd., Kansas City, MO 64131
Region VII	819 Taylor St., Forth Worth, TX 76102
	515 Rusk St., Houston, TX 77002

Region VIII	Denver Federal Center, Denver, CO 80225
Region IX	525 Market St., San Francisco, CA 94105
	300 N. Los Angeles, Los Angeles, CA 90012
Region X	915 2nd Ave., Seattle, WA 98174

National Archives Regional Branches

380 Trapelo Rd., Waltham, MA 02154
Bldg. 22 MOT Bayonne, Bayonne, NJ 07002
5000 Wissahickon Ave., Philadelphia, PA 19144
1557 St. Joseph Ave., East Point, GA 30344
7358 S. Pulaski Rd., Chicago, IL 60629
2306 E. Bannister Rd., Kansas City, MO 64131
4900 Hemphill St., P.O. Box 6216, Fort Worth, TX 76115
Bldg. 48, Denver Federal Center, Denver, CO 80225
1000 Commodore Drive, San Bruno, CA 94066
24000 Avila Rd., Laguna Niguel, CA 92677
6125 Sand Point Way NE, Seattle, WA 98115

DEPARTMENT OF COMMERCE

Headquarters office:
14th & Constitution, NW, Washington, DC 20230

Field Offices
(Arranged alphabetically by city)

505 Marquette Ave, NW, Suite 1015, Albuquerque, NM 87102
412 Hill Bldg., 632 6th Ave., Anchorage, AK 99501
1365 Peachtree St., NE, Suite 600, Atlanta, GA 30309
415 U.S. Customhouse, Gay & Lombard Sts., Baltimore, MD 21202
908 S. 20th St., Suite 200, Birmingham, AL 35205
441 Stuart St., 10th floor, Boston, MA 02116

1312 Federal Bldg., 111 W. Huron St., Buffalo, NY 14202
3000 New Federal Office Bldg., 500 Quarrier St., Charleston, WV 25301
6022 O'Mahoney Federal Center, 2120 Capitol Ave., Cheyenne, WY 82001
1406 Mid-Continental Plaza Bldg., 55 E. Monroe St., Chicago, IL 60603
10504 Federal Office Bldg., 550 Main St., Cincinnati, OH 45205
666 Euclid Ave., Room 600, Cleveland, OH 44114

2611 Forest Dr., Forest Center,
Columbia, SC 29204
1100 Commerce St., Room 7A5,
Dallas, TX 75242
New Customhouse, 19th & Stout Sts.,
Room 165, Denver, CO 80202
817 Federal Bldg., 210 Walnut St.,
Des Moines, IA 50309
445 Federal Bldg., 231 W. Lafayette,
Detroit, MI 48226
203 Federal Bldg., W. Market St.,
P.O. Box 1950, Greensboro, NC 27402
Federal Office Bldg., 450 Main St.,
Room 610-B, Hartford, CT 06103
4106 Federal Office Bldg.,
300 Ala Moana Blvd., P.O. Box 50026,
Honolulu, HI 96850
2625 Federal Bldg., Courthouse,
515 Rusk St., Houston, TX 77002
357 U.S. Courthouse and
Federal Office Bldg., 46 E. Ohio St.,
Indianapolis, IN 46204
11777 San Vincente Blvd.,
Los Angeles, CA 90049
147 Jefferson Ave., Room 710,
Memphis, TN 38103
City National Bank Bldg.,
25 W. Flagler St., Room 821,
Miami, FL 33130
Federal Bldg., U.S. Courthouse,
517 E. Wisconsin Ave.,
Minneapolis, MN 55401
Gateway Bldg., 4th Floor,
Market St. and Penn Plaza,
Newark, NJ 07102

432 International Trade Mart,
2 Canal St., New Orleans, LA 70130
Federal Office Bldg., 26 Federal Plaza,
Foley Square, New York, NY 10007
Capitol Plaza, 1815 Capitol St.,
Suite 703A, Omaha, NE 68102
9448 Federal Bldg., 600 Arch St.,
Philadelphia, PA 19106
Valley Bank Center, 201 N. Central Ave.,
Suite 2950, Phoenix, AZ 85037
2002 Federal Bldg., 1000 Liberty Ave.,
Pittsburgh, PA 15222
1220 SW 3rd Ave., Room 618,
Portland, OR 97204
2028 Federal Bldg., 300 Booth St.,
Reno, NV 89509
8010 Federal Bldg., 400 N. 8th St.,
Richmond, VA 23240
120 S. Central Ave.,
St. Louis, MO 63105
1203 Federal Bldg., 125 S. State St.,
Salt Lake City, UT 84138
Federal Bldg., Box 36013,
450 Golden Gate Ave.,
San Francisco, CA 94102
Federal Bldg., Room 659,
San Juan, PR (Hato Rey) 00918
222 U.S. Courthouse, P.O. Box 9746,
125-29 Bull St., Savannah, GA 31402
Lake Union Bldg., 1700 Westlake Ave. N.,
Room 706, Seattle, WA 98109

GOVERNMENT PRINTING OFFICE
BOOKSTORES AND PROCUREMENT CENTERS

Main office:
North Capitol and H Sts., NW, Washington, DC 20402

Bookstores and Procurement Centers
(* *indicates procurement center*)

* Federal Bldg., 275 Peachtree St. NE,
Atlanta, GA 30303
9220 Parkway East-B, Roebuck Shopping City,
Birmingham, AL 35206
* John F. Kennedy Federal Bldg.,
Sudbury St., Boston, MA 02203
* Everett McKinley Dirksen Bldg.,
219 S. Dearborn St., Chicago, IL 60604
Federal Office Bldg., 1240 E. 9th St.,
Cleveland, OH 44114
* Federal Bldg., 200 N. High St.,
Columbus, OH 43215
* Federal Bldg., 1100 Commerce St.,
Dallas, TX 75242
* Federal Bldg., 1961 Stout St.,
Denver, CO 80202
Patrick V. McNamara Federal Bldg.,
477 Michigan Ave., Detroit, MI 48226
45 College Center, 9319 Gulf Freeway,
Houston, TX 77017

Federal Bldg., 400 West Bay St., Box 35089,
Jacksonville, FL 32202
Federal Office Bldg., 601 E. 12th St.,
Kansas City, MO 64106
* Federal Office Bldg., 300 N. Los Angeles St.,
Los Angeles, CA 90012
Federal Bldg., 519 E. Wisconsin Ave.,
Milwaukee, WI 53202
* 26 Federal Plaza,
New York, NY 10007
* Federal Office Bldg., 600 Arch St.,
Philadelphia, PA 19106
Majestic Bldg., 720 N. Main St.,
Pueblo, CO 81003
* Federal Office Bldg., 450 Golden Gate Ave.,
San Francisco, CA 94102
* Federal Office Bldg., 915 Second Ave.,
Seattle, WA 98104

* Government Printing Office,
710 N. Capitol St., NW, Washington, DC
20402
Dept. of Commerce, 14th & E Sts., NW
Washington, DC 20230
Dept. of State, Rm 2817, North Lobby,
21st & C Sts., NW, Washington, DC 20520

Pentagon, Main Concourse, South End,
Washington, DC 20310
USIA, 1776 Pennsylvania Ave., NW,
Washington, DC 20547
HEW, Room 1528,
330 Independence Ave., SW,
Washington, DC 20201

Appendix 2

Directory of key government installations and offices

Approximately 130,000 government employees are kept busy in about 15,000 "buying activities," handling purchasing for the U.S. government. No one has ever compiled a complete directory of these, although there are a number of brief listings. In fact, each Regional GSA Office can furnish a partial list of buying activities in its own Region, but this list is far from complete.

The offices listed in Appendix 1 can steer you to most of the routine buying of the government. Much of the remaining buying includes some $18 billion of "R&D" at current levels, which is distributed among many agencies, and much of that is readily available to small firms.

All federal agencies are required to have a small business representative or advisor and a minority business representative. In large agencies, there are often individuals assigned full-time to these functions, and there are often several individuals in the agency. In other cases, someone in the agency, often the contracting officer, wears several hats and handles these functions. In any case, in making initial contacts, it is wise to seek out the individual(s) who handle(s) these functions and ask for assistance.

In the following listings, many of the programs are identified specifically. But there are other cases in which the agency has advised us to have those seeking business communicate with the appropriate representative. In many cases, the agency can and will supply a brochure or manual free of charge, to aid the applicant in becoming familiar with the agency's programs and contract or grant opportunities.

The information presented here is accurate at the time of this writing. However, because personnel inevitably change, the names of individuals are not supplied. Relatively few would be useful, in any case, and it is necessary only to know that there is a small business representative or advisor available to help, and that additional, detailed information is available for the asking.

Insofar as possible, too, titles of government publications offered free of charge to assist the small and minority business entrepreneur have been listed in Chapter 9.

At this writing, the Department of Energy is still relatively new (as a Department) and details of its many branches and programs have not yet been published or assembled for publication. Therefore, it is necessary to get this information directly from the agency's small business advisor, whose office address is listed here.

Department of Agriculture
Federal Research, Science and Education
  Administration
Cooperative Research, Science and
  Education Administration
  Both above:
  U.S. Department of Agriculture
  Washington, DC 20250
Competitive Grants Office, Science and
  Eduction Administration
  U.S. Department of Agriculture
  1300 Wilson Blvd.
  Arlington, VA 22209

Department of Commerce
Experimental Technology Incentives Program
  National Bureau of Standards
  Administration Bldg., Room A-739
  Washington, DC 20234
Maritime Administration
  Department of Commerce, Room 4884
  Washington, DC 20230
Programs & Technology Department Office
  National Oceanic and Atmospheric
    Administration (NOAA)
  RD1, Rockville, MD 20852

Department of Defense
Director, Defense Civil Preparedness Agency
  Department of Defense, The Pentagon
  Washington, DC 20301
Director, Defense Communications
  Engineering Center
  Derey Engineering Bldg.
  1860 Wiehle Ave.
  Reston, VA 22090
Director, Command and Control
  Technical Center
  Defensive Communications Agency
  Washington, DC 20301
Director, Defense Communications Agency
  ATTN: MILSATCOM Systems Office
  Code 800
  Washington, DC 20305
WWMCCS System Engineer
WWMCCS System Engineering Organization
  Washington, DC 20305
Defense Nuclear Agency
  Washington, DC 20305
Armed Forces Radiobiology Research Institute
  Defense Nuclear Agency
  Bethesda, MD 20014
Field Command, DNA
  Kirtland AFB, NM 87115

Department of the Air Force
Space and Missile Systems Organization (BC)
  Los Angeles Air Force Station
  Box 92960, Worldway Postal Center
  Los Angeles, CA 90009

Aerospace Medical Division
Directorate of R&D Procurement (BC)
  Aeronautical Systems Div.
  Wright-Patterson AFB, OH 45433
Air Force Electronic Systems Div. (BC)
  Hanscom AFB
  Bedford, MA 01731
Space and Missile Test Center
  Vandenberg AFB
  Lompoc, CA 93437
Air Force Aeronautical Systems Div.
  Wright-Patterson AFB, OH 45433
Air Force Flight Test Center (BC)
  Edwards AFB, CA 93523
Kirtland Procurement Center (BC-39)
  Air Force Contract Management Div.
  Kirtland AFB, NM 87115
Air Force Eastern Test Range (BC)
  Patrick AFB, FL 32925
Rome Air Development Center
  Griffis AFB, NY 13441
Armament Test and Development Ctr. (BC)
  Eglin AFB, FL 32542
Arnold Engineering Development Ctr. (BC)
  Arnold Air Force Station, TN 37389
Directorate of Procurement (BC)
  Air Force Office of Scientific Research
  Bolling AFB
  Washington, DC 20332

Department of the Army
BMD Systems Command
  Box 1500
  Huntsville, AL 35807
HQ DARCOM
  5001 Eisenhower Ave.
  Alexandria, VA 22333
Human Engineering Laboratories (HEL)
  Aberdeen Proving Ground, MD 21005
Army Material Systems Analysis
  Agency (AMSAA)
  Aberdeen Proving Ground, MD 21005
Harry Diamond Laboratories
  2800 Powder Mill Rd.
  Adelphi, MD 20783
Army Materials and Mechanics
  Research Center
  Watertown, MA 02172
Army Natick R&D Center
  Natick, MA 01760
Army Mobility Equipment R&D Command
  Fort Belvoir, VA 22060
ARRADCOM, ATTN: DRDAR-SB
  Dover, NJ 07801
Chemical Systems Laboratory
  ATTN: DRDAR-SB
  Aberdeen Proving Ground, MD 21010
Benet Weapons Laboratory
  ATTN: DRDAR-LCB
  Watervliet, NY 12189

Ballistic Research Laboratories (BRL)
ATTN: DRDAR-BL
Aberdeen Proving Ground, MD 21010
Army Aviation R&D Command
St. Louis, MO 63166
Army Electronics R&D Command
2800 Powder Mill Rd.
Adelphi, MD 20788
Army Communications R&D Command
Fort Monmouth, NJ 07703
Army Missile R&D Command
Redstone Arsenal
Huntsville, AL 35809
U.S. Tank-Automotive R&D Command
Warren, MI 48090
Army Yuma Proving Ground
Yuma Proving Ground, AZ 85364
Office of the Chief of Engineers
Washington, DC 22314
Army Eng. Waterways Experiment Station
Box 631
Vicksburg, MS 39180
Army Cold Regions Research and Engineering Laboratory
Box 282
Hanover, NH 03755
Army Construction Engineering Research Laboratory
Box 4005
Champaign, IL 61820
Army Engineer Topographic Laboratories
Fort Belvoir, VA 22060
Army Coastal Engineering Research Center
Kingman Bldg.
Fort Belvoir, VA 22060
Army Medical R&D Command
(ATTN: SGRD-RP)
Forrestal Bldg.
Washington, DC 20314
Walter Reed Army Institute of Research
Washington, DC 20012

Department of the Navy
Office of Naval Research
Room 718
800 N. Quincy St.
Arlington, VA 22217
Chief of Naval Personnel
Department of the Navy
Washington, DC 20370
Naval Medical R&D Command
National Naval Medical Center
Bethesda, MD 20014
Naval Air Systems Command
Washington, DC 20361
Naval Electronic Systems Command
Washington, DC 20360
Naval Facilities Engineering Command
200 Stovall St.
Alexandria, VA 22322

Naval Sea Systems Command
Washington, DC 20362
Naval Supply Systems Command
Washington, DC 20376
Naval Research Laboratory
4555 Overlook Ave., SW
Washington, DC 20375
Naval Civil Engineering Laboratory
Naval Construction Battalion Center
Port Hueneme, CA 93043
Naval Underwater Systems Center
New London Laboratory
New London, CT 06320
Naval Coastal Systems Laboratory
Panama City, FL 32401
Naval Surface Weapons Laboratory
White Oak Laboratory
Silver Spring, MD 20910
Naval Underwater Systems Center
Newport Laboratory
Newport, RI 02840
Naval Ship Engineering Center
Washington, DC 20362
Naval Air Test Center
Patuxent River, MD 20670
Naval Air Propulsion Test Center
Trenton, NJ 08628
Naval Air Development Center
Warminster, PA 18974
Naval Air Engineering Center
Lakehurst, NJ 08735
Naval Surface Weapons Center
Dahlgren Laboratory
Halgren, VA 22448
Naval Weapons Center
China Lake, CA 93555
Naval Missile Center
Point Mugu, CA 93042
Naval Ocean Systems Center
San Diego, CA 92152
Naval Training Equipment Center
Orlando, FL 32813
Naval Ship R&D Center
Bethesda, MD 20084
Naval Weapons Support Center (Code 50)
Crane, IN 47522
Naval Avionics Facility
6000 East 21st St.
Indianapolis, IN 46218
Naval Explosive Ordnance Disposal Facility
Indian Head, MD 20640
Naval Ordnance Missile Test Facility
White Sands Missile Range, NM 88002
Naval Ship Missile Systems Eng. Station
Port Hueneme, CA 93043
Naval Ordnance Station
Indian Head, MD 20640
Naval Weapons Station
Yorktown, VA 23691
Naval Oceanographic Office
NSTL Branch (Code 4130)
Bay St. Louis, MS 39522

Department of Energy
DOE Div. of Procurement
Railway Labor Bldg., Rm 308
401 First St., NW
Washington, DC 20545

National Institutes of Health
National Institute of Allergy and Infectious
  Diseases
Westwood Bldg., Rm 707
5333 Westbard Ave.
Bethesda, MD 20016
National Institute of Arthritis, Metabolism,
  and Digestive Diseases
Bldg. 31, Rm 2B19
9000 Rockville Pike
Bethesda, MD 20014
National Cancer Institute
Research Contracts Branch
Bldg. 31, Rm 10A20
9000 Rockville Pike
Bethesda, MD 20014
National Institute of Child Health and
  Human Development
Contracts Management Section
Landow Bldg., Rm C619
Bethesda, MD 20014

National Institute of Dental Research
Contracts Management Section
Westwood Bldg., Rm 539
5333 Westbard Ave.
Bethesda, MD 20016
National Institutes of Health,
  Research Contracts Branch
Bldg. 31, Rm 1B32
9000 Rockville Pike
Bethesda, MD 20014
National Heart, Lung, and Blood Institute
Westwood Bldg., Rm 650
5333 Westbard Ave.
Bethesda, MD 20016
National Institute of Neurological
  Diseases and Stroke
Federal Bldg., Rm 1012
7550 Wisconsin Ave.
Bethesda, MD 20014
National Library of Medicine
Bldg, 38, Rm C1
8600 Rockville Pike
Bethesda, MD 20014

Department of Housing and Urban Development
Principal small business opportunities in HUD are in the Office of Development and Research, in connection with the following programs:

Housing Assistance Research
Housing Safety and Standards Research
Housing Economic Data and Analysis
Consumer and Equal Opportunity Research
Community Conservation Research
Community Development Research
Energy Conservation and Standards Research
Data Collection and Analysis

HUD Program Evaluation, Dissemination,
  and Research Support
Office of Procurement and Contracts
Department of Housing and Urban
  Development
451 7th St., SW
Room B-133 (711 Bldg.)
Washington, DC 20410

Department of the Interior
Office of Mineral Information
Bureau of Mines, Dept. of the Interior
2401 E St., NW
Washington, DC 20241
Geological Survey
Department of the Interior
12201 Sunrise Valley Dr.
Reston, VA 22092

Department of Justice
Grants and Contracts Management Div.
Office of the Comptroller
633 Indiana Ave., NW
Washington, DC 20531

Department of Transportation

DOT conducts many studies and researches connected with transportation and its problems. For contracts emanating from the Office of the Secretary, inquire as follows:

Procurement Operations Division
Department of Transportation
Office of the Secretary of Transportation
Washington, DC 20590

There are several other operating divisions in the Department:
Federal Aviation Administration, ALG-380
800 Independence Ave., SW
Washington, DC 20590
National Aviation Facilities Experimental Center, ANA-51
Atlantic City, NJ 08405
Federal Highway Administration
400 7th St., SW
Washington, DC 20590
Federal Railroad Administration
400 7th St., SW
Washington, DC 20590
National Highway Traffic Safety Admin.
400 7th St., SW
Washington, DC 20590
Urban Mass Transportation Administration
400 7th St., SW
Washington, DC 20590
U.S. Coast Guard Academy
New London, CT 06320
U.S. Coast Guard Headquarters (G-FCP)
400 7th St., SW
Washington, DC 20590

Environmental Protection Agency
Contracts Management Division, EPA
Research Triangle Park, NC 27711
Contracts Management Division, EPA
Cincinnati, OH 45268
Headquarters Contract Operations (PM-214), EPA
Washington, DC 20460

National Aeronautics and Space Administration
NASA Headquarters, Contracts Division
Washington, DC 20546

NASA/Ames Research Center
Moffet Field, CA 94035
NASA/Dryden Flight Research Center
Box 273
Edwards, CA 93523
NASA/Goddard Space Flight Center
Greenbelt, MD 20771
Jet Propulsion Laboratory
4800 Oak Grove Drive
Pasadena, CA 91103
NASA/Johnson Space Center
Houston, TX 77058
NASA/Kennedy Space Center
Kennedy Space Center, FL 32899
NASA/Langley Research Center, Langley Station
Hampton, VA 23365
NASA/Lewis Research Center
21000 Brookpark Rd
Cleveland, OH 44135
NASA/Marshall Space Flight Center
Huntsville, AL 35812
NASA/National Space Technology Labs.
Bay St. Louis, MS 39520
NASA/Wallops Flight Center
Wallops Island, VA 23337

National Science Foundation
Applied Science and Research Applications Directorate
National Science Foundation
1800 G St., NW
Washington, DC 20550

U.S. Postal Service
R&D Program Dept.
Advanced Mail Systems Development Office
Postal Technology Research Office
Letter Mail Systems Development Office
General Systems Development Office
Support Services Division
All are at:
11711 Parklawn Drive
Rockville, MD 20852

Appendix 3

Federal information centers

Most of us are aware that the U.S. government operates a great many programs and offers information and other services to the public. But most of us do not have the faintest idea of how to go about tracking down the desired information or service. (In fact, a Washington, D.C., firm, Washington Researchers, makes a business of helping firms locate information and even teaches others how to find it in Washington, D.C.!)

The government has made an effort to help the poor, bewildered citizen by establishing Federal Information Centers, as a function and responsibility of the General Services Administration. The service is designed to aid the public, however, and the public is invited to visit or call any of the offices listed here with whatever questions they have to ask. The intent of the service is to provide answers and guidance. Where the office cannot provide the answer spontaneously, it will track down the information on behalf of the requestor.

Note that in many cases a toll-free tie-line is provided.

Location	Telephone Number	Address	Toll-free Tie-line to
Alabama			
Birmingham	205 322-8591		Atlanta, GA
Mobile	205 438-1421		New Orleans, LA
Arizona			
Tucson	602 622-1511		Phoenix, AZ
Phoenix	602 261-3313	230 N. 1st Ave. 85025	
Arkansas			
Little Rock	501 378-6177		Memphis, TN
California			
Los Angeles	213 688-3800	300 N. Los Angeles St. 90012	
Sacramento	916 440-3344	650 Capitol Mall 95814	
San Diego	714 293-6030	880 Front St. 92188	
San Francisco	415 556-6600	450 Golden Gate Ave. 94102	
San Jose	408 275-7422		San Francisco, CA
Santa Ana	714 836-2386		Los Angeles, CA
Colorado			
Colorado Springs	303 471-9491		Denver, CO
Denver	303 837-3602	1961 Stout St. 80294	
Pueblo	303 544-9523		Denver, CO
Connecticut			
Hartford	203 527-2617		New York, NY
New Haven	203 624-4720		New York, NY
District of Columbia			
Washington	202 755-8660	7th & D Sts., SW 20407	
Florida			
Fort Lauderdale	305 522-8531		Miami, FL
Miami	305 350-4155	51 SW 1st Ave. 33130	
Jacksonville	904 354-4756		St. Petersburg, FL
Orlando	305 422-1800		St. Petersburg, FL
St. Petersburg	813 893-3495	144 1st Ave., S. 33701	

Location	Telephone Number	Address	Toll-free Tie-line to
Tampa	813 229-7911		St. Petersburg, FL
West Palm Beach	305 833-7566		Miami, FL
Georgia			
Atlanta	404 526-6891	275 Peachtree St., NE 30303	
Hawaii			
Honolulu	808 546-8620	300 Ala Moan Blvd. 96850	
Illinois			
Chicago	312 353-4242	219 S. Dearborn St. 60604	
Indiana			
Gary	219 883-4110		Indianapolis, IN
Indianapolis	317 269-7373	575 N. Pennsylvania St. 46204	
Iowa			
Des Moines	515 284-4448		Omaha, NE
Kansas			
Topeka	913 297-2866		Kansas City, MO
Wichita	316 263-6931		Kansas City, MO
Kentucky			
Louisville	502 582-6261	600 Federal Place 40202	
Louisiana			
New Orleans	504 589-6696	701 Loyola Ave. 70113	
Maryland			
Baltimore	301 962-4980	31 Hopkins Plaza 21201	
Massachusetts			
Boston	617 223-7121	John F. Kennedy Federal Bldg. 02203	
Michigan			
Detroit	313 226-7016	447 Michigan Ave. 48226	
Grand Rapids	616 451-2628		Detroit, MI
Minnesota			
Minneapolis	612 725-2073	110 S. 4th St. 55401	
Missouri			
Kansas City	816 374-2466	601 E. 12th St. 64106	
St. Joseph	816 233-8206		Kansas City, MO
St. Louis	314 425-4106	1520 Market St. 63103	
Nebraska			
Omaha	402 221-3353	215 N. 17th St. 68102	
New Jersey			
Newark	201 645-3600	970 Broad St. 07102	
Paterson/Passaic	201 523-0717		Newark, NJ
Trenton	609 396-4400		Newark, NJ
New Mexico			
Albuquerque	505 766-3091	500 Gold Ave., SW 87101	
Santa Fe	505 983-7743		Albuquerque, NM
New York			
Albany	518 463-4421		New York, NY
Buffalo	716 846-4010	111 W. Huron St. 14202	
New York	212 264-4464	26 Federal Plaza 10007	
Rochester	716 546-5075		Buffalo, NY
Syracuse	315 476-8545		Buffalo, NY
North Carolina			
Charlotte	704 376-3600		Atlanta, GA
Ohio			
Akron	216 375-5638		Cleveland, OH
Cincinnati	513 684-2801	550 Main St. 45202	
Cleveland	216 522-4040	1240 E. 9th St. 44199	
Columbus	614 221-1014		Cincinnati, OH
Dayton	513 223-7377		Cincinnati, OH
Toledo	419 241-3223		Cleveland, OH
Oklahoma			
Oklahoma City	405 231-4868	201 NW 3rd St. 73102	
Tulsa	918 584-4193		Oklahoma City, OK
Oregon			
Portland	503 221-2222	1220 SW 3rd Ave. 97204	
Pennsylvania			
Philadelphia	215 597-7042	600 Arch St. 19106	
Allentown/Bethlehem	215 821-7785		Philadelphia, PA
Pittsburgh	412 644-3456	1000 Liberty Ave. 15222	
Scranton	717 346-7081		Philadelphia, PA

Location	Telephone Number	Address	Toll-free Tie-line to
Rhode Island			
Providence	401 331-5565		Boston, MA
Tennessee			
Chattanooga	615 265-8231		Memphis, TN
Memphis	901 521-3285	167 N. Main St. 38103	
Nashville	615 242-5056		Memphis, TN
Texas			
Austin	512 472-5494		Houston, TX
Dallas	214 749-2131		Fort Worth, TX
Fort Worth	817 334-3624	819 Taylor St. 76102	
Houston	713 226-5711	515 Rusk Ave. 77002	
San Antonio	512 224-4471		Houston, TX
Utah			
Ogden	801 399-1347		Salt Lake City, UT
Salt Lake City	801 524-5353	125 S. State St. 84138	
Virginia			
Newport News	804 244-0480		Norfolk, VA
Norfolk	804 441-6723	Stanwick Bldg., E. Virginia Beach Blvd. 23502	
Richmond	643-4928		Norfolk, VA
Roanoke	982-8591		Norfolk, VA
Washington			
Seattle	206 442-0570	915 2nd Ave. 98174	
Tacoma	206 383-5230		Seattle, WA
Wisconsin			
Milwaukee	414 271-2273		Chicago, IL

Appendix 4

Federal supply schedules

EXPLANATION

The Federal Supply Service (FSS), General Services Administration, has three basic buying programs:

The Federal Supply Schedule Program. This is a system of approximately 300 Federal Supply Schedules, which are, in effect, annual supply agreements with a number of suppliers of both goods and services. Some schedules are national agreements with single suppliers; others are multiple-award schedules, entered into with many competitive suppliers. Being on a schedule may therefore qualify you to supply your services or goods on a purely local basis, within the geographical limits set by the schedule (but it is possible to get on schedules for more than one area, in these cases), to be a supplier on a national basis, and even to be virtually the sole supplier of some class of goods or services. These schedules account for about $2 billion annually, at current procurement levels.

The Stock Program. In this program, the FSS buys goods for warehousing and distribution from 20 supply depots and 75 GSA self-service stores.

Special Buying Program. The FSS provides a service to the other federal agencies to assist them in buying items not listed regularly in the schedules or stocked in the stock program.

The Federal Supply Service buys about $3 billion of goods and services every year, accounting for three-fifths of the GSA procurement.

This appendix contains a generalized listing of Federal Supply Schedules in force at the time of this writing (schedules do change, however, and it is necessary to verify the appropriateness of a schedule at the time you wish to apply for inclusion) and a reproduction of a typical multiple-award schedule. For a discussion of the sample schedule, see Chapter 8.

LIST OF SCHEDULES

Schedule Number	Name	Description or Typical Items
NIIS	New Item Introductory Schedule	All types items and services
19	Small Craft and Marine Equipment	Boats, motors, accessories
23	Wheel and Track Vehicles	Snowmobiles, autos, trailers, carts
25 I	Vehicular Equipment Components	Tire chains and clutch facings
25, 28, 29, 38, 39	Parts and Accessories	Automotive, construction, excavating, mining, materials handling, highway maintenance
26 II	Pneumatic Tires and Inner Tubes	Highway, off-highway, industrial
26 IV A	Tires	Industrial, solid and cushion
29 I A	Engine Accessories	Spark plugs, oil filters, and elements
30	Power Transmission Equipment	V-belts
32, 34	Woodworking and Metalworking Machinery and Equipment,	Spare parts and accessories
35 II	Electrical Trash Compactors and Balers	Industrial, institutional, and mobile
35 IV A	Appliances	Household and commercial washers, dryers
36 II A,B	Special Industrial Machinery	Lithographic printing plates and solutions, printing, duplicating, binding equipment
36 II C	Special Industry Machinery	Security shredding machines
36 IV	Special Industry Machinery	Copying equipment, supplies, services
37 I A	Special Industry Machinery	Chain saws
37 I A	Agricultural Equipment	Cattleguards
37 II A	Lawn and Garden Equipment	Lawn mowers, edgers, shredders, and so on
38 I A	Clearing and Cleaning Equipment	Rider- or walker-operated, self-propelled
39 II A	Materials Handling Equipment	Conveyors, hand trucks, towveyer trucks
41 I A	Air Conditioning Equipment	Domestic and window units
41 I B	Air Conditioning Equipment	Central air and export-use window units
41 III A	Appliances	Household refrigerators
41 III B	Refrigeration Equipment	Drinking water dispensers
42 I	Firefighting Equipment and Supplies	Fire extinguishers, accessories
42 II	Safety and Rescue Equipment	Breathing apparatus, safety climbing equipment, welders' protective equipment
42 III	Safety Equipment	Shoe decontamination unit
42 IV A	Safety Equipment	Nonprescription safety glasses
44 I A	Air Treatment and Conditioning Equipment	Air cleaners, portable humidifiers, dehumidifiers, heat pumps
45 IV A	Sanitation Equipment	Industrial incinerators
45 VII A	Plumbing and Heating Equipment	Domestic water heaters, gas and electric
45 VIII A	Plumbing and Sanitation Equipment	Household garbage disposers
46 I A	Water Purification Equipment	Water stills, storage tanks, purity conductivity meters, and reverse osmosis systems
47	Pipe	Culvert, steel and aluminum
47 II A	Pipe	Plastic
49 I A	Maintenance and Repair Shop Equipment	Hydraulic jacks, heat guns, and auger machines
49 I B	Maintenance and Repair Shop Equipment	Motor vehicle and miscellaneous maintenance and repair shop equipment
49 II	Maintenance and Repair Shop Equipment	Ultrasonic cleaning systems and accessories

Schedule Number	Name	Description or Typical Items
51 I A	Hand and Power Tools	Pneumatic, hydraulic, powder-actuated, gasoline engine, and special-purpose drill bits
51 II A	Hand and Power Tools	Electric
52	Measuring Tools	Measuring tapes
54 I A	Prefabricated Structures	Buildings, enclosures, and sound-controlled rooms
54 II A	Scaffolding, Shoring, Work and Service Platforms, Steps	Portable
56 III A	Construction and Building Materials	Solar control film and screens
58 II	Communication Equipment	Message- and data-transmitting equipment and background music systems
58 III B	Communication Equipment	Professional audio and video recording equipment
58 V A	Communication Supplies	Audio magnetic tape, reels and cartridges; video magnetic tape, cassettes, and so on
58 V C	Communication Supplies	Instrumentation recording tape, reels
58 V D	Communication Supplies	Recording tapes, audio cassettes, reels
58 VI	Communication Equipment	Telephone, intercom P.A. systems
58 VII	Communication Equipment	Radio transmitting–receiving equipment
58 IX	Communication Equipment	Telemetry, laser, radionavigation, radar, underwater sound, signal data
59 III	Electronic Components	Microelectronic circuit devices
61 I	Batteries	6- and 12-volt lead acid, automotive
61 II	Batteries	Heavy duty, storage
61 III	Batteries	Dry cell
61 IV A	Batteries	Automotive, storage, wet-charged
61 V A	Power and Distribution Equipment	Portable generators
61 V B	Power and Distribution Equipment	Nonrotating battery chargers
61 VII A	Transformers	For refrigerators
62 I	Lighting Fixtures and Lamps	Household
62 II	Lighting Fixtures and Lamps	Light sets, emergency and auxiliary
62 III	Lighting Fixtures and Lamps	Fluorescent and incandescent
62, 67	Lamps	Electrical and photographic
63	Alarm and Signal Systems	Transit and traffic signals, miscellaneous alarms and signals
65 I A	Drugs and Pharmaceuticals	Drugs and pharmaceutical products
65 I B	Drugs and Pharmaceuticals	Drugs and pharmaceutical products
65 II B	Medical and Veterinary Equipment	Surgical instruments and supplies
65 II C	Dental Equipment and Supplies	Operatory and laboratory
65 II D	Medical and Dental Equipment	Monitoring, electronic, patient aids, tables, physiotherapy equipment
65 III A	Medical and Dental Supplies	Gloves, medical and surgical
65 IV	Medical and Dental Supplies	Prescription opthalmic lenses, glasses
65 V A	Medical and Dental Supplies	Film, X-ray, 90-second processing
65 V B,C	Medical and Dental Supplies	X-ray film, medical and dental
65 VI	Medical and Dental Supplies	Antibacterial deodorant soap
66 I A	Instruments and Laboratory Equipment	Measuring and drafting instruments
66 I B	Instruments and Laboratory Equipment	Magnifiers and reducing glasses, lettering sets, electronic distance-measuring equipment
66 II B	Instruments and Laboratory Supplies	Glass, plastic, metal lab ware; lab distillation and demineralizing systems
66 II C	Instruments and Laboratory Equipment	Microscopes, centrifuges, pH meters

Schedule Number	Name	Description or Typical Items
66 II D	Instruments and Laboratory Supplies	Industrial radiographic X-ray film
66 II E	Instruments and Laboratory Equipment	Analytical balances and scales
66 II F	Instruments and Laboratory Equipment	Amplifiers: low frequency, power, pulse
66 II G	Instruments and Laboratory Equipment	Graphic recording instruments
66 II H	Instruments and Laboratory Equipment	Measuring and test instruments
66 II I,J	Instruments and Laboratory Equipment	Microwave and low-frequency instruments
66 II L	Instruments and Laboratory Equipment	Power supplies, transducers, servos
66 II M	Instruments and Laboratory Equipment	Spectrophotometers, densitometers, and so on
66 II N	Instruments and Laboratory Equipment	Analyzers, chromatographs, colony counters, dilutors, pipetters
66 II O	Instruments and Laboratory Equipment	Laboratory apparatus, furniture, refrigerators, freezers
66 II Q	Instruments and Laboratory Equipment	Oceanographic, environmental, weather
66 III	Instruments and Laboratory Equipment	Time recorders, date and time stamps
66 V A	Instruments and Laboratory Equipment	Solar and wind energy systems and components
66 VI A	Laboratory Equipment	Glassware and supplies
67 II B	Photographic Supplies	Film, chemicals, paper
67 III B	Photo Equipment	Cameras, projectors, developing equipment
67 IV A	Microphoto Supplies and Mobile Projection Stands	Direct-positive and thermal developing, duplicating film, mobile projection stands
68 I A	Chemicals and Chemical Products	Bulk sodium chloride
68 I B	Chemicals, Chemical Products	Calcium chloride
68 I C	Chemicals, Chemical Products	Bleach, laundry and household
68 II A	Chemicals, Chemical Products	Herbicides
68 III A	Chemicals, Chemical Products	Medical gases
68 III C	Chemicals, Chemical Products	Dry ice
68 III D	Chemicals, Chemical Products	Liquefied petroleum gases
68 III E & F	Chemicals, Chemical Products	Refrigerant fluorocarbons and sulfur hexafluoride
68 III G	Chemicals, Chemical Products	Helium
68 III H	Chemicals, Chemical Products	Fire-extinguishing fluorocarbons
68 III K	Chemicals, Chemical Products	Oxygen, aviator's breathing
68 III L	Chemicals, Chemical Products	Industrial gases in cylinders
68 III M	Chemicals, Chemical Products	Industrial gases, liquid, bulk, cylinders
68 V	Chemicals, Chemical Products	Boiler feedwater and a-c compounds
68 VI	Chemicals, Chemical Products	Sanitizers, deodorants, disinfectant cleaners
69	Training Courses, Aids, Devices	Teaching, reading, test-scoring machines
70 X	Data Processing Storage and Related Equipment	Storage, handling, transport equipment for data processing supplies
70 XI	Data Processing Supplies	Edp ½" tape, 1600 and 6250 bpi
71 I A	Household Furniture	Ranch style
71 I B	Household Furniture	Early American and 18th-Century English
71 II A	Household Furniture	Upholstered living room
71 II B	Household Furniture	Modular multiple and individual seating
71 III	Household Furniture	Danish, traditional, and modern
71 V A	Office Furniture	Tables, folding legs; folding chairs, wood and metal

Schedule Number	Name	Description or Typical Items
71 V B	Office Furniture	Bulletin boards and key cabinets
71 V C	Office Furniture	Steel vertical blueprint filing cabinets, roll drawing files
71 V D	Office and Field Furniture	Map and plan filing cabinets, modular steel, folding end table
71 V E	Office Furniture	Contemporary steel filing cabinets, shelf files, card files
71 V F	Office Furniture	Freestanding partitions
71 VI A	Office Furniture	Executive traditional wood
71 VII A	Household Furniture	Metal indoor-outdoor, rec room, lobby
71 VII B	Household Furniture	Metal frame dormitory
71 VIII A	Office Furniture	Executive unitized wood
71 X A,B	Furniture	Special purpose, classroom, auditorium
71 XI A,B	Office Furniture	Security filing cabinets, safes, vaults
71 XII A	Office Furniture	Executive, modern, wood and metal
71 XIII A,B	Library Furniture	Wood and metal
71 XIV A	Shop Furniture	Desks, benches, tables
71 XV	Household Furniture	Traditional wood, dinette tables and chairs
71 XVI B	Household Furniture	Motel-type and sofa beds
71 XVII	Hospital Furniture	Patient's room
71 XIX	Furniture	Contemporary wall units, office use
71 XX	Household Furniture	Contemporary oak
71 XXI	Office Furniture	Acoustical partitions
71 XXII	Furniture	Lounge and reception room, recliners
71 XXIII	Household and Office Accessories	Artificial plants, planters, urns, art
71 XXV	Furniture	Storage cabinets
71 XXVI A	Casual Style and Household Furniture	Rattan, plastic, outdoor metal casual
71 XXVII A	Furniture *	Office and household, centurion by Federal Prison Industries
71 XXVII B	Office Furniture *	Contemporary centurion by Federal Prison Industries
71 XXVIII A	Office Furniture	Lateral files, special sizes and uses
71 XXIX A	Office Furniture	Storage and sorting cabinets, bins
71 XXX A	Office Furniture	Cabinets and desks, card punch and programmer
71 XXXI A	Furniture	Directory boards
72 I A	Household and Commercial Furnishings	Carpets, rugs, carpet tiles, cushions
72 I B	Household and Commercial Furnishings	Floor coverings: tile, linoleum, vinyl
72 I C	Household and Commercial Furnishings	Entranceway carpet mats, mattings
72 I D	Household and Commercial Furnishings	Special-purpose carpet
72 II	Household and Commercial Furnishings	Window shades: cloth, vinyl, fiberglass
72 III A	Commercial Furnishings	Shopping handcarts, nesting
72 V	Household and Commercial Furnishings	Draperies, bedspreads, drapery hardware, cubicle curtains, shower curtains
72 VI A	Household and Commercial Furnishings	Venetial blinds
72 VII A	Household and Commercial Furnishings	Plastic trash receptacles

*Supplied exclusively by Federal Prison Industries, part of the Bureau of Prisons, Department of Justice.

Schedule Number	Name	Description or Typical Items
73 III	Food Service, Handling, Refrigeration, Storage, and Cleaning Equipment	Cabinet/shower (nonrefrigerating, nonheating), cooking equipment, dishwashing equipment, food preparation equipment
73 IV A	Appliances	Household gas ranges
73 IV B	Appliances	Commercial and household electric ranges
73 V A	Appliances	Household dishwashers
74 I	Office Machines	Electric typewriters, composing, photo-composing, and word-processing machines
74 II, III	Office Machines	Adding, calculating, dictating, miscellaneous
74 IV	Visible Record Equipment	Book, cabinet, individual style frames, posting and ledger trays, tub files, and so on
74 V	Office Machines	Manual typewriters, portable and nonportable
74 VIII	Office Machines	Electric erasers, embossing, and stencil-cutting machines
74 XIII A	Word-Processing Supplies	Magnetic data recording cards
75 I C	Office Supplies	Special-use papers, overlay sheets, and so on
75 I D	Office Supplies	Plotting paper and supplies
75 II A	Office Supplies	Pencils, marking tapes, chart supplies, and so on
75 II B	Office Supplies	Looseleaf binders, label tapes, staplers, map tacks, and so on
75 IV A,B	Office Supplies	Rubber stamps
75 IV C	Office Supplies	Pre-inked rubber stamps
75 V	Office Supplies	Envelopes, mailing
75 VII	Office Supplies	U.S. government national credit cards
75 VIII A	Office Supplies	Tab cards, aperture cards, copy cards
75 IX	Office Devices	Contemporary desk accessories
76 I	Publications	Dictionaries, encyclopedias, maps, and so on
76 II	Publications	Law, tax, reporting periodicals
76 III A	Publications	Medical, trade, text, technical
76 III B	Publications	Medical, trade, text, technical
77 I	Home Entertainment Equipment	Phono records, cassettes, 8-track tapes
77 II	Musical Instruments	Instruments, amplifiers, accessories
77 III	Home Entertainment Equipment	TV, radio, phonographs, recorders
78 I A	Recreational, Athletic Equipment	Athletic and sporting goods
78 I B	Athletic, Recreational Equipment	Indoor recreational, gym equipment
78 I C	Athletic, Recreational Equipment	Outdoor
79 I A	Cleaning Equipment, Supplies	Vacuum cleaners, shampooers, polishers
79 I B	Cleaning Equipment, Supplies	Vacuum cleaners, shampooers, polishers
79 II A	Cleaning Equipment, Supplies	Detergents
80 I A	Paint	Tree-marking paint
80 II A	Paint	Gloss and semi-gloss latex
81 I A	Packaging, Packing Supplies	Cushioning materials
81 II A	Packaging, Packing Supplies	Steel and nonmetallic strapping
84 II A	Clothing and Furnishings	Special-purpose clothing
84 II B	Clothing and Furnishings	Footwear and special-purpose clothing
84 III A	Clothing and Furnishings	Men's and young men's
84 III B & C	Clothing and Furnishings	Misses', women's, boys', girls', infants'
84 IV	Jewelry	Civilian career service emblems, plaques
84 V A	Clothing and Footwear	Athletic and recreational
87 IV	Agricultural Supplies	Seeds
87 V	Agricultural Supplies	Fertilizers and hydrated lime
89 I	Subsistence	Nonperishable
89 IV A	Subsistence	Freeze-dried foods
93 II	Nonmetallic Fabricated Materials	Reflectorized fabric, sheeting, tape
99 III	Miscellaneous Supplies	Cutout letters, numbers, striping tape
99 IV A	Signs	Signs and components, mounting fixtures
99 VI A	Trophies and Awards	Trophies, awards, plaques, pins, cups
733	Transcripts	Stenographic reporting services

Schedule Number	Name	Description or Typical Items
733 III	Services	Visual arts, graphics
739 I A	Services	Rental and servicing of portable toilets
739 VI B	Services	Rental of measuring and test instruments
739 VII A	Services	Microfilming, surveys, filming, film processing, aperture card mounting, roll-to-roll duplicating, microfiche
751	Motor Vehicle Rental/Traveler's Pocket Guide	Without driver
781 I & II	Professional Film Processing and Videotape Processing	Motion picture, filmstrip and slide, videotape duplication
782	Distribution of Audiovisual Materials (Free Loan)	Motion picture films, videotapes, cassettes, filmstrips, slides, audiotapes
807 I A	Services	Clinical laboratory tests (human or animal), electrocardiogram analysis, tissue microslide preparation, rental and servicing of specialized medical equipment
823	Services	Lending library

FEDERAL SUPPLY SCHEDULE
Multiple Award

FSC 76   PART I
CLASSES 7610 & 7640
PUBLICATIONS
DICTIONARIES, ENCYCLOPEDIAS, OTHER REFERENCE
BOOKS AND PAMPHLETS, MAPS, ATLASES, CHARTS,
AND GLOBES

FEBRUARY 1, 1979 - JANUARY 31, 1980

ISSUED MARCH 9, 1979

GENERAL SERVICES ADMINISTRATION

FEDERAL SUPPLY SERVICE   O1SC 7601

GSA DC-01902753

76, I

CONTENTS	ORDERING INSTRUCTIONS

GENERAL INSTRUCTIONS

1. **INFORMATION CONTAINED IN THIS SCHEDULE.** This Schedule lists contractors to whom awards have been made. Contractors who were listed in the previous Schedule but have not been awarded contracts are not listed herein and, if awarded contracts, will be published in cumulative editions to this Schedule. New information will be identified by a vertical line in the right hand margin. Ordering offices should review this Schedule to determine: special item numbers; item name and description; contractor's address, telephone number, and contract number; effective date of award; and ordering instructions.

2. **INFORMATION CONTAINED IN THE CONTRACTOR'S PRICELIST/CATALOG.** Ordering offices should review the pricelist to determine: ordering address; payment address; delivery point; delivery time; discounts; prices; business size; foreign items; maximum order limitations; models offered; and, if applicable, warranties, terms and conditions of rental, maintenance, and/or repair; export packing and point of production.

3. **GEOGRAPHIC COVERAGE.** The 50 States, Washington, DC, and Puerto Rico.

4. **MANDATORY USERS.** All departments and independent establishments, including wholly-owned Government corporations, in the executive branch of the Federal Government (except the U.S. Postal Service) and the DC Government.

5. **NONMANDATORY USERS.** The following activities are authorized to use this Schedule on a nonmandatory basis: (i) Federal agencies other than those covered by the mandatory use provision and nonappropriated fund activities as prescribed in FPMR 101-26.000, (ii) Government contractors authorized in writing by a Federal agency pursuant to 41 CFR 1-5.9, and (iii) mixed ownership Government corporations (as defined in the Government Corporation Control Act). Contractors are encouraged to honor orders from these activities. In the event the contractor is unwilling to accept such an order, the contractor will return it by mailing or delivering it to the ordering office within seven working days after receipt. Failure to return an order will constitute acceptance whereupon all provisions of the contract shall apply with respect to such order.

    NOTE: Questions regarding agencies/activities authorized to use this Schedule should be directed to the Schedules Information Center. (See Paragraph 1a, ORDERING INSTRUCTIONS)

6. **MULTIPLE AWARDS.** Multiple award Federal Supply Schedules cover contracts made with more than one supplier for comparable items at either the same or different prices for delivery to the same geographic area.

7. **CATALOGS AND PRICELISTS.** If catalogs and/or pricelists have not been received and are required or if additional copies are required, ordering offices should communicate directly with the contractor for copies of such material. See LIST OF CONTRACTORS for telephone numbers.

8. **INCORPORATION OF FORMS.** The following forms apply to this Schedule:

    a. Standard Form 32, General Provisions (Supply Contract), April 1975 edition, with the following modification: Article 15 is amended by deleting the words "at hard labor".

    b. GSA Form 1424, GSA Supplemental Provisions, June 1977 edition, except Clause 4, Variation in Quantity, is deleted and no variation in quantity is permitted in deliveries.

    c. GSA Form 2891, Instructions to Users of Federal Supply Schedule, May 1977 edition; except paragraph 9, PAYMENTS is deleted and paragraph 20 of the ORDERING INSTRUCTIONS is substituted.

ORDERING INSTRUCTIONS

1. **GSA ASSISTANCE.**

    a. For information of a general nature write or call:

    > GENERAL SERVICES ADMINISTRATION (FPS)
    > SCHEDULES INFORMATION CENTER
    > WASHINGTON, DC   20406
    >   Telephone: (703) 557-8177
    > AUTOVON: 225-9684

    b. For additional copies of Schedules or for copies of the Federal Supply Schedule Program Guide, write or call:

    > GENERAL SERVICES ADMINISTRATION (8BRC)
    > PUBLICATIONS DISTRIBUTION CENTER
    > DENVER, CO   80225
    >   Telephone: (303) 234-4195

    c. Contracting Officer mailing address:

    > GENERAL SERVICES ADMINISTRATION (1FPQ)
    > CONTRACTING OFFICER (FSC 76 PART I)
    > J W McCORMACK P O & CTHSE BLDG
    > BOSTON, MA   02109

2. **PROMPT PAYMENT DISCOUNTS.** Discount terms should be shown on all ordering documents.

3. **POINT OF DELIVERY.** At destination within the area defined in GENERAL INSTRUCTIONS, Paragraph 3, Geographic Coverage.

4. **TIME OF DELIVERY.** See contractor's catalog/pricelist.

5. **IMPREST FUNDS (PETTY CASH).** The contractor agrees to accept cash payment for purchases made under the terms of the contract in conformance with FPR 1-3.604.

6. **SMALL REQUIREMENTS.** No ordering activity is obligated to place orders amounting to $50 or less.

7. **MINIMUM ORDER.** See contractor's catalog/pricelist under "Small Requirements" for lowest value order which will be accepted.

8. **MAXIMUM ORDER LIMITATIONS.** Purchase orders cannot exceed the amount(s) shown in the contractor's pricelist/catalog.

9. **INSPECTION.** This Schedule provides for inspection at destination.

10. **PACKAGING AND PACKING.** Standard commercial practice (Level C of Federal Standard 102).

    If special or unusual packing is required, such packing requirements should be arranged with the contractor by the ordering activity.

11. **BUY AMERICAN DIFFERENTIALS.** Buy American differentials must be applied by the ordering activity before placing an order if foreign and domestic products are listed under the same special item number and both products will satisfy the requirement.

12. **RECEIVING DOCK HOURS.** State on the purchase order the time (local daylight or standard) that material can be received at destination.

13. **RECEIVING DOCK LIMITATIONS.** If there are limitations on size (height, width, or length) or weight of vehicle that can be accommodated at delivery point, state them on the purchase order.

14. **DELIVERY ADDRESS.** If delivery address is vague, include instructions on the purchase order that will assist the carrier in reaching the delivery point.

15. **JUSTIFICATION.** When orders are placed at other than the lowest price available under a special item number and (1) the cost is more than $500 per line item, ordering activities must justify the purchase of the higher priced item; (2) the cost is $500 or less per line item, ordering activities should refer to their agency procurement regulations to determine if justification is required.

16. COPIES OF INVOICES. If more than one copy of the invoice is required, state clearly on purchase orders the number of invoices needed.

17. AGENCIES SUBMITTING REQUISITIONS TO GSA FOR PURCHASE. For items contained in this Schedule, the requisition, if citing National Stock Numbers, must also contain Special Item Number, as shown in the Schedule, manufacturer's name or manufacturer's code, brand name, model, and/or part number.

18. LATEST EDITIONS REQUIRED. All books shall be the latest edition and shall be identified. In the event a revised or new edition is published during the contract period, the following provisions shall apply:

(a) CONTRACTOR will notify the contracting officer of the change 60 days prior to the publication date or as soon as information is available.

(b) If the list price of the new edition remains the same as the one contracted for, there shall be no change other than to note that the new edition is available. If there is a list price change, the Government will compute the discount reflected from the list price and apply the same percentage discount indicated in the contractor's pricelist/catalog to the new list price, to reach the new contract price. No revision or amendment to the contract will be issued and the contractor is obligated to perform on a continuing basis.

(c) Upon publication of a new or revised edition, the earlier edition will no longer be on contract and contractor is expressly prohibited from shipping same. If orders are received showing the old edition and/or price and the computed price of the new edition is not more than 25% higher than the previous edition, the contractor is authorized to ship without prior approval of the ordering office. No amendment to the purchase order is required and payment will be made on properly computed invoice in accordance with sub-paragraph (b) above. If increase in price is more than 25%, contractor is to promptly notify ordering office of the availability of the new edition and price, and upon approval shall ship new edition. Amendment to the purchase order is required and payment will be made accordingly.

19. OUT-OF-STOCK. Contractors will be obligated to notify ordering offices, within delivery time specified in contract, of books which are out-of-stock at publisher's warehouse, advising approximate availability date. Ordering offices shall instruct contractors within 20 days after date of notification to "Back Order" or "Cancel". However, contractor shall not be requested to "Back-Order" unless books are expected within 60 days after date of notice. If instructions are not received by contractor within the time specified, item shall be automatically canceled from order.

20. PAYMENT. Advance payment for periodicals and subscription items is authorized by the Act of June 12, 1930, 46 Statute, 580, as amended by Public Law 87-91 (31 USCA 530) enacted July 20, 1961. Therefore, contractors shall be paid for such items by ordering offices, upon submission of properly certified invoices or vouchers, at prices stipulated in contractor's pricelist/catalog, less deductions, if any, as provided. "Subscription" items include any publication that covers a series printed on a periodic basis or any series of a predetermined number of issues the price of which is set in advance:

(a) Partial Payment. Partial payment of invoices WILL BE MADE without undue delay provided the items have been received. It is not necessary for complete delivery to be made before partial payment is due. Payment of invoices will not be withheld because of failure of the contractor to supply books which are out-of-print, out-of-stock, to be published at a later date, or in case of shortages, i.e., discrepancies between invoices and receiving documents. In such cases, items in question will be deleted on the voucher by indicating the item number and reason for deduction. Contractor will be advised of such deduction. This information will be placed on the face of the voucher at the time the voucher is prepared for payment. INVOICES WILL NOT be returned to the contractor for correction due to any of the above mentioned conditions. Payment for items received subsequent to administrative deductions taken on partial payment of invoices may be effected by cross-referencing the voucher on which the administrative deduction was taken when effecting prior payments, after receipt of invoice from supplier.

(b) Time Discount. In the event it is necessary to return invoices to the contractor for correction, such invoices must be returned by the fiscal officer within the time discount period specified. The discount will be computed from date of delivery or from date a correct invoice is received in the office specified by the Government, whichever is later.

(c) Shortages or Damage in Transit. Contractor shall be notified within 15 days of shortage or damage in shipment. Prompt notification is necessary so that carrier's records may still be available.

21. BLANKET PURCHASE ARRANGEMENTS. Blanket Purchase Arrangements are authorized under this Schedule. The overall dollar value of a Blanket Purchase Arrangement may exceed the contract maximum order limitation; however, no single order or series of orders placed within a short period of time under the Blanket Purchase Arrangement may exceed the contract Maximum Order Limitation.

76, I

LIST OF SUPPLIES AND SERVICES

INDEX NO.	SPECIAL ITEM NO.	SUPPLIES OR SERVICES	INDEX NO.	SPECIAL ITEM NO.	SUPPLIES OR SERVICES
		LISTED BELOW EACH ITEM DESCRIPTION ARE THE CONTRACTORS TO WHOM AWARDS HAVE BEEN MADE.	8	462-8	ENCYCLOPEDIAS. Grolier Educational Corp MacMillan Professional & Library Serv Div
1	462-1	ALMANACS. Federal Employees News Digest Inc Uniformed Services Almanac Inc (06839)	9	462-9	BOOKS, GEOGRAPHY. Follett Publishing Co G & C Merriam Co
2	462-2	BOOKS, FICTION. Follett Publishing Co MacMillan Professional & Library Serv Div	10	462-10	BOOKS, HISTORY. Follett Publishing Co MacMillan Professional & Library Serv Div
3	462-3	BOOKS, INSTRUCTION. Copley & Assoc Emerson Books Inc Follett Publishing Co Govt Marketing News Inc Instructional Resources Corp National Learning Corp Palmer/Paulson Assoc Geo Watson & Co	11	462-11	BOOKS, MEDICAL. Geo F Cram Co Inc G & C Merriam Co MacMillan Professional & Library Serv Div
			12	462-12	PAMPHLETS, INSTRUCTION. Dray Publications
4	462-4	BOOKS, REFERENCE. Carroll Publishing Co Marshall Cavendish Corp Emerson Books Inc The Feminist Committee Follett Publishing Co Govt Marketing News Inc Houghton Mifflin Co MacMillan Professional & Library Serv Div G & C Merriam Co Micro Form Review Inc Political Research Inc Procurement Assoc Inc Reginald Bishop Forster & Assoc Inc Undine Corp Uniformed Services Almanac Inc (06873)	13	462-13	PAMPHLETS, REFERENCE. Dray Publications
			14	462-14	PAMPHLETS, TECHNICAL. Dray Publications
			15	462-15	SAFETY POSTERS. Dray Publications L G Harkins & Co Inc
5	462-5	BOOKS, TECHNICAL. Eastman Kodak Co Emerson Books Inc H M Gousha Co MacMillan Professional & Library Serv Div National Standards Assoc	16	462-16	BOOKS, TEXT. S W Bond Emerson Books Inc Follett Publishing Co MacMillan Professional & Library Serv Div National Learning Corp
6	462-6	DICTIONARIES. Carroll Publishing Co G & C Merriam Co	17	462-17	ATLASES. Follett Publishing Co G & C Merriam Co MacMillan Professional & Library Serv Div Nystrom
7	462-7	DIRECTORIES. Joyner & Assoc Inc MacRae's Blue Book Co Micro Form Review Inc National Standards Assoc Oxbridge Communications Reginald Bishop Forster & Assoc Inc	18	462-18	GLOBES, CELESTIAL, TERRESTRIAL, WORLD. Geo F Cram Co Inc Nystrom
			19	462-19	MAPS (EXCEPT TRAINING AIDS). Geo F Cram Co Inc Nystrom

76, I

LIST OF CONTRACTORS

CONTRACTS AWARDED AS A RESULT OF NEGOTIATION PURSUANT TO SECTION 302 (C)(10) OF THE FEDERAL PROPERTY AND ADMINISTRATIVE SERVICES
ACT OF 1949, 63 STAT. 393, AS AMENDED (41 U.S.C. 252 (C)(10))

Listed in the Contract Number column is the business size indicator "s" for small business and "o" for other than small business,
"a" for minority business enterprises, and "b" for other than minority enterprises

CONTRACT GS-01S-	CONTRACTOR, ADDRESS & TELEPHONE	CONTRACT EFFECTIVE	CONTRACT GS-01S-	CONTRACTOR, ADDRESS & TELEPHONE	CONTRACT EFFECTIVE
s/b 06901	S W BOND BOX 253 MINOT, ND 58701 (701) 839-5513	13 FEB 79	s/b 06897	L G HARKINS & CO INC 239 FOURTH AVE PITTSBURGH, PA 15222 (412) 281-3229	8 FEB 79
s/b 06898	CARROLL PUBLISHING CO 1058 THOMAS JEFFERSON ST NW WASHINGTON, DC 20007 (202) 333-8620	8 FEB 79	o/b 06852	HOUGHTON MIFFLIN CO DICTIONARY DIV 2 PARK ST BOSTON, MA 02107 (617) 725-5172	13 FEB 79
s/b 06889	MARSHALL CAVENDISH CORP 147 W MERRICK RD FREEPORT, NY 11520 (516) 546-4200	8 FEB 79	s/b 06855	INSTRUCTIONAL RESOURCES CORP 251 E 50TH ST NEW YORK, NY 10022 (212) 688-4646	8 FEB 79
s/b 06900	COPLEY & ASSOC SA 2030 M ST NW - SUITE 602 WASHINGTON, DC 20036 (202) 223-4934	9 FEB 79	s/b 06858	JOYNER & ASSOC INC 11250 ROGER BACON DR RESTON, VA 22090 (703) 437-5060	15 FEB 79
s/b 06859	GEO F CRAM CO INC 301 S LA SALLE ST INDIANAPOLIS, IN 46206 (317) 635-5564	13 FEB 79	o/b 06851	MacMILLAN PROFESSIONAL & LIBRARY SERVICES DIV OF MacMILLAN PUBLISHING CO INC 866 THIRD AVE NEW YORK, NY 10022 (212) 935-5620	13 FEB 79
s/b 06854	DRAY PUBLICATIONS INC ROUTE 5 DEERFIELD, MA 01342 (413) 773-5491	8 FEB 79	s/b 06838	MacRAE'S BLUE BOOK CO 100 SHORE DR HINSDALE, IL 60521 (312) 325-7880	13 FEB 79
o/b 06834	EASTMAN KODAK CO 343 STATE ST ROCHESTER, NY 14650 (716) 724-4423	9 FEB 79	o/b 06842	G & C MERRIAM CO 47 FEDERAL ST SPRINGFIELD, MA 01101 (413) 734-3134	8 FEB 79
s/b 06895	EMERSON BOOKS INC REYNOLDS LANE BUCHANAN, NY 10511 (914) 739-3506	9 FEB 79	s/b 06893	MICRO FORM REVIEW INC 520 RIVERSIDE AVE WESTPORT, CT 06880 (203) 266-6967	13 FEB 79
s/b 06831	FEDERAL EMPLOYEES NEWS DIGEST INC BOX 457 MERRIFIELD, VA 22116 (703) 533-3031	7 FEB 79	s/b 06843	NATIONAL LEARNING CORP 212 MICHAEL DR SYOSSET, NY 11791 (516) 921-8888	13 FEB 79
s/b 06832	THE FEMINIST COMMITTEE 3921 LAND O'LAKES DR NE ATLANTA, GA 30342 (404) 231-0988	8 FEB 79	s/b 06856	NATIONAL STANDARDS ASSOC 4827 RUGBY AVE WASHINGTON, DC 20014 (301) 951-0333	13 FEB 79
s/b 06844	FOLLETT PUBLISHING CO 1010 W WASHINGTON BLVD CHICAGO, IL 60607 (312) 666-5858	8 FEB 79	o/b 06835	NYSTROM DIV OF CARNATION 3333 ELSTON AVE CHICAGO, IL 60618 (312) 463-1144	13 FEB 79
o/b 06840	REGINALD BISHOP FORSTER & ASSOC INC 121 W FRANKLIN MINNEAPOLIS, MN 55404 (612) 871-1395	13 FEB 79	s/b 06896	OXBRIDGE COMMUNICATIONS 183 MADISON AVE NEW YORK, NY 10016 (212) 689-8524	9 FEB 79
o/b 06903	H M GOUSHA CO BOX 6227 SAN JOSE, CA 95150 (408) 296-1060	13 FEB 79	s/b 06857	PALMER/PAULSON ASSOC 7400 WAUKEGAN RD NILES, IL 60648 (312) 647-7466	13 FEB 79
s/b 06899	GOVERNMENT MARKETING NEWS INC 1001 CONNECTICUT AVE - SUITE 1019 WASHINGTON, DC 20036 (202) 293-6225	9 FEB 79	o/b 06833	POLITICAL RESEARCH INC TEGOLANO AT BENT TREE 16850 DALLAS PARKWAY DALLAS, TX 75248 (214) 386-5827	8 FEB 79
o/b 06841	GROLIER EDUCATIONAL CORP SHERMAN TURNPIKE DANBURY, CT 06816 (203) 792-1200	9 FEB 79			

76, I

LIST OF CONTRACTORS - Continued

CONTRACT GS-01S-	CONTRACTOR, ADDRESS & TELEPHONE	CONTRACT EFFECTIVE	CONTRACT GS-01S-	CONTRACTOR, ADDRESS & TELEPHONE	CONTRACT EFFECTIVE
s/b 06893	PROCUREMENT ASSOC INC 733 N DODSWORTH AVE COVINA, CA 91724 (213) 966-4576	13 FEB 79	s/b 06873	UNIFORMED SERVICES ALMANAC INC BOX 76 WASHINGTON, DC 20044 (703) 532-1631	13 FEB 79
s/b 06860	UNDINE CORP 221 E 78TH ST NEW YORK, NY 10021 (212) 355-2689	13 FEB 79	s/b 06894	GEO WATSON & CO 913 RIDGE RD GREENBELT, MD 20770 (301) 345-8891	8 FEB 79
s/b 06839	UNIFORMED SERVICES ALMANAC INC BOX 76 WASHINGTON, DC 20044 (703) 532-1631	13 FEB 79			

CROSS-REFERENCE TO RELATED SCHEDULES

FSC	PART	SECTION	RELATED ITEMS
			PUBLICATIONS:
76	II	-	law, tax, and reporting periodicals
76	III	A	medical, trade, text, and technical books; and pamphlets
76	III	B	medical, trade, text, and technical books; and pamphlets

-0-

ik

Appendix 5

Your marketing library

Chapter 9 contains a list of publications you can get without charge from government agencies; it's by no means a complete list, but a representative sample. Here are a few of the books and other documents which should be a permanent part of your marketing library, especially if you write proposals.

United States Government Manual (current year), GPO bookstore.

GPO Style Manual, GPO bookstore.

A *good* dictionary.

The free marketing guides from as many government agencies as possible.

The *Commerce Business Daily* (Department of Commerce or GPO), subscription to.

Directory of minority businesses, your area (SBA).

Proposal Preparation Manual, DOT Report No. DOT-RSPA-DPB-50-78-16 (National Technical Information Service, Springfield, VA 22161).

Small Business Guide to Federal R&D (The National Science Foundation, Office of Small Business R&D, 1800 G Street, NW, Washington, DC 20550).

The *Government Marketing News,* subscription to (a monthly publication on proposal writing, available from Government Marketing News, Box 6067, Wheaton, MD 20906).

Program Guide, Federal Supply Schedule, Stock No. 022-005-0012-0 (GPO bookstore).

If you write proposals, you should keep the following information on file. These items should be readily available so that you do not need to begin a search for them in the frantic last hours of proposal writing.

Up-to-date resumes of incumbent, permanent staff.

Resumes of available special consultants.

Copies of all your own past proposals, particularly the successful ones.

Copies of all competitor proposals you can acquire.

Information on all competitors, such as annual reports, brochures, capability statements, and so on.

Standard capability statements for your own organization.

Federal Contracts Opportunities Report, subscription (biweekly publication) and/or *Federal Grants Opportunities Report* (also biweekly), The Proposal Writer's Kit, four 60-minute audio cassettes (recorded seminar presentation) and a guidance manual, Plus Publications, Inc., 2626 Pennsylvania Avenue, NW, Washington, DC 20037.

Appendix 6

How to get on mailing lists for surplus bids

Property the government finds surplus is sold, sometimes by holding public auctions, more frequently by soliciting sealed bids. The property is enormously variable, reflecting the variety of government purchasing, and includes all kinds of equipment, raw materials, land, timber, buildings, furniture, and other goods. Some of it is in excellent condition, and in some cases may even be new and unused, while some is in such poor condition that its chief value lies in what may be salvaged.

Sales of surplus are listed in the *Commerce Business Daily* almost every day of the year. However, you can have your name placed on mailing lists so that you will automatically receive solicitations to bid for those items or classes of items you indicate some interest in.

The two federal agencies that handle most of the surplus sold are the General Services Administration and the Department of Defense. In the case of the General Services Administration, each of its regional offices (see listing in Appendix 1) conducts surplus sales in its own region, and you must address a request to the GSA office in each region of interest.

To get on the list for GSA surplus sales, address your letter(s) to:

General Services Administration
Federal Supply Service
Personal Property Division
(Use address(es) from Appendix 1 list)

To apply for DOD surplus sales, request an application form from:

DOD Surplus Sales
P.O. Box 1370
Battle Creek, MI 49016

GSA also sells surplus strategic materials—minerals and metals. To get details and have your name added to its mailing list, write to:

Minerals and Ores Branch
Office of Stockpile Disposal
General Services Administration
18th & F Streets, NW
Washington, DC 20405

Appendix 7

Organization charts of major agencies

The following are the official charts of the major federal agencies, as published by the U.S. government. No presentation of an agency is quite so enlightening as its organization chart. From these charts, you can tell rapidly what the reporting order is, how high in the agency hierarchy any given office or officer is, and how much importance the agency attaches to its various functions and missions. Whether you are already doing business with one of the agencies, preparing to make preliminary marketing contacts, or writing a proposal to the agency and seeking intelligence to aid the proposal effort, study of the agency's organization chart is always a helpful first step.

DEPARTMENT OF COMMERCE

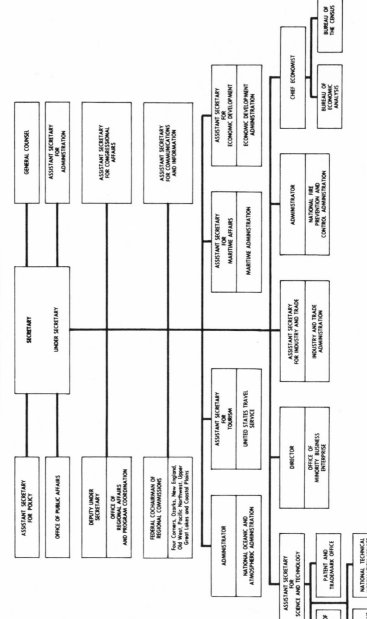

DEPARTMENT OF DEFENSE

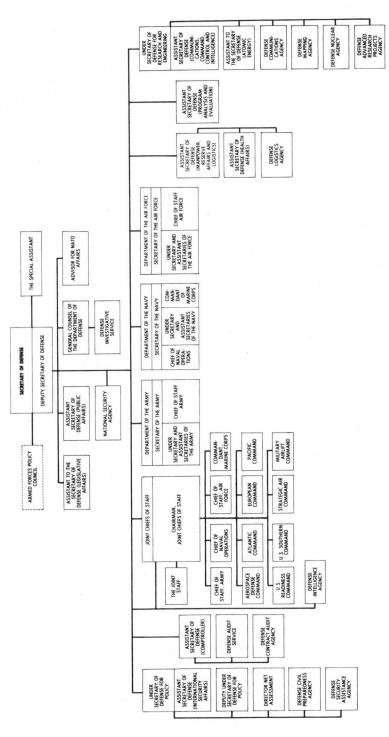

DEPARTMENT OF THE AIR FORCE

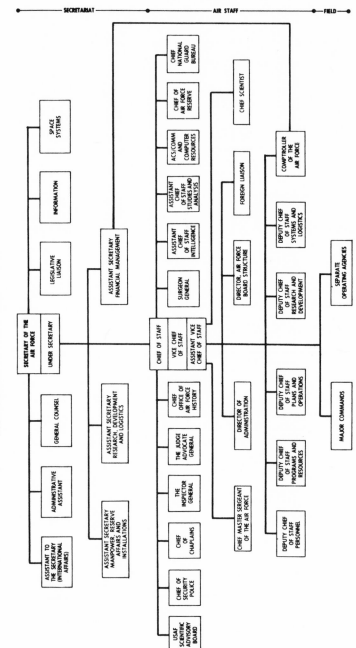

SECRETARIAT ────── AIR STAFF ────── FIELD

DEPARTMENT OF THE ARMY

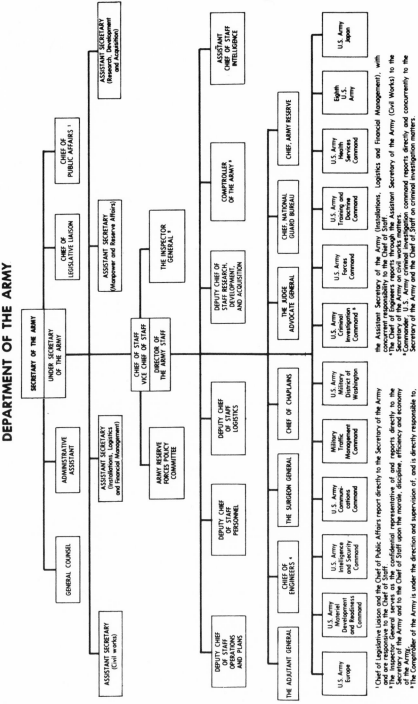

SECRETARY OF THE ARMY

UNDER SECRETARY OF THE ARMY

GENERAL COUNSEL

ADMINISTRATIVE ASSISTANT

CHIEF OF LEGISLATIVE LIAISON [1]

CHIEF OF PUBLIC AFFAIRS [1]

ASSISTANT SECRETARY (Civil works)

ASSISTANT SECRETARY (Installations, Logistics and Financial Management)

ASSISTANT SECRETARY (Manpower and Reserve Affairs)

ASSISTANT SECRETARY (Research, Development and Acquisition)

CHIEF OF STAFF
VICE CHIEF OF STAFF
DIRECTOR OF THE ARMY STAFF

ARMY RESERVE FORCES POLICY COMMITTEE

THE INSPECTOR GENERAL [2]

ASSISTANT CHIEF OF STAFF INTELLIGENCE

DEPUTY CHIEF OF STAFF OPERATIONS AND PLANS

DEPUTY CHIEF OF STAFF PERSONNEL

DEPUTY CHIEF OF STAFF LOGISTICS

DEPUTY CHIEF OF STAFF RESEARCH, DEVELOPMENT, AND ACQUISITION

COMPTROLLER OF THE ARMY [3]

THE ADJUTANT GENERAL

CHIEF OF ENGINEERS [4]

THE SURGEON GENERAL

CHIEF OF CHAPLAINS

THE JUDGE ADVOCATE GENERAL

CHIEF, NATIONAL GUARD BUREAU

CHIEF, ARMY RESERVE

U.S. Army Europe

U.S. Army Materiel Development and Readiness Command

U.S. Army Intelligence and Security Command

U.S. Army Communications Command

Military Traffic Management Command

U.S. Army Military District of Washington

U.S. Army Criminal Investigation Command [5]

U.S. Army Forces Command

U.S. Army Training and Doctrine Command

U.S. Army Health Services Command

Eighth U.S. Army

U.S. Army Japan

[1] Chief of Legislative Liaison and the Chief of Public Affairs report directly to the Secretary of the Army and are responsive to the Chief of Staff

[2] The Inspector General serves as the confidential representative of and reports directly to the Secretary of the Army and to the Chief of Staff upon the morale, discipline, efficiency and economy of the Army.

[3] The Comptroller of the Army is under the direction and supervision of, and is directly responsible to, the Assistant Secretary of the Army (Installations, Logistics and Financial Management), with concurrent responsibility to the Chief of Staff

[4] The Chief of Engineers reports through the Assistant Secretary of the Army (Civil Works) to the Secretary of the Army on civil works matters.

[5] Commander, U.S. Army criminal investigation command reports directly and concurrently to the Secretary of the Army and the Chief of Staff on criminal investigation matters.

DEPARTMENT OF THE NAVY

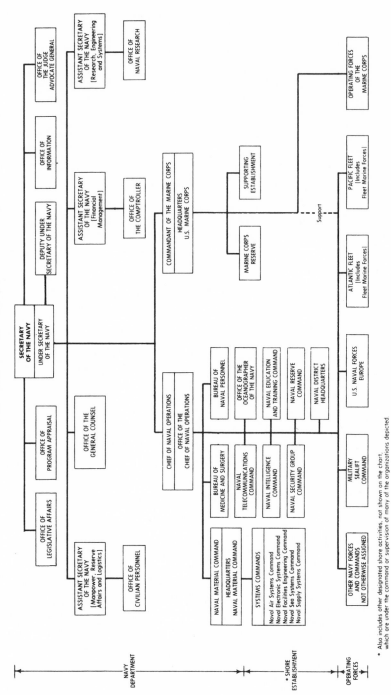

* Also includes other designated shore activities, not shown on the chart, which are under the command or supervision of many of the organizations depicted.

NAVY DEPARTMENT

* SHORE ESTABLISHMENT

OPERATING FORCES

SECRETARY OF THE NAVY
UNDER SECRETARY OF THE NAVY

OFFICE OF LEGISLATIVE AFFAIRS

OFFICE OF PROGRAM APPRAISAL

OFFICE OF INFORMATION

OFFICE OF THE JUDGE ADVOCATE GENERAL

ASSISTANT SECRETARY OF THE NAVY [Manpower, Reserve Affairs and Logistics]

OFFICE OF CIVILIAN PERSONNEL

OFFICE OF THE GENERAL COUNSEL

DEPUTY UNDER SECRETARY OF THE NAVY

ASSISTANT SECRETARY OF THE NAVY [Financial Management]

OFFICE OF THE COMPTROLLER

ASSISTANT SECRETARY OF THE NAVY [Research, Engineering and Systems]

OFFICE OF NAVAL RESEARCH

CHIEF OF NAVAL OPERATIONS
OFFICE OF THE CHIEF OF NAVAL OPERATIONS

COMMANDANT OF THE MARINE CORPS
HEADQUARTERS U.S. MARINE CORPS

NAVAL MATERIAL COMMAND
HEADQUARTERS NAVAL MATERIAL COMMAND

SYSTEMS COMMANDS

Naval Air Systems Command
Naval Electronic Systems Command
Naval Facilities Engineering Command
Naval Sea Systems Command
Naval Supply Systems Command

BUREAU OF MEDICINE AND SURGERY

NAVAL TELECOMMUNICATIONS COMMAND

NAVAL INTELLIGENCE COMMAND

NAVAL SECURITY GROUP COMMAND

BUREAU OF NAVAL PERSONNEL

OFFICE OF THE OCEANOGRAPHER OF THE NAVY

NAVAL EDUCATION AND TRAINING COMMAND

NAVAL RESERVE COMMAND

NAVAL DISTRICT HEADQUARTERS

MARINE CORPS RESERVE

SUPPORTING ESTABLISHMENT

Support

OTHER NAVY FORCES AND COMMANDS (NOT OTHERWISE ASSIGNED)

MILITARY SEALIFT COMMAND

U.S. NAVAL FORCES EUROPE

ATLANTIC FLEET [includes Fleet Marine Forces]

PACIFIC FLEET [includes Fleet Marine Forces]

OPERATING FORCES OF THE MARINE CORPS

DEPARTMENT OF ENERGY

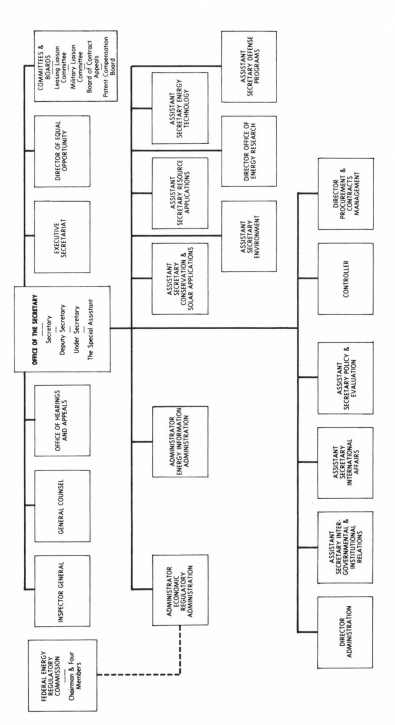

DEPARTMENT OF HEALTH, EDUCATION, AND WELFARE

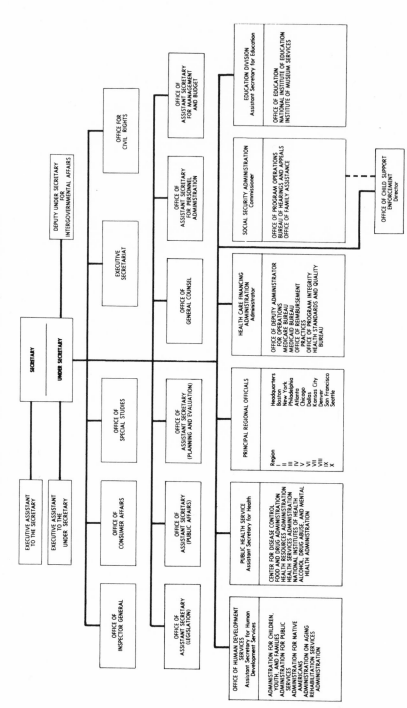

DEPARTMENT OF HOUSING AND URBAN DEVELOPMENT

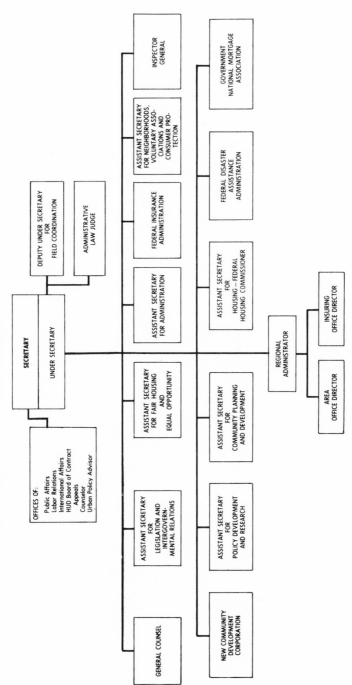

DEPARTMENT OF THE INTERIOR

SECRETARY
UNDER SECRETARY

SOLICITOR

EXECUTIVE ASSISTANT

OFFICE OF CONGRESSIONAL AND LEGISLATIVE AFFAIRS

EXECUTIVE SECRETARIAT

OFFICE OF PUBLIC AFFAIRS

ASSISTANT SECRETARY
POLICY, BUDGET, AND ADMINISTRATION

OFFICE FOR EQUAL OPPORTUNITY

OFFICE OF HEARINGS AND APPEALS

OFFICE OF TERRITORIAL AFFAIRS

ASSISTANT SECRETARY
LAND AND WATER RESOURCES

BUREAU OF RECLAMATION

BUREAU OF LAND MANAGEMENT

OFFICE OF WATER RESEARCH AND TECHNOLOGY

ASSISTANT SECRETARY
INDIAN AFFAIRS

BUREAU OF INDIAN AFFAIRS

ASSISTANT SECRETARY
FISH AND WILDLIFE AND PARKS

U.S. FISH AND WILDLIFE SERVICE

NATIONAL PARK SERVICE

HERITAGE CONSERVATION AND RECREATION SERVICE

ASSISTANT SECRETARY
ENERGY AND MINERALS

BUREAU OF MINES

OFFICE OF MINERALS POLICY AND RESEARCH ANALYSIS

OFFICE OF SURFACE MINING RECLAMATION AND ENFORCEMENT

U.S. GEOLOGICAL SURVEY

NATIONAL MINE HEALTH AND SAFETY ACADEMY

OCEAN MINING ADMINISTRATION

DEPARTMENT OF JUSTICE

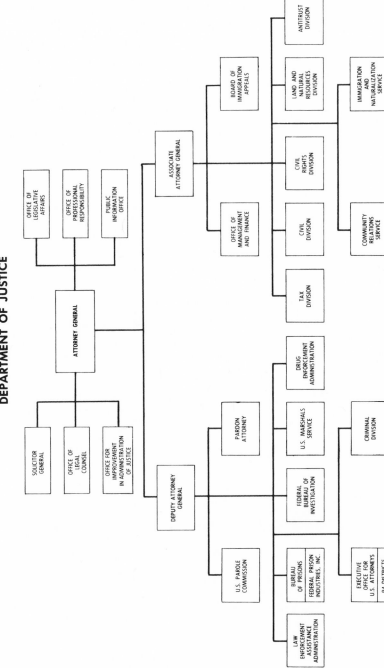

DEPARTMENT OF LABOR

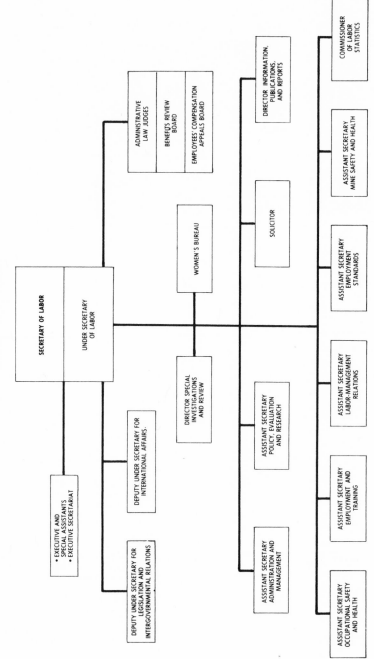

DEPARTMENT OF TRANSPORTATION

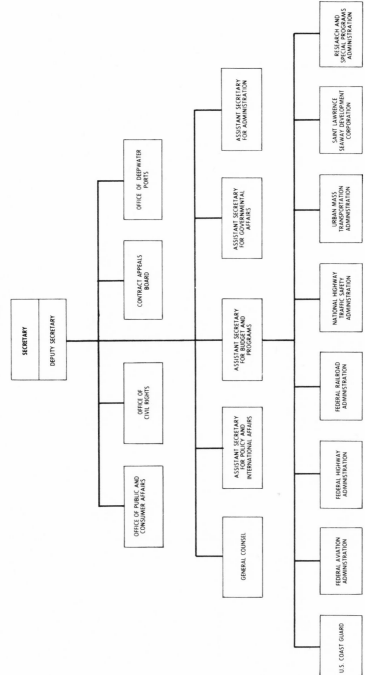

SECRETARY

DEPUTY SECRETARY

OFFICE OF PUBLIC AND CONSUMER AFFAIRS

OFFICE OF CIVIL RIGHTS

CONTRACT APPEALS BOARD

OFFICE OF DEEPWATER PORTS

ASSISTANT SECRETARY FOR ADMINISTRATION

ASSISTANT SECRETARY FOR GOVERNMENTAL AFFAIRS

ASSISTANT SECRETARY FOR BUDGET AND PROGRAMS

GENERAL COUNSEL

ASSISTANT SECRETARY FOR POLICY AND INTERNATIONAL AFFAIRS

U.S. COAST GUARD

FEDERAL AVIATION ADMINISTRATION

FEDERAL HIGHWAY ADMINISTRATION

FEDERAL RAILROAD ADMINISTRATION

NATIONAL HIGHWAY TRAFFIC SAFETY ADMINISTRATION

URBAN MASS TRANSPORTATION ADMINISTRATION

SAINT LAWRENCE SEAWAY DEVELOPMENT CORPORATION

RESEARCH AND SPECIAL PROGRAMS ADMINISTRATION

ENVIRONMENTAL PROTECTION AGENCY

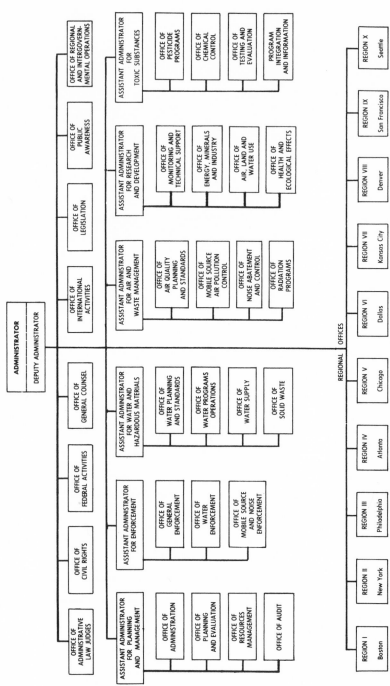

GENERAL SERVICES ADMINISTRATION

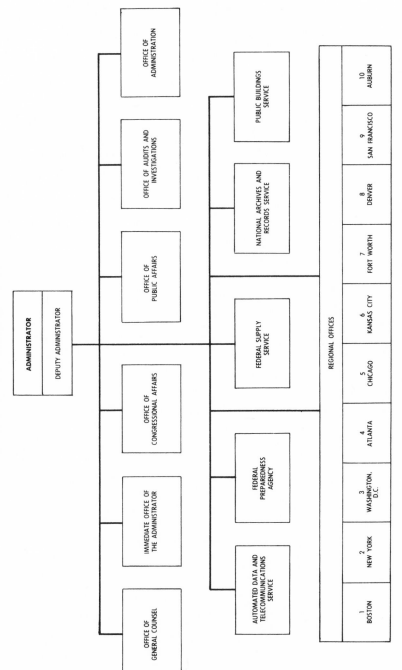

ADMINISTRATOR

DEPUTY ADMINISTRATOR

OFFICE OF GENERAL COUNSEL

IMMEDIATE OFFICE OF THE ADMINISTRATOR

OFFICE OF CONGRESSIONAL AFFAIRS

OFFICE OF PUBLIC AFFAIRS

OFFICE OF AUDITS AND INVESTIGATIONS

OFFICE OF ADMINISTRATION

AUTOMATED DATA AND TELECOMMUNICATIONS SERVICE

FEDERAL PREPAREDNESS AGENCY

FEDERAL SUPPLY SERVICE

NATIONAL ARCHIVES AND RECORDS SERVICE

PUBLIC BUILDINGS SERVICE

REGIONAL OFFICES

| 1 BOSTON | 2 NEW YORK | 3 WASHINGTON, D.C. | 4 ATLANTA | 5 CHICAGO | 6 KANSAS CITY | 7 FORT WORTH | 8 DENVER | 9 SAN FRANCISCO | 10 AUBURN |

UNITED STATES POSTAL SERVICE

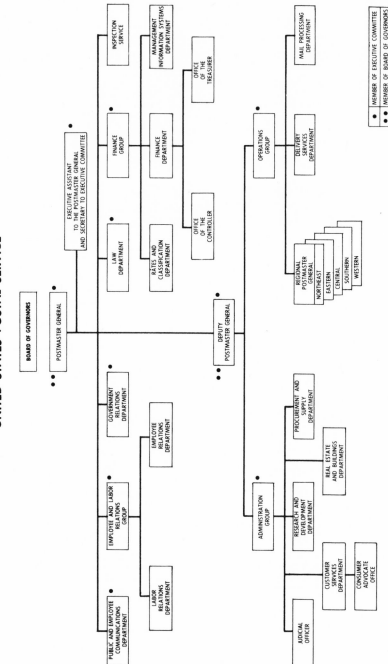

BOARD OF GOVERNORS

POSTMASTER GENERAL

EXECUTIVE ASSISTANT TO THE POSTMASTER GENERAL AND SECRETARY TO EXECUTIVE COMMITTEE

PUBLIC AND EMPLOYEE COMMUNICATIONS DEPARTMENT

EMPLOYEE AND LABOR RELATIONS GROUP

LABOR RELATIONS DEPARTMENT

EMPLOYEE RELATIONS DEPARTMENT

GOVERNMENT RELATIONS DEPARTMENT

LAW DEPARTMENT

RATES AND CLASSIFICATION DEPARTMENT

FINANCE GROUP

FINANCE DEPARTMENT

OFFICE OF THE CONTROLLER

OFFICE OF THE TREASURER

INSPECTION SERVICE

MANAGEMENT INFORMATION SYSTEMS DEPARTMENT

DEPUTY POSTMASTER GENERAL

ADMINISTRATION GROUP

JUDICIAL OFFICER

CUSTOMER SERVICES DEPARTMENT

CONSUMER ADVOCATE OFFICE

RESEARCH AND DEVELOPMENT DEPARTMENT

REAL ESTATE AND BUILDINGS DEPARTMENT

PROCUREMENT AND SUPPLY DEPARTMENT

OPERATIONS GROUP

REGIONAL POSTMASTER GENERAL
NORTHEAST
EASTERN
CENTRAL
SOUTHERN
WESTERN

DELIVERY SERVICES DEPARTMENT

MAIL PROCESSING DEPARTMENT

• MEMBER OF EXECUTIVE COMMITTEE

•• MEMBER OF BOARD OF GOVERNORS

VETERANS ADMINISTRATION

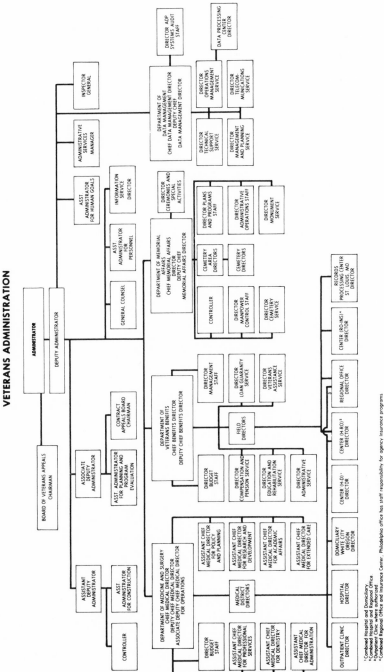

[1] Combined Hospital and Domiciliary.
[2] Combined Hospital and Regional Office.
[3] Outpatient Clinic where authorized.
[4] Combined Regional Office and Insurance Center. Philadelphia office has staff responsibility for agency insurance programs.

Appendix 8

Glossary

---

advertised bid/procurement (also formally advertised)
sealed bid with public opening, using IFB (information for bid) form; bids must be read aloud; award to low bidder

AEC
Atomic Energy Commission

AMC
Army Materiel Command

below the line
cost items on which no profit is taken

best and final offer
invitation to cut price offered in proposal, often with presentation and/or discussions, sometimes considered final negotiation

BIA
Bureau of Indian Affairs (Department of the Interior)

bidder's conference
pre-proposal conference held to answer questions from prospective bidders; usually used for very large procurements where there are many questions or where the customer finds it difficult to explain all in RFP

bid set, bid package
solicitation, including IFB or RFP, work statement, specifications, other information required for bid

B/L
bill of lading, government bill of lading; when contract so stipulates, government will pay freight costs by providing shipping documents

BOA

basic ordering agreement; term contract, with unit prices, under which customer may order goods or services on demand, as stipulated and priced

CBD

Commerce Business Daily

CIA

Central Intelligence Agency

COB

close of business (specific time varies among agencies); often given, with a date, as the deadline for submittal of bids or proposals

CPAF

cost-plus-award-fee contract; type of contract with incentive fees to reward good performance and cost reductions

CPFF

cost-plus-fixed-fee contract, well known as "cost-plus" type of contract

CPSC

Consumer Product Safety Commission

CSA

Community Services Administration, part of GSA, remnant of old Office of Economic Opportunity (OEO)

DACA

days after contract award; often used in scheduling to stipulate milestones or due dates for project products or functions

DC

District of Columbia

DCAA

Defense Contract Audit Agency; auditing agency of Defense Department, often utilized by other agencies to audit contractors' accounts or verify overhead rates

DOC
Department of Commerce

DOD
Department of Defense

DOE
Department of Energy

DOI
Department of the Interior

DOJ
Department of Justice

DOL
Department of Labor

DOT
Department of Transportation

EEOC
Equal Employment Opportunity Commission

EPA
Environmental Protection Agency

FAA
Federal Aviation Commission (part of DOT)

FCC
Federal Communications Commission

FDA
Food and Drug Administration

FOB
Free on Board; stipulation in solicitation requiring contractor to pay
freight (include in cost estimates) to destinations given

FOI
Freedom of Information (Act)

FRA
Federal Railroad Administration (part of DOT)

FSC
Federal Stock Code; government identifying number for standard commodity

FSS
Federal Supply Service, part of GSA

FTC
Federal Trade Commission

GAO
General Accounting Office; arm of Congress, conducts investigations, studies, prepares reports for congressional members; headed by Comptroller General of the United States

GPO
Government Printing Office

GSA
General Services Administration; main supply arm of government (nonmilitary)

HEW
Department of Health, Education and Welfare (now being reorganized)

HUD
Department of Housing and Urban Development

ICC
Interstate Commerce Commission

IFB
information for bid; form used for formally advertised procurement

IG
Industrial Group; used to classify supplies by major groups

indef qty
indefinite quantity; usually used for BOAs and other term contracts where unit prices are established for ordering supplies

labor-hour contract
similar to BOA, but contract rates established for labor classes

LEAA
Law Enforcement Assistance Administration; division of DOJ

NASA
National Aeronautics and Space Administration

NBS
National Bureau of Standards; part of DOC

NHTSA
National Highway Traffic Safety Administration; part of DOT

NIDA
National Institute of Drug Abuse; part of HEW

NIH
National Institutes of Health; part of HEW

NIMH
National Institutes of Mental Health; part of HEW

NIOSH
National Institute of Occupational Safety and Health; part of HEW

NLM
National Library of Medicine; part of HEW

NOL
Naval Ordnance Laboratory

NRL
Naval Research Laboratory

NSA
National Security Administration

NSF
National Science Foundation

NSN
National Stock Number; number assigned to standard commodities; often used as specification in procurement

OE
Office of Education; part of HEW

OEO
Office of Economic Opportunity

OFPP
Office of Federal Procurement Policy; part of OMB

OMB
Office of Management and Budget

OMBE
Office of Minority Business Enterprise; part of DOC

OPM
Office of Personnel Management; replaces former Civil Service Commission

OSHA
Occupational Safety and Health Administration; part of DOL

PBS
Public Buildings Service; part of GSA

PHS
Public Health Service; part of HEW

RFP
request for proposal

RFQ
request for quotation

SBA
Small Business Administration

T&M
time and material (contract); similar to BOA and labor-hour contracts

USA
U.S. Army

USAF
U.S. Air Force

USCG
U.S. Coast Guard

USDA
U.S. Department of Agriculture

USMC
U.S. Marine Corps

USN
U.S. Navy

USPS
U.S. Postal Service

VA
Veterans Administration

Index

DATE DUE